Marvel's Black Widow from
Spy to Superhero

T0276877

Marvel's Black Widow from Spy to Superhero

Essays on an Avenger with a Very Specific Skill Set

Edited by SHERRY GINN

McFarland & Company, Inc., Publishers
Jefferson, North Carolina

ALSO OF INTEREST AND FROM MCFARLAND
Power and Control in the Television Worlds of Joss Whedon, by Sherry Ginn (2012), *Who Travels with the Doctor? Essays on the Companions of* Doctor Who, edited by Gillian I. Leitch and Sherry Ginn (2016), *The Multiple Worlds of* Fringe: *Essays on the J.J. Abrams Science Fiction Series,* edited by Tanya R. Cochran, Sherry Ginn and Paul Zinder (2014), *The Worlds of* Farscape: *Essays on the Groundbreaking Television Series,* edited by Sherry Ginn (2013), *The Sex Is Out of This World: Essays on the Carnal Side of Science Fiction,* edited by Sherry Ginn and Michael G. Cornelius (2012)

LIBRARY OF CONGRESS CATALOGUING-IN-PUBLICATION DATA

Names: Ginn, Sherry, editor.
Title: Marvel's Black Widow from spy to superhero : essays on an
    Avenger with a very specific skill set / edited by Sherry Ginn.
Description: Jefferson, North Carolina : McFarland & Company, Inc.,
    Publishers, 2017. | Includes bibliographical references and index.
Identifiers: LCCN 2016035660 | ISBN 9780786498192 (softcover : acid
    free paper) ∞
Subjects: LCSH: Black Widow (Fictitious character)
Classification: LCC PN6728.B5194 M37 2017 | DDC 741.5/973—dc23
LC record available at https://lccn.loc.gov/2016035660.

BRITISH LIBRARY CATALOGUING DATA ARE AVAILABLE

ISBN (print) 978-0-7864-9819-2
ISBN (ebook) 978-1-4766-2716-8

Cover images © 2017 iStock

Printed in the United States of America

McFarland & Company, Inc., Publishers
  Box 611, Jefferson, North Carolina 28640
  www.mcfarlandpub.com

For Tanya, Heather, and Gillian
and all of the other female fans of science fiction

Table of Contents

a size 14—and the NFL is now one of the richest organizations in the world. I live in NASCAR country and NASCAR has not only rebranded itself into a female-friendly sport, but a family-friendly one as well. Why Disney would want to exclude women from its marketing plans just does not make sense.

A Positive Role Model for Female Power

After my last viewing of Marvel's *The Avengers*, I was finally able to artic-ulate something I have been trying to speak to for about fifteen years. It has to do with power. It goes beyond the idea that women want "strong" female characters and all of the arguments raging on the internet for and against the "Strong Female Character." Beginning somewhere around the turn of this century, I began talking about female characters on science fiction television (SFTV). My remarks generally revolved around Ambassador Delenn and Commander Susan Ivanova of *Babylon 5*; Beka Valentine of *Gene Rodden-berry's Andromeda*; Major Kira Nerys and Lt. Commander Jadzia Dax of *Star Trek: Deep Space Nine*; Officer Aeryn Sun of *Farscape*; and Zoe Washburn of *Firefly* and *Serenity*. In one of my first presentations years ago, an audience member was disturbed that all of these characters were not only capable of using violence in their encounters with men and other women, but that they frequently did so. That audience member wanted to find strong female char-acters that did not resort to violence to solve problems or to prove their strength. We are still looking for those characters today, at least a decade later.[2]

Since that presentation, we have seen even more strong female charac-ters—such as Black Widow, Gamora, River Song, Agents May and Carter—on television and film that use many strategies to solve problems, including violence. What I can articulate much better now is that these women can give a punch but they can also take one. These women are on the receiving end of violence as well as giving it. What I see is a different mind-set from the all-too-pervasive violence *against* women occurring in various countries around the world. It is true that in these films and TV series men aggress against female characters, *but* the women are not afraid of them. The men in these situations are aware that the women will fight back, and hard. In reality, men who are violent against women are violent because they can be. They have learned that they can hurt women and get away with it, for a wide variety of reasons. They know that women fear them and that gives them power. However, in the world of science fiction, there are wonderfully drawn female characters who do not give their male counterparts either physical or psychological power over them. Aeryn Sun is not afraid of men; nor is Zoe or Delenn or Ivanova or Kira. Certainly Black Widow is not. These characters live in worlds where women do not have to be afraid of men, where women have agency, where women have power. And that gives hope to us all.

Black Widow, as presented in the Marvel Cinematic Universe (MCU), is not without her faults; she is, after all, human. Nevertheless, she has characteristics that make her a superhero in her own right. Like Wonder Woman, Black Widow has no special powers other than strength, agility, and speed. However, Trina Robbins notes that Wonder Woman's message—and Black Widow's, too, I argue—is that with training any woman or girl can become a "wonder woman" (57)—not that any of us would want to undergo the type of training that created Black Widow. Unlike many of the female characters that populate the world of comics, MCU's Widow has not been relegated (yet, but see below) to the three stereotypical types of heroines found in comics: love interest, sidekick, or damsel to be rescued. It is true that the Widow's story in the comics involves all three, especially the love interest. She has been involved with a number of men but this is not the case in the MCU, which makes it distressing to hear her character being referred to as a "slut" by actors portraying her male colleagues.[3] Frankly, I think that Black Widow

Black Widow (Scarlett Johansson) and Captain America (Chris Evans) discuss strategy as they prepare to do battle following Nick Fury's "death." From *Captain America: The Winter Soldier* (Photofest).

likes to flirt with her comrades and one of the reasons is because she can. She's a pretty equal match for most of them and they are all "safe." Thor and Iron Man are in relationships, Hawkeye is married, Captain America still carries a torch for Peggy Carter, and Bruce Banner (The Hulk) is the stereotypical absent-minded scientist who doesn't understand or recognize flirting. I also do not think that she is in awe of any of them. After all, she refers to them as "boys" quite frequently and none of them objects.

People also have expressed misgivings over the way Black Widow's character is portrayed in the film *Captain America: The Winter Soldier*. What I particularly liked was the fact that Black Widow and the Captain interacted with one another as comrades, as partners. He treated her no differently than he treated any of the other Avengers (from that film) or the other characters in this film. He did not treat her like a fragile female who needed his protection, and he did not treat her as if she were a sex object or potential sex partner. My impression is that he respected her as a fellow soldier.

The recent controversy over the portrayal of Black Widow in *Age of Ultron* has only added fuel to the fire with respect to female fans and their desire for positive role models. Fans were dismayed that Black Widow's relationship with Hawkeye was relegated to friendship and a wife appeared out of nowhere. This is even more remarkable given that Joss Whedon wrote the scripts for both movies, with the second contradicting the first, especially with respect to Romanoff and Barton's relationship. An internet firestorm also erupted over Black Widow's relationship with the Hulk, especially given several scenes where she appears to lose her agency, such as when he has to rescue her from her captors and when she discusses her inability to have children and how that makes her less of a woman. Yes, it shows how her ability to control her own destiny was taken from her, but it also suggests that women want children and not being able to have them makes them unnatural in some way—as if they are not "real" women.

Black Widow's status as a positive role model has been denigrated as well (see O'Rourke for example). One reason is her past history as an assassin, seductress, and Soviet spy. She comes with a lot of baggage, though much of her past was not within her control. Interestingly, those who note that her sterilization at the hands of her Red Room masters shows her lack of control over her body and her life do not seem to take note that her entire life and everything about her body and mind were the result of the conditioning she received as a young girl. Black Widow's defection from the Soviet Union and her eventual membership in the Avengers Initiative suggests that even the most hardened criminal can be rehabilitated. I argued the same with respect to Officer Aeryn Sun of *Farscape*, who was a member of a brutal paramilitary organization called the Peacekeepers. Not only did Aeryn renounce her Peacekeeping background, she eventually became their leader, guiding them into a new way of being. Aeryn is a positive role model because she became something more than she was; something better, we might say. I argue that the same is true of Black Widow.

The fantasy, science fiction, and horror genres are continuing to do well not only at the box office but also on the small screen. Attendance at Dragon Con reached an all-time high in 2015, as it did at Ottawa Comiccon (both of which I attended). Other cons are also seeing record-breaking attendance numbers and the monetary potential of fans of what was once considered to be "fringe" has captured the attention of toy-makers, costumers, artists and artisans, not to mention producers, writers, and directors. Whether corporate America will also take notice is another question. This collection of essays serves notice that Black Widow is a popular character and fans want more of her. These essays only scratch the surface of the Widow's life and character, but each essay thoughtfully explores topics relevant to Black Widow in both the comic and cinematic universes.

Malgorzata Drewniok examines how Natasha Romanoff uses language in Joss Whedon's *The Avengers*. Although a capable fighter, Natasha has also been trained in seduction and espionage. All of these contribute to her skill set. Nevertheless, Drewniok analyzes Romanoff's use of language in the film to show that when Romanoff's opponents focus on her appearance and her reputation, they so do at their own peril, as illustrated by her scenes with the Russians and Loki. Furthermore, Romanoff's use of language shows that she considers herself to be a member of the Avengers, as do the people who work with her and for whom she works, such as Agent Coulson and Director Fury.

In response to the controversy as to whether "Strong Female Character" is a positive or negative appellation, Heather M. Porter proposes a new title for women in film: "Complete Female Character." She defines the term in her essay and then examines female characters that have appeared in Phases One and Two of the Marvel Cinematic Universe. She notes that all of the major female characters—Pepper Potts, Darcy Lewis, Jane Foster, Maria Hill, Peggy Carter, Scarlet Witch, and Black Widow—are presented as "complete." Nevertheless, female fans that want to purchase merchandise featuring these characters find few items to choose from and indications from Marvel, Disney, and other studios connected with these franchises have little to no interest in marketing to such fans.

Samira Nadkarni's essay is related to Porter's in that both are disappointed by the lack of a film about Black Widow—despite fans' repeated calls for one—as well as merchandise related to her character. Nadkarni examines how fans' engagement with the character and disgust over the ways in which "she" has been treated by people in charge of production at Marvel and Disney Studios led to the creation of "fanvids." These vids examine Black Widow's story-line using various media sources, including scenes from properties in Scarlett Johansson's oeuvre. Fans have also created trailers and promotional materials to advertise the film that many are demanding to see, *Budapest*, which details part of the history of Black Widow and Hawkeye.

Valerie Estelle Frankel traces Black Widow's history from her first appearance in *Tales of Suspense* to her more recent incarnations in comics devoted exclusively to her story. Early writers presented her as a femme fatale, Frankel notes, and her costumes were excessively tight, form-fitting, and glamorous. In addition, Black Widow's story was written in terms of the men in her life, men who treated her badly—if not outright abusively—as well as in terms of men she wanted to emulate, like Spiderman. Recent writers, such as Nathan Edmondson and Paul Cornell, present Black Widow in more positive ways, although traces of her past with respect to the men in her life and her costumes can still be observed.

Jillian Coleman Benjamin also examines Black Widow's history from her beginnings in comics through her appearance in *The Avengers*. Benjamin's essay analyzes depictions of the Widow in terms of the sexism apparent in her story as well as in the stories of other female characters within the comic universes. In many respects Joss Whedon liberated Black Widow in his first film of the MCU, and Benjamin notes "the reception that his movie has received is a signal to Hollywood and the movie-making industry that destruction of sexist archetypal roles isn't destructive to profit."

My own essay probes the training regimen undergone by a young Natasha Romanoff and how that training led to the birth of Black Widow. I describe how brainwashing and other mind control techniques were used in the Red Room; these methods are based on sound psychological theory and are used constantly and continuously in "real life." The essay also looks at other instances of mind control in works set in the MCU, such as *Agent Carter*, and in other works by Joss Whedon, such as *Firefly* and *Dollhouse*.

Lewis Call discusses Black Widow's role in both Avengers films, detailing how she becomes an integral part of the team and why her role is so important to it. He analyzes her actions in terms of third-wave feminism: her combination of both masculine and feminine personality traits, her ability to "kick ass and take names" when necessary, her willingness to subvert personal desires to complete a task, and her recognition of when individual action is more important for solving problems and when collective action is. Call also examines the controversy about Black Widow's portrayal in *Avengers: Age of Ultron* and proposes that the relationship between Black Widow and Hulk illustrates one of mutual dominance and submission.

In his essay on the aesthetics of the films in which Black Widow appears, David Kociemba first describes the action genre and how female characters figure in that genre. Elements of a traditional action film include torture scenes, martial arts, a death that unifies a group, and some type of emotional bonding. All of the elements are contained within Marvel's *The Avengers* and, as Kociemba discusses, showcase Black Widow. The essay makes clear that actions during the film indicate she "is not only becoming a different Black Widow, but also joining a tradition of just female warriors that speak to gender-integrated audiences about power and responsibility."

Finally Tanya R. Cochran discusses fans of Black Widow and, more specifically, fans of Scarlett Johansson's portrayal of Black Widow. She examines the discourse around a stand-alone Black Widow film—something that Marvel is apparently unwilling to produce—using desire path analysis. This term refers to a physical pathway that emerges when over time enough pedestrians, cyclists, or others deviate from a designated route and erode the terrain. Such a path indicates that the use of space may not correlate with those who planned how the space would be used. Fans of Black Widow, through their creation of movie trailers and other fanvids, inform Marvel of their desire for a film centered on Black Widow, starring Johansson.

These essays celebrate Black Widow. Her evolution over the course of her tenure in the Marvel Universes—from assassin to avenger, spy to superhero—yields a character that many people, male and female, admire. We can only hope that the future will bring us more Black Widow.

NOTES

1. The purist in me wishes Black Widow would be given her "true" name. Specifically, her name is Natalia Alianovna Romanova. Natasha or Tasha is a nickname or diminutive for Natalia. She was born in Stalingrad, USSR, in 1928 (comics) or Volgograd in 1984 (MCU). In Russian, women's middle names or patronymics, and their surnames, are feminized to indicate gender. Her father's name would be Alian, with an "a" added to her family name, Romanov, anglicized as Romanoff. Her parents are presumed to be deceased; a brother, also presumed deceased, is introduced in the book *Forever Red*, published in 2015. Interested readers can find her biographies on the Marvel Comics Wiki pages. They have bios for the comics' Black Widow and the MCU's Black Widow (see Works Consulted).

2. As I write this in the winter of 2016, there are still no plans for a Black Widow film. Still, I am heartened by the fact that Marvel is reintroducing its Black Widow comics (although she has supposedly turned against her former Avenger allies according to the press release).

3. Comments by Jeremy Renner and Chris Evans set off a firestorm on the internet once fans of Black Widow heard and read about their juvenile remarks. Anyone interested can Google "Black Widow slut" and find articles with comments about this issue.

WORKS CONSULTED

Black Widow [Marvel Cinematic Universe character]. *Marvel.* The Walt Disney Company. Accessed 13 February 2016.

Bowman, Sabienna. "9 Things Black Widow Fans Can't Stand Hearing, Because Natasha Romanoff Is Truly a Flawless Queen." *Bustle.* 30 April 2015. Accessed 13 February 2016.

Edmunds, T. Keith. "Heroines Aplenty, but None My Mother Would Know." *Heroines of Comic Books and Literature: Portrayals in Popular Culture.* Eds. Maja Bajac-

Carter, Norma Jones, and Bob Batchelor. Lanham, MD: Rowman & Littlefield, 2014, 211–219. Print.

Ginn, Sherry. "Examining the Psychology of Aeryn Sun: The Pin-Up Girl for Frontal Assault." Unpublished manuscript.

Ginn, Sherry. *Our Space, Our Place: Women in the Worlds of Science Fiction Television.* Lanham, MD: University Press of America, 2005. Print.

Marnell, Blair. "Natasha Romanoff Takes on S.H.I.E.L.D. in BLACK WIDOW #1 (Preview)." *Nerdist.* 7 February 2016. Accessed 13 February 2016.

O'Rourke, Morgan B. "*The Ultimates* as Superheroes in the Age of Social Media and Celebrity." *The Ages of the Avengers: Essays on the Earth's Mightiest Heroes in Changing Times.* Ed. Joseph J. Darowski. Jefferson, NC: McFarland, 2014, 120–138. Print.

Robbins, Trina. "The Great Women Superheroes." *The Superhero Reader.* Ed. Charles Hatfield, Jeet Heer, and Kent Worcester. Jackson: University Press of Mississippi, 2013, 53–60. Print.

Romanova, Natasha [Marvel Universe character]. *Marvel.* The Walt Disney Company. Accessed 13 February 2016.

Stohl, Margaret. *Black Widow: Forever Red.* Los Angeles: Marvel Press, 2015. Print.

A "very specific skill set"

Black Widow's Use of Language
in The Avengers

Malgorzata Drewniok

Language is one of the most distinctive features of Joss Whedon's work. It has been particularly scrutinized in *Buffy the Vampire Slayer* (1997–2003)— the language used in this series has been extensively examined by scholars, including Karen Eileen Overbey and Lahney Preston-Matto, Michael Adams, and Jesse Saba Kirchner, as well as Susan Mandala, Charlotte Bosseaux, and myself. Mandala has also examined the language of *Firefly*.

It is likely that when working on films Joss Whedon has much less creative liberty than on his TV shows. He is, however, credited as a co-author of the story and the author of the screenplay for *The Avengers* (2012), hence we might safely assume that he had a major influence on the dialog in the film even if (perhaps) not all the words were exactly how he might have wanted them.

This essay examines the character of Black Widow in the film. It is not her first appearance in a Marvel universe movie, but only in *The Avengers* has she been shaped by Joss Whedon. I am particularly interested in Natasha's language behavior in five pivotal scenes: her first appearance when captured by Russian rebels; her meeting with Bruce Banner; her meeting with Steve Rogers and Banner on the Helicarrier; her conversation with Loki; and her conversation with Hawkeye, when he recovers from Loki's influence. I evaluate how her "very specific skill set" is treated by Whedon and expressed in the language Natasha is made to use. As this is a relatively short essay, and because I am interested in Whedon's language in particular, I do not focus on Black Widow's other appearances (comics and films).

Conversation analysis is part of linguistic studies and focuses on the conversation behavior of characters in a given exchange. The elements examined are: who is the powerful participant and who is powerless; who initiates the conversation; who controls the topic; and who says more. Language choice is also an important consideration—lexis (vocabulary) as well as grammar (structure, tenses). Apart from conversation behavior, I would also like to examine the pragmatic side of these five scenes, that is, power relations and strategies to keep or change these. A pragmatic analysis concentrates on politeness and impoliteness strategies employed by the participants.

Through examining Natasha's conversational behavior and politeness/ impoliteness strategies I show how Joss Whedon succeeded in expressing Black Widow's special skills. A viewer unfamiliar with the character's background might suspect at the beginning of the film that Natasha's power is that of seduction; her linguistic behavior, however, shows it is in fact her ability to manipulate an opponent through language.

The Scenes in Question

As I have already mentioned, this essay focuses on five scenes from *The Avengers* featuring Natasha Romanoff. The first scene is shown at the beginning of the film, at the point when Agent Coulson starts assembling the Avengers. Here Natasha has been "captured" by Russian rebels and is tied to a chair. There are three armed thugs standing in front of her, hence one might assume she is in need of rescue; however, towards the end of the scene it is revealed she has been in charge all along.

The second scene is set in India where S.H.I.E.L.D. sends Romanoff to find and recruit Bruce Banner. His sensitivity to gamma radiation could prove priceless in finding the Tesseract. We witness an exchange between reluctant Banner and determined Romanoff. The third scene is a natural follow-up to the second: this time Natasha joins Steve Rogers and Bruce Banner on the deck of the Helicarrier and welcomes them aboard.

The fourth scene could be considered one of the most powerful scenes in the film. It is later in the film, when the Avengers have captured Loki, but have failed to obtain any information from him. Romanoff approaches him and they speak. On the face of it, Loki seems to rattle Natasha, but in the end she gets the information she wants.

The final scene is more intimate than the others. This is the moment when Natasha talks to Hawkeye in the infirmary. The connection between the two is palpable, and viewers might wonder whether this is the real Natasha Romanoff they finally get a glimpse of. She seems to lower her guard and speak to Barton as a friend, not as a fellow agent.

These five scenes are different from each other, but they can be grouped into three types. The first type is Natasha being business-like, clearly acting on behalf of S.H.I.E.L.D. and it includes two scenes—Natasha's first meeting with Bruce Banner and her appearance on the Helicarrier when Rogers and Banner meet. The second type includes two scenes that showcase Natasha's "very specific skill set," namely the scene with the Russian rebels and her exchange with Loki. The third shows a more human Natasha; this is her conversation with Hawkeye in which we can suspect she has let down her guard.

"Gentlemen, you might want to step inside"

I start with the third scene chronologically, the one on the Helicarrier, because it shows Natasha Romanoff in the most neutral way. She is presented as a S.H.I.E.L.D. agent, bringing a message for Agent Coulson from the bridge. She wears civilian clothes rather than her trademark black leather, but still carries a weapon. Although like Steve Rogers, she has been around for longer than you would expect given her young looks, her way of speaking is rather modern. Coulson introduces her to Rogers, who greets her with "Ma'am"; she responds only with a non-committal "hi," as if assuming familiarity despite the fact that they have never met. Then she asks Rogers about Coulson's Captain America trading cards. Although she knows Rogers' background (that he is from a different time), she does not provide much explanation, opting for an ellipsis (an omission of parts of the sentence without harming the meaning): "They're vintage, he's very proud." For the audience this ellipsis is successful; the meaning is perfectly clear. However, it is lost on Rogers; you can see he is confused (but he does not ask for clarification, perhaps to save face).

It is also worth noticing how Natasha refers to Coulson. When she arrives on the deck she speaks to him matter-of-factly, perhaps not like a subordinate, but with respect. However, when Coulson is gone and she asks Rogers about the cards, she says, "There was quite the buzz around here, finding you in the ice. I thought Coulson was gonna swoon." Note the use of "swoon" which is normally used in reference to females. This is consistent with Coulson's representation as an over-excitable fan in an earlier scene on the plane taking Rogers and him to the Helicarrier. Such mixing of action and humor has been Whedon's signature, notes David Lavery.

"Just you and me"

Before arriving on the Helicarrier, Natasha is sent to recruit Bruce Banner. She is not thrilled by this task (note her exclamation: "My God" at the end of her phone conversation with Coulson), but she goes all the same. It is clear she is very alert in this scene; this is expressed by her body language and her choice of words. Note her opening line, when she reveals her presence in the shack: "You know, for a man who's supposed to be avoiding stress, you picked a hell of a place to settle." This echoes the words of Whedon's most well known strong, female character, Buffy Summers. In "Prophecy Girl" (1.12), Buffy reluctantly faces the Master, the leader of vampires in Sunnydale. An old prophecy implies Buffy will die in this fight, so she is understandably scared. To boost her confidence, she uses language (often described as her main weapon; see Overbey and Preston-Matto). Buffy says: "Y'know, you really oughtta talk to your contractor. Looks like you got some water damage." Later her words are even more similar to Natasha's: "You know, for someone who's all powerful, you sure do like to hide." Buffy employed banter to boost her confidence and distract the Master, and it seems Whedon is making Agent Romanoff do the same. We know she is quite apprehensive about facing Banner.

Both Buffy and Natasha's comments are seemingly off-hand, as if they could care less, but we can safely read more into them. Natasha reveals her presence with this line, which also implies she is in charge. She knows about Banner whereas he does not know who she is. When he asks her whether the whole place is surrounded, she lies saying it is just the two of them. This lie might have a few reasons. On the one hand Natasha wants to keep it cool and keep face; she does not want to admit she has significant back-up outside. On the other, this might also be her strategy to appease Banner. She wants to persuade him to join S.H.I.E.L.D. peacefully, not by force. Throughout the film Whedon makes sure the Avengers treat Banner respectfully. It is visible here, and it is also shown later when Director Fury explains he just needs Banner as consultant, when Steve Rogers says he does not care for Banner's alter ego, and when various characters address him repeatedly as "doctor." When Banner asks her about her intentions, Natasha reveals she works for S.H.I.E.L.D.:

> BANNER: S.H.I.E.L.D. How did they find me?
> NATASHA: We never lost you, doctor. We've kept our distance, even helped keep some other interested parties off your scent.

Note the choice of personal pronouns in this exchange. Banner refers to S.H.I.E.L.D. as "they"; Natasha opts for "we." She presents herself as an active member of the Agency. This is very conspicuous when we look at her next turn. When Banner asks why S.H.I.E.L.D. kept an eye on him, she replies: "Nick Fury seems to trust you. But now I need you to come in." This time she chooses "I" which points to the fact that she is following orders. Note also that she refers to the S.H.I.E.L.D. Director with his first name and surname, but without the title. This is unusual in the Marvel cinematic and televisual universe in which he is usually referred to as just "Fury" or "Director Fury." This attitude is similar to the scene I discussed above, the scene on the deck of Helicarrier. She is respectful and she follows orders, but at the same time she is not one for honorifics. With Coulson she does not say, "Director Fury needs you on the bridge," but uses "they" instead. Similarly, she does not title Fury in her conversation with Banner. She must also assume Banner has knowledge of S.H.I.E.L.D. and its director; this is to do with Marvel universe continuity.

It is also worth mentioning the wordplay in this particular exchange. Banner asks how S.H.I.E.L.D. *found* him. Natasha replies they never *lost* him. The verb "to find" implies that something was lost, or hidden, or not discovered yet. "To lose" means to have something and then not have it anymore, misplace it for example. By this clever wordplay Natasha admits S.H.I.E.L.D. has had an eye on Banner since his earlier disappearance. This choice of words is not only entertaining, but also economical. Natasha saves words and time, which is of the essence in this particular situation. In fact, all five scenes discussed here show that Natasha is not wordy, but concise.

Later in the scene Natasha explains why S.H.I.E.L.D. needs Banner's help. It is worth considering her conversation strategies here. Instead of explaining at length and talking over the exchange (i.e., speaking the most and not letting Banner speak), she lets him be in control, asking questions. This approach backfires when Banner gets impatient and accuses Romanoff of lying to him. At this point it is clear she is scared he will transform into the Hulk, and she lets her guard down. Banner never believed she came to him on her own, but he appreciates her efforts at civility; this is expressed in his apology: "I'm sorry, that was mean. I just wanted to see what you'd do." His apologetic attitude is supported by a lopsided smile and a shrug. This scene leaves Natasha rattled. However, it also gives us a glimpse of her skills and her business-like attitude. Her language strategies might not work completely successfully with a person like Banner who can transform into the Hulk at any moment. She is more successful with predictable humans and with the caged Loki later.

"Are you kidding? I'm working!"

In the scenes above Natasha Romanoff is matter-of-fact, very business-like. She acts on behalf of S.H.I.E.L.D., follows orders, and is respectful, even if her language choices might sometimes be rather colloquial ("swoon") and informal ("hi"). She is aware of her position in the S.H.I.E.L.D. hierarchy, but treats Fury and Coulson as equals all the same. The next two scenes I want to examine showcase her "special skill set" much more clearly.

The scene with the Russian rebels is rather entertaining. It is a classic Whedon scene, one that encapsulates his mission to empower women on screen. When he created *Buffy* according to Billson, Whedon wanted to flip the classic horror scene in which a helpless girl walks into a dark alley and is attacked. The very first episode of *Buffy* featured such a scene, but with a twist: the girl (Buffy) fights back and defends herself against a vampire (Angel). The scene in *The Avengers* gives homage to Whedon's idea. Natasha is shown tied to a chair, shoeless, and seemingly vulnerable to whatever torture Luchkov has prepared for her. However, at the end of the scene she walks away free without much struggle.

Because she is first presented as helpless, it is not surprising that it is Luchkov who starts the conversation. By admitting he imagined this evening differently, he reveals how he sees her: as a seductress. Natasha gives him a slight warning: "I know how you wanted this evening to go. Believe me, this is better." With the knowledge of Natasha's identity, it is easy to read this. Most viewers familiar with the Marvel universe could imagine what would have happened at the end of Natasha and Luchkov's encounter. But there is also a slight innuendo here: this could be read as a warning that the Russian would perhaps not have been able to keep up with her sexual prowess (or be metaphorically consumed like a mantis or a spider after mating).

As it is, being tied to a chair, Romanoff cedes the power over the conversation to Luchkov. He is in charge, he asks the question ("Who are you working for?"). In reality, she is in true control. By asking whether she works for Lermontov, Luchkov reveals information which Natasha probably seeks. And she leads him on, mentioning Solohob:

> LUCHKOV: Who are you working for? Lermontov, yes? Does he still think we have to go through him to move our cargo?
> NATASHA: I thought General Solohob was in charge of the export business.
> LUCHKOV: Solohob? A bagman, a front…. Your outdated information betrays you. The famous Black Widow. And she turns out to be simply another pretty face.
> NATASHA: You really think I'm pretty?

It might be safely assumed that Natasha offers Solohob's name as a red herring. Luchkov finds it funny that she has wrong information, but in fact this is her strategy: to let him think she does not really know the details of his activity. When he dismisses her as just "another pretty face," she plays on. She implies she is out of her depth to put her captor at ease and make him lower his guard. Unfortunately her cover is blown by the phone call from Agent Coulson. When she exclaims: "Are you kidding? I'm working!" the power positions are reversed. Natasha admits she was just playing along, especially when she says: "I'm in the middle of an interrogation and this moron is giving me everything." This not only blows her cover, but also makes for good entertainment—her words do not correspond with her physical position (being tied to a chair); on the face of it, Luchkov is interrogating her, not the other way round.

At the end of the scene, when Natasha leaves the derelict building she has been held in, Coulson tells hers to recruit "the big guy." She assumes he means Tony Stark/Iron Man for whom she worked in the past (*Iron Man 2*, 2010), but it turns out Coulson wants her to talk to Banner. This little moment is not only important for story continuity (commenting on the fact that Natasha knows Stark), but also acts as a comic relief of sorts. She has just learned Clint Barton, whom she cares for, has been compromised, and she is visibly worried. And although her realization that she is to talk to Banner does not fill her with joy (her exclamation "Bozhe moi" ["My God"]), the misunderstanding about "the big guy" could be entertaining for the viewers.

"You're a monster!"

The scene with Russian rebels gives us a taste of what Natasha is capable of. Her skills are even more showcased when she talks to Loki. Just like with Banner and Luchkov, she lets Loki control the conversation. He is the one who speaks first; she does not announce her arrival. Although she asks the first two questions (about what happened to Barton), he thinks he is in control, because he has something she wants. Then Loki asks about her intentions. Like Luchkov earlier, Loki sees Natasha as a stereotypical woman, implying she wants to save the man she loves. And yet she denies any emotional attachment: "Love is for children. I owe him a debt." Again, just like Buffy, Romanoff reverts to a sharp retort to save face and to manipulate the conversation in the direction she wants. This is very clever; Loki clearly takes the bait when he says: "Tell me." At this point their conversation is more informal; she pulls up a chair and superficially lowers her guard. But although she appears to be quite open with him, he reacts rather violently. Interestingly, this is not because he does not believe her, but because he does. He goes along with her story, but aims to hurt her by reminding her of all the blood she has spilled. Loki still believes she is a creature run by emotions. By revealing he knows about her past, he not only implies she is a monster, but also—more subtly—that Barton has been broken: "Barton told me everything. Your ledger is dripping, it's gushing red, and you think saving a man no more virtuous than yourself will change anything?" Loki is now angry. He seems to despise Natasha and her "petty" concern. He is now employing no mitigation in his impoliteness, attacking her to cause as much damage as he can, describing how he wants to kill Barton. Loki falls victim to his vanity here, just like Luchkov earlier. They both think they have power over this seemingly vulnerable young woman. Too late do they realize she has played them. When Loki finishes his rant, Natasha turns around visibly distressed and calls him a monster. This is the moment when Loki lets his guard down, and comments with a laugh: "Oh no, you brought the monster." Thus he reveals his plan. The way he provoked Natasha is, in his eyes, the way to destroy the Avengers, by unleashing the Hulk. Soon he sees Agent Romanoff composed again and the penny finally drops.

Like in the scene with the Russians, Natasha offers more than one layer of acting. The superficial lowering of the guard is actually a performance. With Loki more layers can be peeled away. She arrives as an agent of S.H.I.E.L.D. She then acts as an independent player who wants to "wipe the red from her ledger." Finally, she seemingly lets her guard down and shows distress. And all this is a very calculated manipulation of Loki. He has shaken her; she admits it in her conversation with Barton later. However, she exposed herself for a reason: to get information out of Loki. This is her way of acting as an Avenger. On the Helicarrier everyone is looking for answers: Banner and Stark work in the lab; Captain America searches the store rooms; and Natasha puts her "special skill set" to use.

"Clint, you're gonna be alright"

The final scene I examine is one just before the final battle, the Battle of New York. Natasha talks to Barton in the infirmary as he tries to make sense of what has happened to him. She starts off soothing: "You're gonna be alright," but it is clear it will take more than some reassuring for Barton to recover. Like in the scenes before, Natasha lets her interlocutor talk. Barton explains how he feels, but although she wants him to get better, she knows there is no time, that they have to keep fighting to save the world from Loki. Once again we get a piece of Whedon's humor:

> BARTON: Why am I back? How did you get him out?
> NATASHA: Cognitive recalibration. I hit you really hard in the head.

Natasha first uses a technical term, and then explains in more simple words; this results in a rather comic explanation. The words here are carefully chosen: "cognitive recalibration" sounds technical and implies Natasha knew what she was doing; "I hit you hard in the head" is supposed to relieve the tense situation—Natasha did what she had to do to save Barton. For a while their conversation focuses on what happened to Barton. He is serious and still a bit confused, whereas Natasha sounds supportive and warm. But this changes at the end of the exchange, when Barton comments on Natasha's visibly changed behavior and attitude:

Hawkeye (Jeremy Renner) and Black Widow (Scarlett Johansson) in the infirmary of the S.H.I.E.L.D. Helicarrier. He is recovering from his "brainwashing" by Loki. From *Marvel's The Avengers* (Photofest).

> *NATASHA:* Now you sound like you. [Natasha sits next to Barton]
> *BARTON:* But you don't. You're a spy, not a soldier. Now you want to wade into a war. Why? What did Loki do to you?
> *NATASHA:* He didn't, I just… [She pauses]
> *BARTON:* Natasha.
> *NATASHA:* I've been compromised. I got red in my ledger. I'd like to wipe it out.

Note that Barton clearly defines Natasha's identity and skills: he calls her a "spy, not a soldier." That is poignant in this scene and the whole film. Viewers familiar with *Iron Man* 2 (2010) will remember her as Tony Stark's assistant, a S.H.I.E.L.D. agent under cover. In that appearance she was more someone who followed Fury's orders and, although not explicitly presented as a soldier, she was clearly placed close to Stark to protect him, not spy on him. In contrast, Whedon's *The Avengers* (2012) emphasizes Natasha's "specific skill set," namely being a spy. This is perhaps best illustrated by the above-mentioned scene with the Russian rebels.

Barton notices a change in Natasha and it worries him. Although they have fought many a battle together, he sounds convinced that she is not expected to be a soldier. Therefore, he rightly guesses that Loki has had something to do with Natasha's transformation. She is reluctant to admit Loki managed to hurt her, but when she finally puts it in words, she repeats her words from her conversation with Loki. This is significant. The first time she mentioned red in her ledger, she referred to her debt to Barton. And as I said earlier, this could have also been means of avoiding discussing her feelings for him. Here, although she uses the same words as before, her meaning is different. There are at least two readings: first, her desire to take revenge on Loki for abusing her verbally; and second, atoning for all the blood she spilt by saving the world from Loki. Either way this line—"I got red in my ledger. I'd like to wipe it out"—is memorable because it is repeated. This is another of Whedon's characteristic uses of language; he has used such repetition elsewhere, especially in *Buffy*. For example, in *Buffy*'s Season One finale ("Prophecy Girl"), her white prom dress is commented on twice ("By the way, I like your dress"): first, in a menacing way, by the Master who leaves her to drown; and second, as a compliment, by Angel when Buffy is revived and marches to face the Master again. Another, even more conspicuous example is evil Willow repeating "Bored now" in "The Wish" (3.09) and when the good Willow impersonates evil Willow in "Doppelgangland" (3.16) but fails to repeat the signature line, instead saying: "I'm bored" (for a more detailed discussion of this see Drewniok "'I feel strong'").

From the five scenes that I have examined, this one seems to be the only one in which Natasha really lets her guard down. She trusts Barton, and although she does not necessarily want to talk about it, she opens up enough to express that something is wrong, that the conversation with Loki has rattled her.

Conclusion

Whedon said that *The Avengers* is at the end of the day "a human story that … people can relate to on a lot of levels" (O'Hehir). Lavery also observes, quoting Maureen Ryan, that the film "actually deepened most of the characters in important and exciting ways." I believe that, in Natasha Romanoff, Whedon gave us not only a relatable character, but also another strong female lead. It is commonly known that Whedon fought with Marvel to include Black Widow in *The Avengers*. Although the focus of the film might be on the male superheroes and the antagonist, it is Natasha who is the key in pivotal moments of the story. She is the one who persuades Banner to help S.H.I.E.L.D. She manipulates Loki to reveal his plan. She fights in the battle alongside others, and it is she who gets to the top of Stark Tower to eventually find herself in the position to close the portal. In *Iron Man 2* she was an agent

(3) they talk about something other than a man. This test seems simple to pass, but one would be surprised at how many films do not, including *The Avengers*. There are also many films with poor depictions of women that pass by having two females talk about things like their wardrobe or nail polish. This dichotomy is mentioned in an article by Luke Owen, who states, "some films that fail the test actually portray women better than the ones that pass." As Stefan Solomon notes,

> The major issue with the Bechdel test is that it only demands small modifications to the narrative events in the movies we watch, and doesn't ask for any deep, structural changes. Ultimately, the test ends up telling us that the *content* of a film is more important than its *form*; that is to say, we are being told that what is most important about women on screen is simply *what* they do, not how they are *shown* to do it.

Though the majority of my own research is quantitative, it is not just the quantity that counts. My previous research on violence and sex has shown the quality of that quantity is also important. As Sarah from *Cinesnark* says regarding female characters, "I'll take two great heroines over nine useless bimbos any day of the week."

The question is thus: what is a good female character? The term "strong female character" is the most oft-used description when the quality of female characters is discussed. Carina Chocano indicates that "'strong female character' is one of those shorthand memes that has leached into the cultural groundwater and spawned all kinds of cinematic clichés." She lists numerous examples, from the "alpha professionals whose laser like focus on career advancement has turned them into grim, celibate automatons" to "gloomy ninjas with commitment issues," and points out that "'strong female characters,' in other words, are often just female characters with the gendered behavior taken out. This makes me think that the problem is not that there aren't enough 'strong' female characters in the movies—it's that there aren't enough realistically weak ones."

There is no consensus on a definition of this "Strong Female Character." Is she a woman ready to kick ass and take names, or is she a well-written character? Many people can name strong female characters, such as Buffy the Vampire Slayer, Veronica Mars or Katniss Everdeen, or their characteristics, such as independent, intelligent, or brave, but I have yet to find a definition or a conclusive check list of these people, we just "know them when we see them."[3] Tasha Robinson tells us, "the 'strong' refers to the quality of character development and plot importance, whether a given character has an inner life of her own, and a story worth telling. And worthwhile stories—about *any* characters, not just women—often revolve more around vulnerability, mistakes, and flaws than about impeccable skills." This is a good example of how this term is in need of a definition. To even talk about the Strong Female Character one must first define what is meant by the word strong: does one mean physical strength or strength of personality, or just an overall descriptor of a character? This is just the start of the problem with this term, as Sophia McDougall observes:

[I]t is not enough to redefine the term. It won't do to add maybe a touch more nuance but otherwise carry on more or less as normal. We need an entirely new approach to the problem, ... We need [sic] get away from the idea that sexism in fiction can be tackled by reliance on depiction of a single personality type, that you just need to write one female character per story right and you've done enough.

I agree with her observation and, as such, propose not a new character type but an overall examination criterion and terminology, the Complete Female Character.

The Complete Female Character (CFC) is an onscreen female that is just as fleshed out as any male character. As Sophia McDougall humorously pointed out in her discussion on the Strong Female Character, male characters aren't required to fit into a certain set of guidelines as female characters often are. She adds, "What happens when one tries to fit other iconic male heroes into an imaginary 'Strong Male Character' box? A few fit reasonably well, but many look cramped and bewildered in there. They're not used to this kind of confinement, poor things. They're used to being interesting across more than one axis and in more than two dimensions." This is how all characters should feel when they are pushed into these small boxes of stereotypes and required characteristics. This is why the definition I propose for a Complete Female Character is very broad and allows the characters to show their traits in a variety of ways.[4] As such I propose six qualities for a Complete Female Character. She is a named, speaking character with a backstory, and she possesses skills and traits, agency, flaws, and emotional resonance.

The first quality of a Complete Female Character is that she is a named, speaking character; this means that she is not just the girl that hangs all over a male hero and does not talk. By being a speaking character, I mean, more broadly, that she can communicate. Some characters may be deaf and only communicate through sign language or for another reason only through the aid of technology, but they can still communicate. The second quality of such a character is that she has a backstory, because in the real world everyone has a backstory. Even babies who are barely hours old have a backstory about what brought their parents together to make them. One cannot expect characters to have materialized out of nowhere and be whomever they are with no backstory.[5] Even characters that are created on a computer have a history, as is shown in Joss Whedon's television series *Dollhouse*. Topher Brink, the scientist who imprints personalities on Dolls who have had their own personalities wiped, explains, "I can create amalgams of those personalities, pieces from here or there but it's not a 'greatest hit,' it's a whole person" (*Dollhouse*, "Ghost," 1.1). Along with having a backstory, this character has to have traits and skills. These are features that define them beyond their looks, as a character with no traits or skills has no defining personality beyond being an object to look at and hang clothes on.

The fourth quality of a Complete Female Character is agency. These characters have purpose, drive, and some reason for their existence; they take action, they push the plot and themselves forward. As Silverstein and Kang state,

> a female character should have the wits and a big enough part in the story to propel and shape the plot significantly on her own accord … it would not count if, say, a female character's kidnapping triggered the plot because, obviously, that wouldn't be something she made happen, just something that happened to her.

The difference in action because of a character versus the action of a character is a key piece in the agency of a character. In discussing the difference in agency between Buffy in *Buffy the Vampire Slayer* and Bella in *Twilight*, Kirsten Stevens points out that

> unlike Bella who, as the focus of other people's looking, does not initiate action, Buffy embodies the action of speech. Buffy, no longer the heroine of sensibility is one of agency, one who creates the action and advances the story. While Bella relies on being saved and inspiring the men around her into action, Buffy creates the action, more often than not saving the men in her life.

The fifth quality of a Complete Female Character is that the character must be flawed. No one is perfect, even Mary Poppins was only "practically perfect in every way." As Shana Mlawski states in her article on examining how strong female characters are bad for women, "Good characters, male or female, have goals, and they have flaws. Any character without flaws will be a cardboard cutout. Perhaps a sexy cardboard cutout, but two-dimensional nonetheless." Characters need flaws and weaknesses; this helps motivate them to move past their flaws and weaknesses to achieve something greater. *Dollhouse* character Topher sums this up saying, "achievement is balanced by fault, by a lack, you can't have one without the other. Everyone who excels is overcompensating, running from something, hiding from something" ("Ghost"). What these first five qualities have in common is that they are all characteristics of real people.[6]

It is the final quality that makes an onscreen character real for audiences. A Complete Female Character must have emotional resonance. The Oxford dictionary defines resonance as "the ability to evoke or suggest images, memories, and emotions." As it applies here, that would be an onscreen character that creates an emotional response in the audience. Jack O., in an article on writing characters with this quality, states "influencing readers by evoking emotion with your writing, is an important part of content marketing. When you get your readers to feel deeply, they become more interested in your content, more loyal to your brand, and ultimately more likely to buy from you."

Characters with this quality have a form of audience relatability, the character has something about them that allows them to connect to the audience because if they don't, why are they even there? The character of Haymitch said it best in *Hunger Games: Mockingjay Part 1*,

> Let's everybody think of one incident where Katness Everdeen genuinely moved you. Not where you were jealous of her hair style or her dress went up in flames or she made a halfway decent shot with an arrow and not where Peeta made you like her, no I would like you all to think about one moment where she made you feel something real.

This feeling something "real" is what makes audiences relate to character. In an interview with Access Hollywood, Scarlett Johansson touches on this as well, "Let's be honest. Like the audience is attracted to men, women alike; characters that have substance and are rooted in some truth and have something visceral that we can connect to and associate with. That is part of the audience going experience." With these six qualities in mind let's look at a few of the main female characters in the Marvel Cinematic Universe.

The Complete Female Character in the Marvel Cinematic Universe

There were many female characters presented in the MCU over the course of Phase Two. For the sake of space, this essay will limit its examination to female characters that are featured in at least two films and the two most prominent with respect to screen time and involvement in the story arc of each film if more than two female characters are presented. Based on these parameters this essay examines the following characters chronologically in order of their introduction to the MCU: Pepper Potts, Black Widow, Jane Foster, Darcy Lewis, Peggy Carter, Maria Hill, and Scarlet Witch. Each character will be examined for how she reflects the Complete Female Character, as all of these characters are named and have speaking roles.

Pepper Potts was introduced in the first MCU film *Iron Man*. She is first seen kicking Tony Stark's latest conquest out of his Malibu mansion. She is featured in all three *Iron Man* films, moving up from Tony's assistant to the CEO of Stark Industries. After Tony decides to step aside, he appoints her to run the company that, as of the last movie, she continues to do. Pepper's backstory has her coming out of the secretarial pool to spend years as Tony's assistant. She has a variety of skills, from business knowledge to legal expertise, and is one of the few people who stands up to Tony. She is presented as a love interest to Tony, but also has her own story and agency. Pepper does her best to keep Stark Industries running well even when Tony doesn't care. She takes control of situations and doesn't let anyone intimidate her, such as in *Iron Man 2,* when she takes control after Hammer's Tech goes awry at the Stark Expo. One could consider her flawed because of her attraction to Tony, but that also makes her relatable. Though she exudes confidence, she doubts herself occasionally and is concerned with how she is perceived by others, which drives her to succeed.

Black Widow has one of the most complex backstories in the MCU as we know it, but it is also one we have only scratched the surface of, as most of her life story is a cover for her being a spy. Natasha Romanoff was trained in the Red Room and became a spy for the KGB. We know from *The Avengers* that she "got onto S.H.I.E.L.D.'s radar in a bad way" and that Agent Barton was sent to kill her but he "made a different call." From there she worked for S.H.I.E.L.D. until the fall of the agency, after which she went off to "find herself." By the time of *Avengers: Age of Ultron* she has rejoined the team and become the only member who can tame the Hulk. She is a very gifted agent with espionage skills; she speaks multiple languages and often uses other people's perceptions of her against them. Black Widow is driven to make amends for her past. Her general cockiness and dark past can be seen as the faults that drive her forward along with being what makes her a relatable character. Black Widow's vulnerability behind a hard mask along with her concern for her team is just the start of her emotional resonance. Being one of only two humans in the superhero group of the Avengers makes her a character to whom the audience can relate.

The Thor films presented audiences with a variety of female characters from the scientist Jane Foster and her assistant Darcy Lewis, to the Asgardian warrior Lady Sif and the Queen of Asgard, Frigga, but here I will only go into detail on Jane and Darcy. Jane Foster is an astrophysicist studying an atmospheric disturbance with her intern Darcy Lewis who is studying for a degree in political science when we meet them in *Thor.* Jane is intelligent, conducts her own research, and makes her own scientific equipment. Darcy is headstrong and speaks her mind. Jane is driven by her own curiosity and doesn't allow her research being stolen (by S.H.I.E.L.D.) to stop her search for answers to the anomalies she has found. This curiosity often causes her to act rashly, first by pushing ahead to get the data back by trusting a man she doesn't know in the first film and then investigating the anomalies in the warehouse and touching an unknown artifact which leads to her being possessed by the Ether in the second film. Darcy is driven to help her friend; she is loyal to a fault. Both of the characters have emotional resonance as illustrated by their attempts to understand an alien world that has been thrust onto our own. Jane's attraction to Thor is also something the audience can relate to.[7]

Peggy Carter was an officer in the British Guard before joining the Strategic Scientific Reserve to help defeat Hydra and the Nazis in World War II. She has military skills, can handle a gun, and has strategic "know how."

Being a woman entrenched with the military in the 1940s, she is often disregarded by the men around her, which forces her to have to fight even harder to be acknowledged. She at times lets her emotions get the better of her, like her jealousy with regard to Steve Rogers. The struggles she faces as a woman discounted by her male comrades makes her relatable to her audience and her reactions to their prejudices make her even more real.[8]

Agent Maria Hill appears for the first time in *The Avengers*. We do not have much of her backstory outside of her work for S.H.I.E.L.D., as when she is introduced she is only known as Nick Fury's second-in-command. She is a leader who is good under pressure and can assess a situation and make decisions quickly and effectively. She is driven to protect the world and S.H.I.E.L.D. and, when Hydra takes over, she is driven to stop them and restore order. Her extreme locality to Nick Fury without question can be seen as a flaw. The little time she appears on film does limit our knowledge of her and even her appearance in *Agents of S.H.I.E.L.D.* adds little additional information.

Wanda Maximoff, a.k.a. Scarlet Witch, appears unnamed in the post-credit sequence of *Captain America: The Winter Soldier*, but becomes a prominent character in *Avengers: Age of Ultron*, where we quickly learn a lot about who she is and where she comes from. Her complex and sordid history gives her many skills as well as her agency. Wanda and her twin brother Pietro watched their family die as children and spent three days staring at a Stark missile that never went off waiting to see if they would be killed as well. This drive for revenge against Stark leads them to volunteer for von Strucker's experiments on giving people superhuman powers using Loki's scepter. Wanda attained a number of mental powers including telekinesis, mental manipulation, and mind reading. The revenge she seeks can be considered as weakness as it often clouds her judgment of people, as indicated by her alliances with von Strucker and Ultron. Finding strength in her pain is a major aspect of her character that makes her relatable.

We can see that there are multiple Complete Female Characters in the MCU, but as mentioned before, quantity is also important. A film can have a fantastic female character, but if she is only on screen for a couple of minutes and/or is only in two scenes, is that enough, especially if it accounts for a small percentage of the film? To answer this question, I also examined the amount of time these characters are a part of the MCU. Two measurements can be used to evaluate quantity: screen time and number of scenes. Screen time is simply how long a character is shown on screen, and it can be compared to total running time or to other characters' time on screen. In an article for *Vulture*, Gilbert Cruz conducted such an analysis for characters in *The Avengers* and found that Black Widow received the third most screen time, at 33 minutes and 35 seconds, just after Iron Man with 37:01 and Captain

America with 37:42. After the release of *Age of Ultron, Vulture's* Dee Locket analyzed screen time for each Avenger, and found that Black Widow received the third most screen time in the film (33:07) once again behind Iron Man (45:34) and Captain America (50:25). One can also scrutinize the number of scenes in a film and determine how many of them contain a particular character, and I conducted this analysis for each Complete Female Character in the MCU.

For this analysis I defined a scene as a continuous block of storytelling, either set in a single location or following a particular character. The end of a scene is typically marked by a change in location, style, or time. A scene was counted when an action occurred in a single location for a continuous time, such as a group of people fighting in one location, or when a single character chases or runs through multiple locations without a break in action or time, such as when a hero chases a bad guy out of a building or through the streets. Establishing shots, such as building exteriors with no cast in them, transitions such as sunsets or sunrises with no cast in them, beauty shots or transportation shots, such as a car driving without seeing cast, were included in the scene that they were setting up. Reactionary closeups or cutaways were included in the scenes in which they occurred and were not counted as a break in the scene. Montages that established all characters for a set space of time were counted as one scene, such as the montages of the characters' reactions when Fury announced Coulson's death in *Avengers*. Montages that established the passage of time for a set group of characters with a set action in one location were also counted as one scene, such as the *Iron Man 2* montage of the Russian building his suit. If additional characters entered or the action changed, a new scene was counted.

For a character to be counted as included in a scene, they must participate in the scene and not just be in the background unengaged in the action of the scene. To participate in a scene the character must speak, be featured, perform an action or perform the same action as other characters in the scene. For example, in *Captain America: The First Avenger* when all the characters are gathered at a conference table and the general is giving a briefing, we see all of our characters. Everyone listening is participating, but the barely identifiable secretaries moving in the background are not. Closeup reaction shots of characters, such as those when Coulson dies, are also examples of participation in a scene. All scenes were counted in the MCU films, excluding *The Incredible Hulk* (2008), *Guardians of the Galaxy* (2014), and *Ant Man* (2015) as none of their female characters appear in any additional films. The participation of female characters in each of the scenes was tabulated by character. Then the total number of scenes each character appeared in was divided by the total number of scenes in the film to determine the percentage of scenes in which she appeared, per film.

The results of this analysis revealed some interesting trends between characters and different properties in the MCU. Pepper Potts appeared as a main character in three of the MCU films, with a small cameo in the *Avengers*. In the three *Iron Man* films she appeared in 26, 25, and 24 scenes respectively or approximately 25 percent of the scenes per film. Agent Peggy Carter was in 32 scenes of *Captain America: The First Avenger*, which was 35 percent of the movie's scenes, but her cameo in *The Winter Soldier* only accounted for one percent of the scenes in that film. When the films *Thor* and *Thor: Dark World* are analyzed a different skew occurs in the data. Jane Foster appears in 32 and 47 scenes respectively, which account for 35 and 43 percent of the total number of scenes. Darcy is in 24 scenes in each movie, 26 and 22 percent, respectively. These data indicate that Complete Female Characters get a particular number of scenes depending upon which superhero's movie they are in. Thus approximately 25 percent of scenes in *Iron Man*, 30 percent of *Captain America* and over 30 percent of *Thor* contain a Complete Female Character. Black Widow's numbers continue this trend as she appears in the other properties, starting in *Iron Man 2* at 21 percent, continuing to *Avengers* with 27 percent, then to 30 percent in *Captain America: The Winter Solider* and to *Age of Ultron* with 27 percent. Once again, these data show how individual female characters are treated in the MCU, but other overall numbers in each film tell a slightly different story.

The overall numbers include all Complete Female Characters in each film and all scenes in which they appear. These data can be seen in Table 1.

Black Widow (Scarlett Johansson) prepares to fire her weapons against the Chitauri on the streets of New York. From *Marvel's The Avengers* (Photofest).

A glance at these numbers reveals the trend of increasing inclusion of these characters in the films, starting with 27 percent in *Iron Man* and reaching a peak, at 58 percent, in *Thor: Dark World*. The *Iron Man* films contain the lowest number of scenes with a Complete Female Character with the peak at 37 percent in the second film, which included Black Widow. When the numbers for Lady Sif are included in the analysis of Thor films, the total for the two jumps to 49 percent, with the second film reaching the peak of 58 percent. *The Avengers* was the first non-Thor film to reach over 40 percent of scenes including a CFC. The second film to near this number was Black Widow's third appearance, *Captain America: The Winter Solider*. The current trend continues into *Age of Ultron* where the numbers show that Black Widow increases the scene count of Complete Female Characters wherever she appears.

Table 1. Average Number of Scenes Containing Complete Female Characters (CFC) by Movie in the Marvel Cinematic Universe, Phases One and Two*

Film	Total number with a CFC	Percentage of Scenes with a CFC
Iron Man	26	27%
Iron Man 2	36	37%
Thor	45	49%
Captain America: The First Avenger	32	35%
Marvel's The Avengers	71	43%
Iron Man 3	24	24%
Thor: Dark World	64	58%
Captain America: The Winter Soldier	57	40%
Avengers: Age of Ultron	103	50%

*The Incredible Hulk *and* Guardians of the Galaxy *are intentionally omitted from this chart because neither movie contains female characters that reoccur in additional films at this time. Even though Peggy Carter appears in one scene in* Ant Man, *that film was also excluded.*

Conclusion

The Marvel Cinematic Universe franchise with its twelve films to date has made over $3.5 billion domestically in box office receipts, according to Box Office Mojo. The number of people, including young children, who see these movies means we need to be concerned about how females are portrayed in this universe. In an article for *The Washington Post*, Alexandra Petri tell us that fiction matters. You don't have the luxury of getting to know most people. But fictional characters you can learn inside and out. You see them in situations most people never get to face; you watch them grow and change; you get glimpses of their interiors that most people, even the people you're closest to, never afford you. You internalize them and make them a part of yourself. They, and their stories, accompany you wherever you go.

A report for The Geena Davis Institute by Stacy L. Smith and Marc Choueiti on gender disparity found that females accounted for 29.2 percent of characters with distinct speaking roles when inspecting characters in films. Put differently, 2.42 males are depicted for every 1 female. MCU doesn't seem to be doing much better on that front, but it does appear to be slowly increasing the number of female characters and how many scenes these characters are in. If we are internalizing and taking cinematic characters with us, as Petri suggests, maybe audiences can finally start taking more female characters along also.

The future of the MCU characters will be evident soon, as the next phase begins. MCU characters are getting richer, more complex, and the MCU is becoming more inclusive of female characters; this can be seen most often where Black Widow goes. Will she have her own movie? The jury is still out on that. However, this trend of increased female inclusion in the films of the MCU does not carry over to the merchandizing. Currently if you want to use action figures or other toys to reenact the increasing number of scenes that Black Widow and the other CFCs are getting, you are going to have a difficult time doing so. Peter Brett comments in his article for *The Mary Sue* that "when comics and game designers exclude or otherwise diminish the role of female characters, they are really telling girls they are not welcome. That sure, they can play, but they can't have full immersion. Full immersion is for boys only." The Marvel Cinematic Universe is slowly changing this. Now it is time for merchandizing to catch up.

Notes

1. The Marvel Cinematic Universe consists of three Phases of Movies. Phase One started in 2008 with *Iron Man* and includes: *The Incredible Hulk* (2008); *Iron Man 2* (2010); *Thor* (2011); *Captain America: The First Avenger* (2011); and concludes with *The Avengers* (2012). Phase Two picked up after *The Avengers* starting with *Iron Man 3* in 2013 and includes: *Thor: The Dark World* (2013); *Captain America: The Winter Soldier* (2014); *Guardians of the Galaxy* (2015); *Avengers: Age of Ultron* (2015); and concludes with *Ant Man* (2015). Phase Three is scheduled to launch in 2016 with *Captain America: Civil War* and the current release schedule includes, in anticipated release order through 2019: *Dr Strange*; *Guardians of the Galaxy Volume 2*; *Untitled Spiderman Film*; *Thor: Ragnarok*; *Black Panther*; *Avengers: Infinity War Part 1*; *Ant Man and the Wasp*; *Captain Marvel*; *Avengers: Infinity War Part 2*; and *Inhumans*. This universe has counterparts on both the network ABC and the online streaming service Netflix. ABC airs two shows spun off of the MCU, *Marvel's Agents of S.H.I.E.L.D.*, which entered its third season in the fall of 2015, and *Agent Carter,* which

saw its second and last season in the 2015–2016 television season. Netflix has launched a set of series based on the comic book heroes called the Defenders, which launched with *Daredevil* (2015) and is to be followed by series featuring Jessica Jones, Iron Fist, and Luke Cage that is planned to cumulate in a series featuring an ensemble of these characters called *The Defenders*. All of these series occur in the same universe as the MCU, with some so far just referencing events in the films, like *Daredevil*, while in others entire plots take place in concurrence with the events in the films, such as *Agents of S.H.I.E.L.D.*

2. Fans who have gotten tired of waiting have created their own videos about Black Widow. See Nadkarni, this collection.

3. As I have pointed out in a previous essay on wisdom and intelligence in the television series *Fringe*, when anyone cannot define something they tend to resort to Supreme Court Justice Potter Stewart's definition of pornography: I know it when I see it.

4. It was pointed out during a discussion at the 2015 PCA/ACA national conference, where portions of the paper on which this essay is based were presented, that some of these definitions are a little "squishy," or soft definitions, not hard and fast rules. After further examining these definitions I did change one from reliability to emotion resonance which includes audience relatability, but stuck with the more soft and open interpretations because I feel that part of the problems with other tests and checklists, along with the term "Strong Female Characters," was trying to make hard and fast rules, which do not really apply in the real world for people and thus don't apply to realistic depictions of people on screen either. In addition, this is the first study of its type and further research will build upon and extend the definitions included herein.

5. Really at the end of the day materializing out of thin air in and of itself is a backstory, an odd story, but a backstory nonetheless.

6. At the Producers Guild conference in 2014, Seth Rogan was a featured panelist and brought up a point about film ratings that has stuck with me on many levels of character analysis and how it relates to the real world. He said life was not PG 13 and went on to give examples of how quickly in a day one's life would get an R rating. The film rating system is a checklist such that if one checks too many boxes one goes up in ratings (say "Fuck" once PG 13, twice R). As I put this scale together I had that idea in mind that this scale should be more flexible and as a character fits in more categories they become more real and like people who would be found in the real world.

7. Thor's attractiveness was often alluded to at first but the subtlety of these comments has gone away to the point where the stone cold Agent May in *Agents of S.H.I.E.L.D.* corrects Coulson's assessment of Thor as "Sure, he's handsome, but," to confirm Skye's assessment, "No, he's dreamy" ("The Well," 1.8).

8. Peggy Carter is further developed in her television series, *Agent Carter*, but for the sake of the current study her appearance in the films are all that is being examined.

WORKS CONSULTED

Bechdel, Alison. "The Rule." Dykes to Watch Out For. Dykes to Watch Out for Comic Strip, circa 1985. Accessed 31 Aug. 2015.

Brett, Peter V. "Dear DC Comics, This Is Why You Shouldn't Leave Creative Little Girls Behind." *The Mary Sue*. The Mary Sue, 16 Sept. 2014. Accessed 1 March 2015. http://boxofficemojo.com//franchises/chart/?id=avengers.htm, http://but-notblackwidow.tumblr.com/.

Chocano, Carina. "A Plague of Strong Female Characters: 'Tough, Cold, Terse, Taciturn and Prone to Not Saying Goodbye When They Hang Up the Phone.'" *The*

New York Times Magazine. The New York Times Company, 1 July 2011. Accessed 16 Feb. 2015.

Cronin, Brian. "Movie Legends Revealed: Black Widow Nearly Beat Iron Man to the Big Screen." *SpinOff Online*. Comic Book Resources, 24 Sept. 2014. Accessed 19 April 2015.

Cruz, Gilbert. "How Much Screen Time Does Each Avenger Get?" *Vulture*. New York Media LLC, 7 May 2012. Accessed 29 Sept. 2014.

Locket, Dee. "*Age of Ultron*: How Much Screen Time Does Each Avenger Get?" *Vulture*. New York Media LLC, 5 May 2015. Accessed 2 Sept. 2015.

MacLeod, Catreece. "The Bechdel Test, or How I Learned to Stop Worrying About It and Love Character Development." *A Voice for Men*, 4 Oct. 2014. Accessed 16 Feb. 2015.

Marston, George. "Johansson Confirms Talks with Marvel Studios Head about Black Widow Standalone Movie." *Newsarama*. Newsarama, 15 April 2015. Accessed 20 April 2015.

McDougall, Sophia. "I Hate Strong Female Characters." *New Statesman*. New Statesman, 15 Aug. 2013. Accessed 2 March 2015.

Mlawski, Shana. "Why Strong Female Characters are Bad for Women." *Overthinking It*. Overthinking It, 18 April 2008. Accessed 27 March 2015.

Mouse, Annie N. "Invisible Women: Why Marvel's Gamora & Black Widow Were Missing From Merchandise, And What We Can Do About It." *The Mary Sue*. The Mary Sue, 7 April 2015. Accessed 20 April 2015.

O., Jack. "Creating Emotional Resonance Through Writing." *Scripted*. Scripted Inc., 21 Feb. 2014. Accessed 23 April 2015.

Orley, Emily. "People Have Noticed 'Avengers' Merchandise is Seriously Lacking Black Widow." *Buzz Feed News*. Buzz Feed, 20 April 2015. Accessed 21 April 2015.

Owen, Luke. "Why the Bechel Test Doesn't Work." *Flickering Myth*. Flickering Myth, 24 July 2013. Accessed 16 Feb. 2015.

Petri, Alexandra. "What Jeremy Renner Really Got Wrong about Black Widow." *The Washington Post*. The Washington Post, 24 April 2015. Accessed 20 April 2015.

Porter, Heather M. "'They teach you that in Whore Academy?' A Quantitative Examination of Sex and the Sex Workers in Joss Whedon's *Firefly* and *Dollhouse*." *The Sex Is Out of This World: Essays on the Carnal Side of Science Fiction*. Ed. Sherry Ginn and Michael G. Cornelius. Jefferson, NC: McFarland, 2012. 86–101. Print.

Porter, Heather M. "'You're a smart boy. But there is much you don't know': A Quantitative Examination of Intelligence, Wisdom and Family Relationships." *The Multiple World of Fringe: Essays on the J. J. Abrams Science Fiction Series*. Ed. Tanya Cochran, Sherry Ginn, and Paul Zinder. Jefferson, NC: McFarland, 2014. 93–107. Print.

Robinson, Joanna. "Why Is Scarlett Johansson Missing from the *Avengers* Merchandise? Black Widow's conspicuous absence is part of a larger, sexist pattern." *Vanity Fair*. Conde Nast, 21 April 2015. Accessed 21 April 2015.

Robinson, Tasha. "The Best New Strong Female Characters Are the Weak Ones." *The Dissolve*. Pitch Fork Media Inc., 8 Dec. 2014. Accessed 3 March 2015.

Romano, Nick. "Black Widow's Plans in the MCU Changes Drastically, Find Out Why." *Cinemablend*. Cinema Blend LLC, 16 April 2015. Accessed 21 April 2015.

Sarah. "When It Comes to Female Superheroes, It's Quality, not Quantity." *Cinesnark*. Word Press, 2 May 2012. Accessed 2 March 2015.

"Scarlett Johansson Shares Tips For Dating The Hulk." Int. Scarlett Johansson and

Mark Ruffalo. *Access Hollywood.* Accesshollywood.com, 17 April 20015. Accessed 20 April 2015.

Silverstein, Melissa, and Inkoo Kang. "Goodbye to Strong Female Characters." *Indiewire.* Indiewire, 30 Dec. 2013. Accessed 15 Oct. 2015.

Smith, Stacy L., and Marc Choueiti. "Gender Disparity on Screen and Behind the Camera in Family Films; The Executive Report." *Geena Davis Institute on Gender in Media.* Geena Davis Institute on Gender in Media, 2010. Accessed 1 March 2015.

Solomon, Stefan. "What the Bechdel Test Doesn't Tell Us About Women on Film." *The Conversation.* The Conversation, 14 Nov. 2013. Accessed 16 Feb. 2015.

Stevens, Kirsten. "Meet the Cullens: Family, Romance, and Female Agency in *Buffy the Vampire Slayer* and *Twilight.*" *Slayage: The Journal of the Whedon Studies Association* 8.1 (Spring 2010). Accessed 27 March 2015.

Front and Center
Examining Black Widow Fanvids

SAMIRA NADKARNI

The big screen oeuvre of the Marvel Cinematic Universe (MCU)[1] consists, at the time of this writing, of ten major motion pictures: *Iron Man* (2008), *The Incredible Hulk* (2008), *Iron Man 2* (2010), *Thor* (2011), *Captain America: The First Avenger* (2011), *The Avengers* (2012), *Iron Man 3* (2013), *Thor: The Dark World* (2013), *Captain America: The Winter Soldier* (2014) and *Avengers: Age of Ultron* (2015). These films provide information about each of their titular characters, primarily acting as standalone tales of the respective superheroes until they are united formally in 2012's *The Avengers* and its sequel *Avengers: Age of Ultron*. Of the six Avengers introduced in the 2012 movie, four characters are provided with their own films, while two—Hawkeye/Clint Barton and Black Widow/ Natasha Romanoff—are not, resulting in repeated allegations of sexism within the Marvel 'verse that would see four male characters be produced as franchise leads with multiple sequels without any hope of its single female Avenger being granted the same possibility.

Despite the lack of response to multiple calls for a Black Widow film (or, in certain cases, because of it), the character has developed a large fan following. Although these fan works range from the creation of fan fiction, fan art, music playlists and blog posts (to name a few) to the manipulation of media content to produce fan videos (or fanvids) whereby Black Widow becomes the focus of the content, this article will focus solely on fan-based creation of video content. I have chosen to use clips easily available on popular sites such as YouTube for the purposes of this article as these are clearly intended for the purposes of mass viewing, though vids themselves exist in a multiplicity of locales that are themselves private and public depending on the vidder's choice of audience. In doing so, this article considers the manner in which this fan-manipulated content produces a conversation with the MCU content itself and its evident socio-political statements, as well as the way in which gender structures these relations.

Issues of Sexism and Diversity in the Superhero Industry

Any discussion of sexism within the MCU is inevitably co-mingled with the common Hollywood assertion that the market demands white male leads in the creation of a successful franchise, a trend predominantly upheld within recent surveys of these films (Lauzen). Additionally, the MCU appears to market a large percentage of its content towards what it presumes to be the primary audience of comic book readers (i.e., white American males) with the result that the majority of representation on screen sees franchise leads and screen time dominated by white men. However, the assertion that comic consumers are largely white males is itself a hotly contested point (Schenker, Berlatsky) and repeated calls for diversity within the MCU would suggest otherwise (McMillan, "Could Fandom" and "Warner Bros."; Dockterman), particularly given the fact that the comics canon in the Marvel 'verse displays far more diversity than the MCU film and television franchise that draws upon its canon (Riesman). Regardless of claims that female-led superhero franchises are less likely to be successful—an argument that tends to circle the box office failures of Halle Berry's *Catwoman* (2004) and Jennifer Garner's *Elektra* (2005) in particular—the increasing emphasis placed on representation of women and/or people of color suggests that the market is not only willing to support these franchises, but has begun to actively demand them.

In clear response to this growing demand, the president of Marvel Studios, Kevin Feige, announced in October 2014 that a Black Panther and a Captain Marvel movie were each in production and set to release in 2018 (Feige, in McMillan, "Could Fandom"). Yet this response follows in the aftermath of numerous instances where sexism formed the basis of the franchise narrative. David Lavery notes in *Joss Whedon, A Creative Portrait* that Whedon had to fight to retain Black Widow as a central character to *The Avengers*, using the justification that "without her the Helicarrier was going to feel like a gay cruise" (170), and this occurred despite Janet van Dyne/Wasp, a founding member of the Avengers in the comics canon, already being written out of the script. Following these events and further calls for increased diversity, came the announcement of Marvel's plan to release *Ant-Man* (2015) with yet another white male as its lead. Notably, early references to the script suggested that Janet van Dyne, his wife and founding member of the Avengers team, would not only be physically absent from the film but that her death would be used as a plot point by which to develop Hank Pym/Ant-Man's narrative, rankling fans (Baker-Whitlaw). In effect, this not only erases van Dyne's own narrative within the MCU, but also subordinates her own contributions as a popular female superhero within the comics' canon to that of her husband, Hank Pym, within the film franchise.

Repeated calls by fans for a titular female superhero film focusing on Black Widow have met with little success so far. The well-publicized line up of upcoming films within the MCU franchise that details forthcoming releases until 2019 shows no listing of a Black Widow film, although *The Avengers: Age of Ultron* did provide further information on her past such that her narrative arc is presented as integral to the functioning of the Avengers (Feige, in Michelle). In effect, the choice to purpose Black Widow's narrative arc only within the ensemble format does indicate a choice to view women's narratives as less important than that of men, and essential only insofar as their own actions may contribute to the functioning of more central male narratives. The easy way in which female and/or person of color narratives are discarded in favor of multiple white male protagonists simply underscores the issues of diversity evident within the Marvel franchise in particular and the comic book movie industry at large; as Whedon puts it, there is a "genuine, recalcitrant, intractable sexism, and old-fashioned quiet misogyny that goes on" (Dibdin).

Fan Response to the MCU

Marvel Studios is not the only media conglomerate that has marketed their responses to fan demands as an indication that the studio heeds audience feedback. The evolving relationship between the fans and producers of content, greatly affected by the growth of social media, is undergoing constant negotiation, and Kevin Feige's responses to heated demands for more diversity is symptomatic of a larger set of responses within the media industry that attempts to utilize marketing strategies and the mobilization of fans in service of their own promotion (McMillan, "Could Fandom"). Feige's revelations in 2010 regarding the possibility of a Black Widow movie indicates to the viewers that Marvel Studios is listening to audience demands and attempting to provide content as per these demands, while making clear that this demand would need to be sustained and the film seemingly "earned" by fans, in contrast to those led by white males. Yet in 2014, Feige announced that a Black Widow film would be unnecessary as her role in the *Avengers* arc would be sufficient to the character's development. He stated that given the character's representation as part of four films in the MCU, Marvel would lack "credit" when providing her with her own titular film. Favoring the originality of introducing a new character, Feige then promoted the forthcoming *Captain Marvel* (2018) film as a response to fan outcry for female-led superhero films (Pahle). This announcement makes evident Marvel's assumption that a single female superhero film will be all the franchise can support at this time despite the dearth of such films, positioning the case such that it appears to be a choice of Black Widow *or* Captain Marvel, rather than Black Widow *and* Captain Marvel. As Nicole Massabrook notes, fans consequently responded by creating the Black Widow Offensive on November 2, 2014, and promoted it on the tumblr "Where is My Black Widow Movie?" (http://whereismy-blackwidowmovie.tumblr.com) and using the twitter hashtag of #BlackWidowMovie. The goal of the offensive is to argue that a token female character is not the solution to the cries for more focused female representation in superhero films. They insist that the *Captain Marvel* movie should be a start, with multiple female superheroes represented on-screen eventually, and Black Widow being amongst these in her own titular film (Massabrook).[2]

In response to this contradictory stance of studios "listening" on the one hand yet barely deviating in their response on the other, female fans performing fandom within the MCU have begun to respond by manipulating and producing their own media content. Mirroring Black Widow's choice to repurpose gendered performances and content provided to her in order to create her own sources of information, these fans refuse traditional assumptions that would see them merely as consumers of content, choosing instead to manipulate existing media and produce the content to their own ends. Gleaning material from three films in which Black Widow appears (i.e., *Iron Man 2*, *The Avengers*, and *Captain America: The Winter Soldier*),[3] and often garnering matter from Scarlett Johansson's filmography that might fit the storyline of defected Russian KGB agent turned S.H.I.E.L.D. operative and Avenger, fans have produced fan-made videos that are either character studies or intended to depict relationships that the source content has failed to provide (detailing relationships that occur between Black Widow and Hawkeye, Bucky Barnes, and Captain America; each of which occurs in the comics' canon).

The fanvids outline the creation of what Francesca Coppa broadly recognizes as an argument: the restructuring of available material to make a distinct point about the contents themselves, as well as the independence of these consumer-producers' choices and methods of interpretation. As E. Charlotte Stevens notes, vidding relies on sharpening and somewhat redefining signifiers—whether film, television, or audio sources—such that these can be represented in the vid's new context and perhaps in variance with the original content's purpose. The vids are therefore not simply a remix of the available content, but also a challenge to the premise of the original that sees Black

Widow as a secondary character, or one amongst many, instead of the content's sole focus. The meaning-making of these vids relies on the coinciding but distinctive elements of the audience's understanding of the canon and its manipulation, as well as the creation and acceptance of these new layers of meaning. In doing so, these vids add and subtract information, and exist both in relation to the original MCU content and also as works to be considered on their own. Vidding thus appropriates elements, transforms them, and purposes them towards an expression of intent.

For example, YouTube user egoscsajszy's "Marvel's Black Widow | Fanmade Movie Trailer" is a character study vid as well as a formal trailer vid. Its content is aimed at using short sequences drawn from Johansson's oeuvre as well as sequence shots from other films that might serve the vidder's narrative purposes, overlaid with audio quotes drawn from *The Avengers, Mission Impossible: Ghost Protocol* (2011), *Captain America: The Winter Soldier,* and Johansson's cameo in Justin Timberlake's music video "What Goes Around Comes Around." These are spliced together to create a simulated trailer that draws on hints provided within the MCU regarding Romanoff's history before and after her S.H.I.E.L.D. recruitment. egoscsajszy states that the fanvid involves

> Natasha Romanoff before she joined S.H.I.E.L.D., and the first few years of her being a S.H.I.E.L.D. agent and trying to put her past behind her. In my scenario, she was kidnapped when she was a young girl, and then trained to be a KGB agent. Then, she got on S.H.I.E.L.D.'s radar and Barton was sent to get her—just when she was involved with the Winter Soldier. The rest is history.

The content is clearly focused on Romanoff's character, opening with scenes of a youthful teen Johansson being kidnapped which are then contrasted with Romanoff as she is known to audiences of the MCU. The early sequenced clips outline her life in Russia, the screams of this sequence overlaid with a clip of Clint Barton's confession about being remade during his encounter with Loki in *The Avengers,* drawing distinct parallels between this secretive KGB training and his own brainwashing. The short bursts of images that follow showcase her in various guises in an effort to detail her strength and efficiency as a solitary field operative, the audio overlay drawn from Romanoff's own confession of her past to Loki in *The Avengers.* These audio and visual elements combine such that these scenes, which are drawn from outside of the MCU franchise, are integrated into the narrative to illustrate the events themselves. Similarly, the quote from the Impossible Missions Force Secretary to William Brandt in *Mission Impossible: Ghost Protocol* regarding the disavowal of the team is overlaid with Romanoff's eventual extraction from the KGB, her encounter with the Winter Soldier, and her introduction to the Avenger Initiative.

The image sequences used are often removed from their original context and reframed within the vid; the narrative audio overlay repositioning scenes that are familiar to audiences of the MCU into new configurations. Thus, the vid's use of clips drawn from *Captain America: The Winter Soldier* erase Captain America's presence and are repurposed instead to play out the events of Black Widow's first encounter with the Winter Soldier, an event which was only verbally recalled in the course of the film. Similarly, Director Fury's speech to Tony Stark welcoming him to the idea of the Avengers Initiative in 2008's *Iron Man* is used as Fury welcoming Romanoff instead. The vid continues and eventually concludes with her conversation with Loki regarding the amount of red in her ledger, returning the audience to the central notion of redemption that informs Black Widow's actions. In effect, this not only indicates the vidder's acknowledgement of the theme running through Black Widow's storyline in the MCU, but also positions the character as deserving of a title role; redemption forming the basis of so many heroic tales.

The sampling and splicing of audio and video clips drawn from disparate sources thus provides a detailed and compelling outline of Romanoff's experiences, adapting multiple texts in order to construct a singular retelling within which Romanoff's emotional life acts as the sole focus. By doing so, the vid repositions the content so as to exclude many of the male protagonists involved in the original content in favor of Romanoff's subjectivity, relying on her female-led narrative to engage the viewer's interest. This effectively expresses the vidder's own interest in a Black Widow film (so much so that they have spent time and effort engaging with multiple sources, forms of media, and film-making software in order to make this interest evident), and also evidences the vid-maker's own audience, who view this content in order to interact with the notion of a film focused almost exclusively on the character of Black Widow.

Similarly reggievass' "Natasha and Bucky—Winter Soldier—I'm Not the One" repurposes video clips from various films, particularly Johansson and Sebastian Stan's filmographies, which are then sequenced and overlaid with 3OH!3's song "I'm Not the One." The vid draws parallels between Natasha Romanoff's training and brainwashing by the KGB and James "Bucky" Barnes' conversion into the Winter Soldier, and the song's lyrics effectively narrate the sequence of events that follow, as the vid plays out each character's capture and conversion into a weapon. As E. Charlotte Stevens notes, the music functions as an authorial intervention on the part of the vidder. The characters are thus given a "voice" using lyrics, instrumentation, and other connotations of the song to animate an otherwise silenced sequence of images. In doing so, reggievass' vid draws fairly explicit parallels between the experiences of both characters as they share this voice, while also implicitly drawing parallels between Romanoff's training by the KGB and Barnes' brainwashing by Dr. Arnim Zola, a Hydra scientist.

This appropriating, hybridizing, and queering of content simultaneously informs a celebration of the character of Black Widow, a critique of the lack of information afforded regarding the character, as well as a construction of a narrative involving the character. It's worth noting that since vidding is the near-exclusive purview of women, and that the media corporations that produce and control the original content are largely the purview of men, that these critiques and/or homages are often both implicitly and explicitly coded by gender (Jenkins 155). That is, female fans creating content based around the character of Black Widow may not only be doing so with a view to expand the limited narrative offered to the single female Avenger, or making a point about their own investiture in a film with her as its central protagonist. Vidding also engages them in an arena that provides them with the means by which to indicate their own expertise and knowledge of the comic book canon or the MCU. This allows them to fight back against the pervasive notion that comic books or their films are solely the purview of men, while also reframing these narratives so as to include women's narratives that have been either sidelined or excluded in the MCU canon. As Tisha Turk and Joshua Johnson have noted, these responses are therefore not merely a reaction to the source content or to the studios themselves, but also to the society and cultural context within which they are produced.

Turk and Johnson add that these fan creators not only form the audience of the media they consume, but have their own audiences in turn. When producing their own video versions of a Black Widow narrative, fans create productions that function not merely as critique or un/intended promotion of the MCU, but also encourage active participation in and transformation of its culture as well as their own. This complexity and relative autonomy engages with the fact that these texts are shifting properties themselves— Black Widow's narrative having been rebooted within the comics' canon as well as for the film franchise—with no official version made distinct. Vidders engage with these canons as well as their own interpretations of the same to produce content for their audiences. As such, vids in this 'verse mirror the manner in which the narratives within the MCU are negotiated by multiple parties, functioning in relation to, yet outside of, the comics canon they draw from, thereby creating their own narrative as a distinct piece of content. The creation of content such as fanvids provides fans (particularly female fans) with access and control to fields of representation, which, as Virginia Kuhn notes, is critical in liberatory politics. The ethos is thus not simply one of passive consumption but one of active engagement; these fans as consumer-producers engage in participatory culture that interprets, extends, or critiques these media sources for an audience of their own.

Working Within and Against Media Cultures

It is important to note that these fanvids are not without their own problems. Both egoscsajszy and reggievass indicate that Romanoff's beginnings in the KGB were the result of kidnapping and extensive indoctrination, the former paralleling it with Loki's brainwashing of Clint Barton and the latter paralleling it with Barnes' brainwashing by Hydra. Loki's depiction as strongly tied to Nazism as well as Dr. Zola's own affiliations with Hydra suggest that the parallel made is one wherein Russian intelligence of the sort that recruited Romanoff is tied to various associations of fundamentalist evil associated with Nazism. And though both incorporate the images and events of *Captain America: The Winter Soldier*, neither choose to capitalize on the parallels the film chose to make between S.H.I.E.L.D.'s infiltration by Hydra and America (and particularly the American military's own increasing power and fundamentalism). As such, the vids evidence a willingness to function within the political framework of the MCU that suggests that Romanoff, as ex-KGB, was likely to be trained at one of the Soviet facilities for young girl spies (much as Dottie Underwood is as per the *Agent Carter* episode "The Iron Ceiling" and as indicated in *Avengers: Age of Ultron* as well as per the revised 2004 comics canon #1–8) before eventually defecting to the American-led S.H.I.E.L.D. Given that this defection is explicitly indicated as Romanoff "going straight" in *Captain America: The Winter Soldier*, the MCU yields an implicit demonization of Russia and its military intelligence while only just beginning to problematize that of the United States, given S.H.I.E.L.D.'s infiltration by Hydra. That the vids repeat this ethos while removing any indication of S.H.I.E.L.D.'s own complicity in neo-imperial American enterprise (as per the film) privileges associations with American morality, suggesting that the makers of these vids and their audiences are far from contesting the socio-political biases within the franchise's portrayal of U.S.-Russian military intelligence activities, and indeed, implicitly endorse this ethos.

Yet it is possible that this endorsement of socio-political ethos likely functions against vidders' calls for a Black Widow film. The events of *Captain America: The Winter Soldier* indicate a shift in the MCU that correlates the growing sense of American neo-colonial fundamentalism with Nazism, though arguably this is performed in favor of rehabilitation of Americana. That is, the "good war" imagery associated with American representation in World War II and the franchise's use of 9/11 symbolism shows that despite the critique evident in the franchise's later stance, the focus is less on decrying these issues and more on separating the "truth" of American values and culture from the growing association of American fundamentalism and militaristic neo-imperialism. José Alaniz notes that the popular conception of superheroes is closely associated with America itself, and superhero iconography is shorthand not only for American popular culture, but also American values (2). The separation of the Avengers that occurs in the aftermath of S.H.I.E.L.D.'s revelation as Hydra-reborn suggests that while the hidden military and those in power may perform neo-imperialism, the American values represented by "true" Americans (and embodied in their superheroes) remains distinct from these.

This repeats much of the comic book ideology evidenced during the Golden Age of comics; as Marco Arnaudo notes, the simplistic propaganda of the comics during World War II saw that

> these characters were easily made into positive, reassuring symbols, intervening in a conflict where the line between good and evil seemed to neatly coincide with nationality (Americans good, Axis bad). At the same time, the close connection with the political system requires the most patriotic heroes to continually monitor the governing bodies and implicitly or explicitly judge their actions [96].

While nationality no longer absolutely indicates good or evil, popular cultural perceptions of current global evils are represented in this frame instead. That is, both *The Avengers* and *Captain America: The Winter Soldier* skew closely to this reading, with Steve Rogers/Captain America plainly and repeatedly stating his discomfort with the wide reach and lack of governing restraint on the American military. In much the same pattern, the *Iron Man* franchise appears to position itself as an internal critique of the capitalism and violent privilege associated with the American "one percent"—though this occurs with limited success, given that the films are largely a critique of American capitalism that itself reinforces American capitalism and the power of the one percent through the character of Tony Stark. It would appear that the franchise's coincidence of "good war" imagery associated with American representation in World War II and its evocation in events following 9/11 alongside this separation of its superheroes from seeming militarism is positioned more in terms of the rehabilitation of the "good war" rather than any true denunciation. As such, given the current state of relations between the United States and Russia (and Russia's own fundamentalism),[4] the creation of a superhero film about an ethnically-Russian female spy within the heart of a franchise so strongly coded with Americana and so closely related to contemporary socio-political issues seems unlikely at best, impossible at worst. By contrast, Carol Danvers/Captain Marvel is easily the safer bet as an American and member of the Air Force, with her 2018 film beginning an arc that will likely act as a narrative bridge to the events of *Inhumans* (2019) as she becomes half-human and half-Kree (as per the Marvel 'verse). If Marvel were to change their current stance and create Black Widow as the titular character of a film at all, it would only occur in the aftermath of the *Avengers* arc (which currently culminates in *Avengers: Infinity War Part 2*, presently scheduled for 2019), nearly nine years after the character was introduced in 2010's *Iron Man 2*.

Additionally, despite the claims of feminism that have begun to be associated with the calls for female-led superhero franchises, many of the fanvids that focus on Black Widow repeat the same pitfalls that concern feminist discourse regarding the depiction of "strong women" in film. That is, in an effort to portray Romanoff's strong, capable potential as an intelligence operative, the clips used tend to favor her ability to fight, which is itself coded as masculine, rather than her more feminine-coded skill at manipulation or infiltration. Indecisive Fangirl's vid "Black Widow/Natasha Romanova Music Video," set to the Iggy Alazea (featuring Rita Ora) song "Black Widow," is essentially a three-minute, seventeen-second montage that collates a number of Romanoff's fight sequences into one narrative frame. The song's repetitive refrain coincides with images of Black Widow fighting a number of assailants, creating a strong link between the sexual theme of the song itself with the physical violence she performs on screen. The vid thus draws on Romanoff's use of the femme fatale persona in her role as an operative for S.H.I.E.L.D., yet the film's portrayal of her skill at information gathering is sidelined in favor of her ability to physically overpower her targets with her use of hand-to hand-combat. By doing so, the vid falls prey to the issue of "strong, female character" that creates a one-dimensional framework within which (1) physical strength is paramount, (2) attractiveness is a necessity, (3) as is the wearing of skin-tight, skimpy, or fetishistic gear, and (4) there are no close female friends or allies which might indicate female interpersonal relationships. The trope of the "strong, female character" thus seemingly offers a symbol of feminism while choosing to undercut values more closely associated with femininity as well as the importance of actual female relationships. This not only forces these characters to solely interact with men, creating a visible hierarchy wherein female-female relationships are absented in favor of male-female relationships, but also uses these "strong, female characters" to indicate certain values in male characters, positioning them through their interaction with these women as seemingly feminist male characters.

It's worth noting that vids that focus solely on the MCU's action sequences featuring Black Widow rarely if ever include clips of conversations between Johansson's character and any other women, despite having access to and/or drawing from Johansson's extensive filmography. Instead, they favor clips wherein she is either shooting or fighting in hand-to-hand combat. As such, this continues to favor a mindset wherein the more masculine attribute of physical strength is favored and women are only heroic or valuable when they conform to this model. In effect, despite attempting to indicate female power in a way that draws attention to the need for female-led films in general and a Black Widow film in particular, these vids recreate certain gendered biases which insist on a single "strong, female character" who rarely if ever interacts with any other women. This is not to say that Romanoff's ability to fight on par with the other, mostly superpowered Avengers isn't worthy of note, but rather that creating it as the sole focus of her character devalues her various other skills—which notably, almost all the other Avengers in the MCU lack.

In effect, women superheroes only achieve the same status as their male counterparts when they perform masculine-coded behavior as Bakedap-pletea's "Black Widow—Do It Like a Dude" suggests. Notably, unlike the Jessie J song that functions as a tongue-in-cheek analysis of male behavior indicating that the singer can perform masculinity despite how ridiculous it might be if it is the price of recognition, the vid appears to be a straight presentation of Romanoff's ability to perform physically. "Do it like a dude" in this case is not simply Romanoff fighting and therefore performing masculinity (as the lyrics make clear), but also beating all opponents in order to make evident her recognition as a member of the Avengers.

In contrast, "One Girl Revolution: Black Widow/Natasha Romanoff" by hisGrLFriday spends at least a third of its time drawing attention to the friendship between Pepper Potts and Romanoff. Drawing clips from the events of *Iron Man 2* and set against Superchick's song "One Girl Revolution (Battle Mix)," the vid is a call for a Black Widow movie that spends a significant amount of time attempting to display an interpersonal relationship between Romanoff and another woman, rather than having the sole focus be her interaction with the men of the MCU or her ability to fight. The sequences which feature Romanoff's interactions with Potts are interspersed throughout the vid so as to indicate a repeated return to this relationship between various assignments. Additionally, given the viewer's likely knowledge of the MCU, this also showcases Romanoff's skills at infiltration as well as her ability to function with ease within the corporate world that would require a specific and highly qualified skill set from her. This is further underlined by the lyrics themselves that indicate strength and hidden depths which should be underestimated at the other character's (and the audience's) own peril. The chorus, that announces Black Widow as a one girl revolution whose voice is yet to be heard, coincides with a deliberate blurring of the video frame in sync with the electric guitar in the background. The use of an artificial effect that normally results from wear after repeated viewings on videotapes suggests not only that these sections of the clip have been repeatedly viewed by the vidder, but draws attention to the importance of these clips. And notably, these sections feature Romanoff's interactions with multiple people (including Potts) as well as her fight scenes; i.e., an interpersonal skill set is evidenced as just as important as her ability to fight.

Conclusion

Regardless of the problematic nature of certain vid portrayals, it remains that these fan responses are revolutionary in the context of a larger media landscape that sidelines female stories in favor of male narratives, and that require that female-led superhero films be justified and demanded in order to become available. Marvel's introduction of *Captain Marvel* as its first female-led film, a whole ten years after the introduction of the MCU and nearly eight years after the calls for a Black Widow female-led film began continues to indicate the dearth of female superhero narratives from an industry that continually claims to be listening to the needs of its fans. Moreover, the studio's decision to play off the creation of a *Captain Marvel* movie against the possibility of a *Black Widow* film clearly outlines the sexist bias that continues to permeate the comic book film industry that would see two female-led superhero films as too much when compared to the sheer number of male-led superhero films within the same franchise. The creation of these vids that not only embrace the myth-building of the MCU, but position Black Widow as a chosen focus, underlines the unwillingness of fans to settle for Marvel's continual sidelining and shadowing of this character. The intense work that comes with sampling Johansson's oeuvre in order to present Romanoff as the focal point of these narrative efforts shows that fans are not only willing to create their own content for audiences hungry for the same, but also highlights the necessity of this material production.

NOTES

1. The Marvel Cinematic Universe is a multimedia adaptation of a shared fictional universe that consists of comics, films, a direct-to-video set of animated films, and, more recently, the TV series *Marvel's Agents of S.H.I.E.L.D.* (2014–present), *Marvel's Agent Carter* (2015–2016), and Marvel's *Daredevil* (2015–present).

2. It is worth noting that the calls for films representing both Captain Marvel and Black Widow focus fannish solidarity and media concentration in a manner that is particularly coded to white American feminism, demanding egalitarian representation in a 'verse that sees few, if any, women of color represented onscreen, let alone women superheroes of color. Although the Marvel 'verse far outstrips the film or television 'verses in terms of its representation of women and/or people of color, that argument has yet to be brought to bear formally on depictions within the big screen adaptations as representation of "women" in these seems to be coded by default to the representation of white women in particular.

3. Although *Avengers: Age of Ultron* had released at the time of this essay, its contents had yet to make their way into fanvids available to view on YouTube.

4. International relations between the U.S. and Russia have suffered particularly in recent years, following Russia's granting of asylum to Edward Snowden, the Ukrainian crisis, and the Syrian Civil War, leading to the possibility of Cold War-esque relations being resumed between the two countries.

Works Consulted

Alaniz, José. *Death, Disability, and the Superhero: The Silver Age and Beyond*. Jackson: University Press of Mississippi, 2014. Print.

Arnaudo, Marco. *The Myth of the Superhero*. Translated by Jamie Richards. Baltimore: John Hopkins University Press, 2013. Print.

Bakedappletea. "Black Widow—Do It Like a Dude." *YouTube*. YouTube, 12 May 2013. Accessed 2 April 2015.

Baker-Whitlaw, Gavia. "Marvel Unceremoniously Snuffs out Female Founding Member of Avengers Team." *The Daily Dot*. The Daily Dot, 30 July 2014. Accessed 22 March 2015.

Berlatsky, Noah. "The Female Thor and the Female Comic Book Reader." *The Atlantic*. The Atlantic Magazine, 21 July 2014. Accessed 2 July 2015.

Booth, Paul. *Digital Fandom: New Media Studies*. New York: Peter Lang, 2010. Print.

Coppa, Francesca. "Women, Star Trek, and the Early Development of Fannish Vidding." *Transformative Works and Cultures* 1 (2008): n. pag. Accessed 28 March 2015.

Dibdin, Emma. "Joss Whedon Criticizes Comic Book Movie Industry for 'Intractable Sexism.'" *Digitalspy*. Hearst Magazines UK, 28 January 2015. Accessed 28 March 2015.

Dockterman, Eliana. "Marvel President Tries to Explain Lack of Female-Superhero Movies." *Time*. Time Inc., 3 August 2014. Accessed 28 March 2015.

egoscsajszy. "Marvel's Black Widow | Fanmade Movie Trailer." *YouTube*. YouTube, 10 June 2014. Accessed 2 April 2015.

Hellekson, Karen, and Kristina Busse, eds. *Fan Fiction and Fan Communities in the Age of the Internet: New Essays*. Jefferson, NC: McFarland, 2006. Print.

hisGrLfriday. "One Girl Revolution: Black Widow/Natasha Romanoff." *YouTube*. YouTube, 11 February 2011. Accessed 5 April 2015.

Indecisive Fangirl. "Black Widow/Natasha Romanova Music Video." *YouTube*. YouTube, 10 August 2014. Accessed 2 April 2015.

Jenkins, Henry. *Convergence Culture: Where Old Media and New Media Collide*. New York: New York University Press, 2006. Print.

Kuhn, Virginia. "The Rhetoric of Remix." *Transformative Works and Cultures* 9 (2012): n. pag. Accessed 28 March 2015.

Lauzen, Martha M. *It's a Man's (Culluloid) World: On Screen Representations of the Female Characters in the Top 100 Films of 2013*. Center for the Study of Women in Television and Film, San Diego State University, 2014. Accessed 24 March 2015.

Lavery, David. *Joss Whedon, A Creative Portrait: From Buffy the Vampire Slayer to Marvel's The Avengers*. London: I. B. Tauris, 2014. Print.

Lewis, Lisa A., ed. *The Adoring Audience: Fan Culture and Popular Media*. Eastbourne, UK: Antony Rowe, Ltd., 2005. eBook.

Massabrook, Nicole. "Why Is Marvel Not Making A 'Black Widow' Movie? Fans Campaign For More Superhero Films After 'Captain Marvel' Announcement." *International Business Times*. IBT Media, 30 October 2014. Accessed 12 April 2015.

McMillan, Graeme. "Could Fandom Shame Marvel Studios Into Being More Diverse?" *The Hollywood Reporter*. Lynne Segall, August 19 2014. Accessed 2 April 2015.

_____. "Warner Bros. and DC Expose Marvel's Achilles Heel: Diversity." *The Hollywood Reporter*. Lynne Segall, 18 October 2014. Accessed 9 April 2015.

Michelle, Kara. "The Making of a Solo Black Widow Movie, Still a Long Wait Ahead for Marvel Fans." *Celebeat*. Celebeat, 5 January 2015. Accessed 9 April 2015.

Misiroglu, Gina Renée, and David A. Roach, eds. *The Superhero Book: The Ultimate Encyclopaedia of Comic-book Icons and Hollywood Heroes.* Canton, MI: Visible Ink Press, 2004. Print.

Murray, Christoper. *Champions of the Oppressed? Superhero Comics, Popular Culture, and Propaganda in America During World War II.* Bristol, UK: Hampton Press, 2011. Print.

Pahle, Rebecca. "Kevin Feige Continues to Say Infuriating Things About a Solo Black Widow Movie, Teases Captain Marvel Instead." *The Mary Sue.* The Mary Sue, 17 March 2014. Accessed 12 April 2015.

reggievass. "Natasha and Bucky—Winter Soldier—I'm Not the One." *YouTube.* YouTube, 4 September 2014. Accessed 2 April 2015.

Riesman, Abraham. "Marvel's Diversity Issue: Screen Output Doesn't Reflect Open-Minded Comics." *Vulture.* New York Media LLC, 9 October 2013. Accessed 12 April 2015.

Schenker, Brett. "Market Research Says 46.67% of Comic Fans are Female." *Comicsbeat.* The Beat, 5 February 2014. Accessed 1 April 2015.

Stevens, E. Charlotte. "Re: Fanvids and Television: History, Pleasure, and Adaptation" (thesis draft). Message to the author. 22 July 2014. Email.

Turk, Tisha, and Joshua Johnson. "Towards an Ecology of Vidding." *Tranformative Works and Cultures* 9 (2012): n. pag. Accessed 5 April 2015.

Tyron, Chuck. *Reinventing Cinema: Movies in the Age of Media Convergence.* New Brunswick: Rutgers University Press, 2009. Print.

"Eyes front, Ivan!"

The Comic Books' Journey through Fashions and Men

VALERIE ESTELLE FRANKEL

When the Black Widow arrives on the scene in 1964, she is hardly an action heroine. In a low-cut emerald dress and alluring veil with more webbing over her cleavage, she bats her eyelashes at her male victims and lures them into traps. Literally everyone she encounters describes her as "beautiful." Upon getting her assignment from her Russian masters—distracting Tony Stark as that comic's villainess—she happily dwells on his good looks and wealth ... clearly "Black Widow" is a reference to her seducing the enemy while wearing furs and jewels, rather than being a killer spider. On the way, she makes a side trip, as she's captivated by a jewelry display. "Cunning and ruthless though she may be, Madame Natasha is a woman ... and as such, she loves pretty things!" the caption by writers Lee and Korok announces (*Tales of Suspense* #53). Still, in her gowns drawn by Don Heck, she goes on to charm Stark, steal his antigravity gun and menace everyone with his creation, rather than one of her own making, until of course, he stops her. On a second encounter, her crocodile tears of repentance earn Tony's forgiveness. She reflects the glamorous playboy on many levels, being as sophisticated and flirtatious as he is.

As she romances Stark, then Hawkeye, acting all the while to save her husband Alexi (until love of Hawkeye causes her to defect against the USSR), her role is tied to romance and men, rather than the independence and power she later develops. As Hawkeye, a circus performer accused of theft, plunges into her getaway car and sees her in an emerald gown adorned with diamonds, he exclaims, "This is *one* dream I don't *ever* want to wake up from," while the caption describes "the daring, dazzling, dangerous *Black Widow!*" (*Tales of Suspense* #57). His desperate love for her makes him her willing pawn.

52

Deep green with furs and diamonds certainly suggests wealth and luxury. Along with money, green is the color of jealousy, one of the Widow's greatest weapons. Included in her wardrobe are a red dress and a black one, all with matching jewelry and elaborate wraps. All are strong colors, uncompromising and powerful, even as she slinks and seduces her way through the masculine world of comics.

Many critics have analyzed excessive femininity as performance, a way of reassuring men by burying aggression, strength, and dominance in sweetness. Psychoanalyst Joan Riviére analyzes this type of disguise in her 1929 essay "Womanliness as Masquerade." She suggests flaunting exaggerated femininity in this manner is a type of mask adopted by a woman "to hide their possession of masculinity and to avert the reprisals expected if she were found to possess it" (38). Any strength must come through lipstick and seduction—this disguise grows so profound that it becomes a definition of femininity in itself.

Soon enough, Natasha's superiors decide, "Lady, you need a costume." In *Tales of Suspense* #64 (1965), she wears a blue skintight suit with a pattern more fishnet than spider web from head to toe, with a black one-piece bathing suit on top. Her blue cape is clasped with a B for Black Widow, but otherwise the outfit isn't particularly iconic. Meanwhile, the bright blue is more anonymous superhero than seductive, and it's a color of peace, serenity, and innocence rather than villainous emerald or black. "Let's face it, even without the cape and its cute monogrammed claps, the costume is still just a wee bit silly, even for the Silver Age of comics," Alan Kistler notes on *The Mary Sue*. Her boots and gloves cling to surfaces, and she sports her weaponized bracelets for the first time. With the new costume, her role changes—she's physically capable of action herself using her gadgetry rather than wheedling men into doing her bidding.

Once again corrupting Hawkeye, she charms him into partnership. However, instead of making him dress like she does, emphasizing his submission, she explains of her own costume, "All that remained was to design a *mask*! And I made one to resemble *yours*, Hawkeye…. For *you* shall again be my partner!" (*Tales of Suspense* #64). They eye each other through identical blue cats-eye slits. In fact, the Russian spy dressing to match a male circus performer indicates she's surrendering power. At the same time, her widow identity becomes more performance than before. It's also unclear what good a normal bow and arrows will do against Iron Man's armor, leaving her plan rather far-fetched and ineffectual.

The Black Widow then leaves *Tales of Suspense* for a villain's role in *The Avengers* #29–30. She continues her seductive skills as she recruits Power Man and the Swordsman as her goons and soon has them fighting over her. Hawkeye too succumbs, thinking, "Even though I *know* she's out to get me,

I can't bear to battle her!" (*The Avengers* #30). Captured by communist leaders and brainwashed so that she forgets her love for Hawkeye, she's revealed as a pawn of the patriarchy once more. "I don't understand it! I know the Avengers are my enemies … and Hawkeye is an Avenger! Yet I cannot get the handsome archer out of my mind!" she thinks in clingy fashion (*The Avengers* #30). In this scene, her costume has been cut down to just a black bathing suit with fishnetting over her arms and chest, with all the bare skin suggesting vulnerability. Her most spiderlike image is the prominent hourglass shape produced by the corset. While she retains blue gloves, cape, belt, and mask, it's an interesting precursor to her black outfit. As she stands vulnerably in her new outfit, she suddenly falls into Hawkeye's arms, crying, "Oh my darling! Did you think I would ever harm you … ever turn *against* you? It was the *Reds!* They *brainwashed* me into betraying you" (*The Avengers* #30). She has shaken the programming off just in time. As Hawkeye campaigns for her to join the Avengers, her dramatic defection from the KGB is inspired by her love for him, another man dictating her life even as she wears a mask that reflects his.

In *The Avengers* #37, Natasha saves the heroes, mostly because unlike them, she's not adverse to killing. Further, unlike telepathic or tricky Marvel women of the Silver Age such as Sue Storm and Jean Gray, Black Widow actually punches people. She shows inner strength, oddly based on her appearance (complete with heavy makeup) rather than gadgets: "Are these the eyes of one who deals in empty words and idle threats?" she asks (*The Avengers* #37). She's gaining power despite her flimsy costume.

Other permutations of her outfit include a mauve grey suit of leotard, fishnets, cape, large gloves, and pointy mask with powder-blue eyeshadow. In *The Avengers* #36–37, she has large "B" earrings and a "W" cape clasp, which are rather silly. Her hair, shorter and longer by turns, is blue-black and generally poofed.

The USSR's new pawn, the Red Guardian, is introduced as the Soviet "counterpart to the accursed Captain America" in *The Avengers* #43. However, as he's garbed in red from head to toe with white belt, boots, and gauntlets, he also reflects Black Widow in her blue. It's soon revealed that he's the Black Widow's husband, Alexi Shostakov, presumed dead. Her backstory indicates that Natasha only joined the KGB after her husband apparently died in a test flight—her entire career has been for the memory of a man. Once again, she comes across as flimsy, tricked and discarded by her country in favor of this more powerful male echo of herself.

After a year's disappearance from the comics, Black Widow returns in *The Avengers* #76 to break up with Hawkeye. Distraught, he protests her reappearing after weeks only to reject him. When he demands a reason, she replies, "Nothing … that I can say! Nothing that won't hurt even more than

Black Widow in an iconic S-shaped pose, designed to showcase her figure. Note the larger than normal breasts and smaller than normal waist. Marvel Comics, *Black Widow and the Marvel Girls*, volume 2, 2010 (editor's collection).

a simple goodbye." She finally says at his insistence that she never loved him, though a tear contradicts her words. This seems like the lazy shorthand that has Captain Marvel running off with the man who impregnated her against her will (also in *The Avengers* comics), much to readers' confusion.

Another image of Black Widow in her iconic S-shaped pose, here wearing a purple skin-tight suit. Marvel Comics, *Black Widow and the Marvel Girls*, volume 1, 2010 (editor's collection).

However, if one takes the Widow's plot arc on faith, one might see her wanting to grow beyond a life of Hawkeye's mission and preferring to quest for her own. Dissatisfied with her dependent, frivolous life, the Widow thus resolves to change.

Beautiful in Black

She dons her trademark skintight black costume in *The Amazing Spider-Man* #86 (July 1970), written by Stan Lee and drawn by John Romita and Jim Mooney, noting, "In order to *erase* every last *vestige* of that past.... I'll begin by designing a new *costume* for myself." She details her entire painful history (problematically, doing so while stripping, and ending in no more than a towel). She washes the black dye from her now blazing long red hair. "I've got to become ... the Black Widow once again," she says. "I've got to do what I do best ... to fulfill my destiny ... to help me forget ... the haunted past!" While she means her husband, the Red Guardian, with this act she throws off his influence and becomes an independent career woman at last.

In the next panel, she dons the tight black outfit, adding, "It may not be as fancy, but this *new* costume will be more in keeping with the *swingy seventies*! ... And with the modern image of the new Black Widow." As she also notes, her costume will "be the envy of my jet set crowd from Jackie [Kennedy] on down!" It's practical, with new wristbands that shoot a "widow's line" wire for swinging, tear gas pellets, and a "widow's bite" electric stinger. She adds a chain belt to hold her "spare web-line" and "the powerlets for my widow's bite." This outfit has no mask, a complication that endangers her secret identity, as she thinks. Still, showing her face suggests a proud statement of purpose, no longer skulking in the shadows.

"At the time, I think this elevated Black Widow to the level of icon," says Nathan Edmondson, the writer behind the current *Black Widow* series. "The suit was like an invitation, a uniform offered to the character as she was escorted into the halls of fame—or infamy, as the case may be. Comics are a medium—and isn't all of storytelling?—that is built upon iconography, and that means, for super heroes, a suit" (qtd. in White). Certainly, this is basically the suit she wears today. In an interview with Matt Blum, Scarlett Johansson notes of the outfit:

It's totally empowering because once you get on the belt and the gloves and the bracelets and your guns and the boots, it looks great. It's bad-ass! And when I have my legs wrapped around some giant stunt guy's head, and feel totally ridiculous hanging on for dear life ... it sells it. [The costume] totally sells things that would otherwise look absolutely absurd. It changes the way you stand; it changes your posture. You're more aware of your body, obviously. I think when you walk on the set everybody's like, yeah, it's the Widow: looks good. I've grown to love it. First, I was terrified of it; and now I embrace it because it embraces me, actually.

Comic book costumes are expressions of purpose. They emphasize that one has powers and plans to use them. Symbolically, black is dramatic, bold, mysterious. It's the color of sadness and isolation as well as toughness, indicating the superspy, spider, widow, and action heroine. Meanwhile, red hair symbolizes uniqueness, sexual freedom, a brazen personality, and a touch of magic. Her lack of a mask is also brazen, yet open and vulnerable.

The comic known for her transformation has a problematic storyline. As a returning villain, she arrogantly declares she will attack Spider-Man to "prove myself his equal or learn the reason why!" (while readers certainly rolled their eyes in disbelief). Her costume suggests reflection, rather than a unique identity, as she invents web-slinging gadgets to mimic Spider-Man's powers. "No matter *how* effective my powers may be … they're just like a female *imitation* of the original wall-crawling, web shooting *Spider-Man*,"

Black Widow with some of her gadgets. Marvel Comics, *The Amazing Spider-man,* **1986 (editor's collection).**

she declares of herself, emphasizing her flimsiness as a web-slinging super-hero (*The Amazing Spider-Man* #86). Although she loses the battle to become Spider-Man, she is beginning to establish an identity.

In fact, Spider-Man, weakened as he is, toys with her, and she finally realizes she cannot win. In this appearance, she is merely a subplot for Spider-Man, who's worried that he is becoming human—a more significant storyline. In *Marvel Team Up* #82–85, she admits an attraction to Spider-Man, further emphasizing her fickleness. Each time she appears, her every act is to ensnare men with her beauty or imitate their powers in a far-weaker copy.

This contradictory storyline of strength and weakness was appearing onscreen around this time in television about sexy action women like *Wonder Woman* and those in *Charlie's Angels*, as well as *The Avengers'* Emma Peel. According to Jennifer K. Stuller:

> Television series in the mid-to-late 1970s attempted to capitalize on the feminist move-ment, and several shows featured women in genre roles that were strong in spirit, if stereo-typically feminine in appearance. This meant devising a way to appeal to the changing social consciousness of women viewers while not alienating men. The solution was the Kick-Ass Babe—a talented and capable woman whose beauty deflected the focus from her otherwise transgressive acts. Women could identify with—or aspire to be—these lovely ladies, while men would not be threatened by depiction of female independence, as they would instead be focused on the eye candy [44].

The Widow's black suit echoes Emma Peel and Modesty Blaise, popular British adventuresses in it for thrills as well. The costume is sleek and prac-tical, as well as sophisticated. It has no symbols, but as the heroine rejects the KGB and the Avengers to follow her own path, this makes strong sense. With the sleek black suit comes power and brazen independence: "Black Widow was a thrill seeker who chose the life of a crime fighter for the excite-ment it brought her. She didn't do it to aid a boyfriend, didn't hide behind a wallflower alter ego, and lived her life with a freedom usually reserved for men" (Madrid 156). She became, however, more seductive than ever.

She ends the comic by removing her black outfit for a sleek pink robe, dismissing her quest for Spider-Man's powers and noting, "I have my own unusual powers, my own style of combat, and my own strange destiny to ful-fill! So whatever dangers lie ahead.... I'll face them my way ... as the *Black Widow!*" (*The Amazing Spider-Man* #86).

Immediately, Black Widow gained her own series in *Amazing Adventures* #1 (1970), written by Gary Friedrich and drawn by John Buscema. By co-headlining *Amazing Adventures* with the Inhumans, Black Widow became the first female Marvel superhero with her own ongoing monthly series. The story also served to make her an independent hero. According to Brett White, author of "Marvel Women of the Seventies: Black Widow":

Black Widow in her black leather suit, holding a gun. Marvel Comics, *Marvel's The Avengers: Black Widow Strikes* #3, 2012 (editor's collection).

In *Amazing Adventures,* Black Widow became a defender of the persecuted, descending from her penthouse above the East River to mix it up with lowlifes, mobsters, and corrupt police officers on behalf of hippies and wayward teenagers. As the lead character in her own ongoing adventures, the Widow gained a level of competence and expertise rarely afforded to guest stars. She even gained a supporting cast of her own in Ivan, her confidant and driver. It's here in these issues that Black Widow goes from being a femme fatale to a force of nature by combining her new weapons with an updated and ferocious fighting style.

As she begins her story curled up in something of a hot pink harem outfit with poofy pants and large jewelry, "Madame Natasha," an "international jet-setter" in a "luxurious penthouse," decides to become a superhero. The jet setter in *Amazing Adventure* has a penthouse pad, chauffeur, maid, "and swinging parties with playboys, princes, and Jackie O. The strips were sharp, hip, and beautifully drawn" (Roach 86).

She becomes a wealthy do-gooder, independent of a man. She goes on missions—though her constantly changing clothes in the car, with a tagline of "Eyes front, Ivan!" reduces her to cheesecake. Readers, while voyeuristically watching this, also get to see her in bed, cuddled in expensive lingerie, or all dressed up for a date. As with her earliest appearances, she appears more seductress than superhero. *Amazing Adventures* #5, a Christmas issue written by Roy Thomas, shows her naked with flapping towel, as she makes her spy plans. "From here on out each issue of *Amazing Adventures* has at least a few panels dedicated to Natasha suiting up, undressing, or showering in an effort to entertain the pre-teen and teenage male demographic" (Paula).

During her adventures, the Black Widow begins to wonder if she is cursed, as all men who get close to her die, a worry seen often through the Bronze Age and the early 90s, a phenomenon referred to as the "Widow's Curse." Her obsession with her relationships with men is once more weakening her. Nonetheless, she keeps her costume and becomes a savior of the persecuted around her. "When her amazing adventures came to an end after eight issues, Black Widow had irreversibly transformed into the powerhouse character we now see today in comics, cartoons, and films," says White.

Daredevil's Girlfriend

She returns in *Daredevil* #81 (November 1971), introduced by the time-traveling android Mr. Kline with the words, "I've brought the woman called *Black Widow* into the plan ... hopefully some sort of *romantic entanglement* may be *precipitated*." As Kline directs her action as femme fatale and love object, she's once more a pawn—and a romantic pawn at that. She dives into the action, long legs flashing in new black spandex—and saves Daredevil (Matt Murdock) from a watery grave.

True, she saves Daredevil's life. But this time her black outfit's so tight that it seems indecent and salacious, even for comics. The issue ends with "the first in a *series* of pulse-pounding pin-ups" by Bill Everett, as it's labeled, with "the beauteous Black Widow" leaping, one leg outstretched, every muscle of her stomach and legs prominent through the painted-on suit (*Daredevil #81*).

Ironically, Daredevil objectifies Natasha less than others—because he can't see her. When she first rescues him from a watery doom, all he perceives is "a looming, blurred figure" rendered to the audience as only a pale blue burst. She in turn guesses, "He must have seen me—recognized me ... unless? Of course, dear Mister *Daredevil* must be ashamed—ashamed to owe his *life* to a *woman*." Off she goes, with another "Eyes front, Ivan" as she changes her wet clothes in the backseat.

While Daredevil is recovering, a bank robbery begins, and Ivan tells Natasha, "Time to play *Gypsy Rose*, Sweetheart." She leaps into the fray, quipping, "We countesses get *around* now days" and "Manhandling little ladies just isn't *in* your *Emily Post*." All she does is performance, often related to these weaker feminine roles. As Daredevil charges into the fight, he makes similar quips on Natasha's behalf, noting, "Since when is it good form to play hockey with a lady's little rounded *head* as a slightly-rounded *puck*?"

Daredevil, having saved the day, collapses, and Natasha thinks, "Don't look too closely at him.... Please—remember that *curse*—and be *careful* ... not to care." Thus she appears so weak-willed that she'll fall for the masked hero even with everything she knows about her ability to have relationships. As she panics about loving another man and thus leading him to his doom, she loses independence. She remains a recurring guest in *Daredevil* comics as he's torn between her and the good girl Karen Page. Natasha, more sidekick than partner, alternates between needing rescuing to being forcefully excluded from fights by a disturbingly paternalistic Murdock.

In #87, Daredevil and the Black Widow become the first major Marvel characters to move outside of the New York City area—specifically, to San Francisco—and the first couple to move in together, though admittedly on different floors of their shared mansion. Daredevil stays in San Francisco until *Daredevil* #109, Black Widow until *Daredevil* #120. Their romantic relationship—superhero and bad girl—is highlighted here, leaving Black Widow in the role of seductress once again, at least on a symbolic level.

Around this time, series writer Gerry Conway was alerted that the comic was coming across as sexist, and he decided to make changes. In *Daredevil* #91, Black Widow complains of Daredevil taking her for granted, ignoring her thoughts and feelings as he fails to ever thank her or consider her wishes. Angry that he doesn't feel their relationship is equal, she storms out, only to smile in surprised delight when several women on the street describe her glowingly as "The Gloria Steinem of the jump-suit set." She is not just Daredevil's sidekick, but at last a superheroine icon.

> In the 8 years we've followed Natasha so far she's been a lot of things: a villain, a love interest, a hero, a femme fatale, a partner … now for the first time she is explicitly presented as a role model for women to look up to. She's her own character, not just a side-character in male heroes' stories, and Conway is sending that message loud and clear. Now, whether or not Marvel adheres to this idea from now on is pretty variable, but this issue is certainly a bright spot in the bronze age of Black Widow [Paula].

From issues #92 through #107, the cover logo was retitled *Daredevil and the Black Widow,* and many recall this as an equal partnership. For example, David Roach explains, "Daredevil and the Black Widow were a good combination: two sleek, elegant figures swinging gracefully through the night sky of San Francisco; this period of the comic is fondly remembered for its sophistication" (86).

Black Widow officially joins the Avengers again in *The Avengers* #111, written by Steve Englehart and drawn by Don Heck. However, she only stays for one issue, *The Avengers* #112, until she misses Matt Murdock and returns in *Daredevil and the Black Widow* #101. On their dual adventures, her frequent insistence that Daredevil hold her comes out as less affectionate and more fainting female. Her black outfit remains, though she occasionally covers it with "street clothes" of a beige trench coat, de-sexing her, instead letting her emotions take center stage.

In #120, he tells her, "Why don't you slip into something barely legal? I want my date to be the most gorgeous thing at the party!" He even spanks her as she calls him a chauvinist in disgust. Certainly, if the writers are trying to make him appear a caveman, they succeed. Natasha obediently dons a low-cut yellow gown and rather bitterly enters the party on his arm. However, as he privately smirks that "I think our horseplay before has lifted Tasha's spirits," she prepares to leave him.

Despite the retitling, she ends the relationship in *Daredevil* #124 (July 1975), fearing that playing "sidekick" is sublimating her identity. "It felt *good—* being the Black Widow again, and not just Daredevil's *partner.* I'd almost forgotten *how* good. I can't give that up *again,* Matt…. I just *can't.*" Based on their interactions, she appears to be right. Ivan arrives and she hops into his backseat once more. Natasha returns for a short run in 1978–1980 (#155–165) and attempts to rekindle her romance with Daredevil. In #158, she rushes off to defend her hero in a loose green dress with kimono sleeves and strappy sandals, hair in giant red ponytails. High kicks and summersaults let readers see a good way up her skirts as she obsesses over her widow's curse. In #161, the villain Bullseye literally ties her to the tracks of a roller coaster, or at least substitutes a Natasha-dummy that doesn't fool Matt's super senses. In #165, she lounges in Matt's office in a green wrap dress cut down nearly to her navel with the hem at her thighs—this may actually be a bathrobe, but either way she appears more Girl Friday than superhero.

Nonetheless, Daredevil ultimately rejects her in favor of fragile good girl Heather Glenn. "Heather needs me. I'm going alone," he says when his love is in danger, possibly because Natasha's hardly serious-looking in that outfit. Matt adds that he and Black Widow are no longer even a team, just "friends" (*Daredevil* #165). Natasha follows him nonetheless and arrives just in time to see Heather whimpering "Don't leave me," as Matt rescues and kisses her. "It wasn't difficult to find you … but it's so very hard to lose you. Goodbye, Matt, and good luck," Natasha thinks (*Daredevil* #165).

Returning to visit Daredevil much later in 2004's *Daredevil: The Man Without Fear: The Widow* (written by Brian Michael Bendis and drawn by Alex Maleev), she appears in numerous cover art pieces, all of them with a jutting rear end or skintight outfit unzipped to her navel. She arrives in his apartment in a burst of henna and "oils you can't buy in America" along with the sound of her "naked skin sliding between the top and bottom silk sheets and right into my bed" as Daredevil thinks. He reflects that when he was younger, he'd dreamed about events like this one. When he enters the room, she's curled up in his bed, only a fishnet stocking and bra strap visible beyond the concealing sheet. Daredevil's first thought is that Nick Fury's sent her to mess with his head. In fact, the government of Bulgaria has offered to exchange her for Madame Hydra, and the Widow is now in hiding. Throughout the story, as numerous assassins prey on her and Daredevil, they all stare at Natasha (often through an assassin's scope) and call her "the smoking hot hottie."

Natasha in turn is literally setting herself up as a spectacle, making sure she's seen alongside Daredevil in the headlines. At one point, nine thugs enter Daredevil's apartment to find Natasha in a towel, which she drops to her waist, teasing the men in French. As they stare with gaping smiles, she calls them "very ugly" and "more stupid than they are ugly." Waiting some distance away, Daredevil thinks, "Gentlemen, you are being screwed with by a world-class superspy whose *expertise* is screwing around with guys just like you …" When the police arrive, she sobs for help. Even they call her "one piece of woman" and sympathize that Matt Murdock is blind. Fury texts Natasha that the pair must play sitting ducks and they do—this time while observed through a long range scope focused carefully on her cleavage. Natasha blows the villains a kiss, observing them as they do her.

She ends the story discovering that the Red Guardian, her ex-husband who was thought to be dead, is (once again) behind the attempts to capture or kill her. He has created a secret stronghold for himself and amassed money and power. Nonetheless, his obsession with Natasha is such that he risks (and loses!) it all only to attack her. The Avengers arrive and take him out.

Leading the Champions

Having lost her mysterious source of funds (and tired of living off Daredevil) Natasha applies to teach Russian at UCLA, a short plaid skirt or plaid vest changing her black jumpsuit into something marginally more professional. As such, she adds a bit of secret identity to her ordinary life as college teacher, in contrast to her supervillainess mask. The other team members who call themselves The Champions are Iceman, Angel, Hercules, and Ghost Rider, with Darkstar joining later as a second female. After the team assembles and fights mythic monsters, #3 ends with Natasha sprawled by the pool in a black bikini and big gold earrings … with Angel beside her in only a speedo. She's objectified, but she's not the only one. The Champions actually appoint Natasha team leader, and they all face her and Ivan's own villains (such as Crimson Dynamo, who is really Yuri Petrovitch, Ivan's son). Natasha has (limited) arcs with the other characters as Darkstar's reformed villain arc mirrors her own, and Johnny Blaze keeps making sexist remarks she must combat. Hercules flirts with Natasha, but they're always interrupted just as things get romantic. Finally with Darkstar's protest "We are too *disparate* a group to remain *united* for long!" they break up after only sixteen issues.

Natasha and Hercules join the Avengers together in the middle of the epic Korvac saga during *The Avengers* #173 (written by Jim Shooter and David Michelinie, and drawn by Sal Buscema). As Hercules postures before party guests and mentions that humans (even Natasha) live in only a blink to his immortal self, trouble blooms in paradise.

Suddenly, a murderous (and externally controlled) Daredevil arrives and tries to strangle Black Widow who begs, "Please! You're hurting me." This is a metaphor for their strained and painful relationship. Soon enough, however, they're kissing, and Hercules takes a hint and leaves. Matt turns down Black Widow in favor of Heather Glenn once more, and then accidentally asks them both out on the same night, revealing his dismissive feelings towards the heroine. She waits angrily to confront him in a buttoned pale green dress that resembles a shapeless bathrobe—the least sexual costume she's possibly ever worn.

While working with S.H.I.E.L.D., Black Widow is briefly captured by Hydra and regresses to her old cover identity of teacher Nancy Rushman. Spider-Man discovers her and tries to help. As the clingy heroine is rescued by a man, she develops a crush … at least as Nancy. Spider Man, on discovering Black Widow's costume in her purse, urges her to try the costume on to trigger her memory. It doesn't. In the end, Natasha is left wondering if maybe she would have been better off being Nancy Rushman forever, because as the superheroine, she's doomed to be eternally alone.

Eighties and Onwards

Her visit to *Daredevil* #187 in 1982 "under the aegis of *enfant terrible* Frank Miller, led to a harsh, 1980-style makeover, replacing the widow's flowing locks with a spiky buzz-cut and sacrificing her hipster belt and groovy bracelets for a grey leotard" (Roach 87). This is a more punk outfit, complete with disco collar on her jumpsuit, but she appears less sophisticated, and more like a mechanic or disco clubber than superheroine with flowing red hair. She's more masculine, and certainly more understated. This uniform is decorated by two spider symbols, a large one on the back and another over her heart, which are reminiscent of Spider-Man, not independence. Thick, slatted yellow bracelets stand out on her wrists, but don't appear particularly superpowered. A high belt with pouches and a jacket likewise do little to dress this up. Symbolically, she's grey—caught between light and dark, the USSR and the U.S., heroism and villainy, in a world that, *Watchman*-style, is starting to question the value and morality of superheroes.

While visiting Daredevil, Natasha has the opportunity to meet Heather. With a magenta blazer and sky blue skirt over stockings and heels, blonde Heather is Natasha's polar opposite. She's also a bad relationship focus for Matt, as she staggers in drunk and tells him, "Love it when you tell me what to do" (*Daredevil* #188). Meanwhile in *The Avengers* #239, Natasha meets Hawkeye's new wife, Mockingbird. She wears a grey-blue jumpsuit that reflects Natasha's, only differentiated by white trim, bell bottoms, and a plunging neckline. Mockingbird also has a pointy black and white mask mirroring Hawkeye's and long blonde hair. Pink is a sexual color, while masks suggest concealment and mystery. Blue for both is a sign of innocence and peace, unlike raging Natasha. While Natasha is polite to Mockingbird, her mirror image, she schemes to break up Daredevil and the girlish Heather—a scheme that succeeds.

Follow-up appearances include respectful art from George Pérez (also famed for a sympathetic and empowered Wonder Woman) and some amount of cheesecake from artists Bob Layton and Luke McDonnell as she changes clothes in a four-issue limited run in the anthology comic *Marvel Fanfare* (1983). In *Alpha Flight*, she works with the Avengers. Her cover poses are worthy of the Hawkeye Initiative; with her grey suit she wears more clothing than the other women combined. Likewise, *Marvel Graphic Novel* #61 "The Coldest War" by Gerry Conway and George Freeman has disturbing nudity. She then becomes a sidekick for Iron Man, starting with *Iron Man* #269 by John Byrne and Paul Ryan, which appears to require her waking in her penthouse, naked in bed, followed by changing and exercising. "While superwomen of the 1970s had at the very last represented a restrained progressiveness, most of their followers in the 1980s (with the exception of a notable few) further exaggerated perceived contradictions between femininity and feminism" (Stuller 54). Thus the Widow alternated between power and camp, emphasizing her independence while seducing her male audience.

In *Daredevil* #236 Ann Nocenti and Barry Windsor-Smith portray her sympathetically, as she works in a man's clubhouse and must deal with their sexist quips about how she "used to tumble with that spandex exhibitionist, Daredevil," call her assignment "women's work," and speculate her "little heart" will take over and she'll fall for him. Black Widow silently takes the criticism to maintain her cover. In a plain white shirt with blue skirt and red belt, she's more ordinary than ever, giving a nod to everyday women without superpowers or stand-out costumes who must deal with this heckling while in a man's world (rather like Nocenti herself).

Natasha's Flashbacks

Uncanny X-Men #268, penned by Chris Claremont and drawn by Jim Lee, tells a flashback story of young Natasha being kidnapped by Nazis to be trained as an assassin by the Hand. Alpha males Captain America and Wolverine team up to save her. Cap insists she's "just a kid!" and indeed, her student robes are bright red and then pink, enveloping her to the point of swaddling. Her eyes are large, with hair short and tussled. Despite her youth, she's made a master assassin for the Hand, even as Cap protests.

In the present, Natasha sees Wolverine and faints into his arms, butt hanging out in her tight grey jumpsuit. She awakens in bed, in a set of green pastel frilly underwear as Logan tells her, "I took the precaution of removin' your widow's bit, Tash, when I put you to bed." Even if she was already wearing frilly underwear, it seems the creators felt the need for Wolverine to strip Black Widow in the story. Jubilee, spying through the window and emphasizing that viewers too should be watching the undressed Widow, asks, "Is it like my imagination … or is every old buddy Wolvie's got in the whole world … some incredibly fabulously gorgeous *babe*?!" Natasha touchingly calls Logan her "Little Uncle," but the outfit they've stuck her in—to say nothing of her rescue by the all-masculine Wolverine—casts doubt on this relationship, while he calls her the condescending "princess." She's soon undercover in a black minidress, incredibly short and low-cut. Once again, she's been reduced to scantily-dressed sidekick.

Back in Black

After a few years, she was back in black, but often in a suit so tight, with features so augmented, that her breasts jutted out like shiny balloons nearly the size of her head. She resumed her gold utility belt but this time put it around her thigh instead of her waist, a popular style for superheroes of the nineties. For a brief time, the suit was navy blue with eight red stripes around the abdomen, for a blatant spider costume, though this was quickly discarded.

Her return to black coincided with the girl power era, itself ambiguously empowering. Susan J. Douglas writes,

> The warrior women in thongs insisted that females could, and should, combine force and aggression with femininity and sexual display. On the one hand, this was welcome, given how often our culture emphasizes that female sexuality is dangerous and shameful. On the other hand, they reaffirmed the sexual objectification of women and girls, and suggested women could be as strong as any man as long as they were poreless, stacked, and a size two [99].

The action hero of this time was powerful, but her exaggerated sexiness was problematic. "No matter how strong we got, it was more important to be slim and beautiful and to know how to deploy femininity as a weapon" (Douglas 99). The Widow was the perfect image.

Around the twenty-first century, she resumed the seventies outfit but lowered or unzipped the neckline, sometimes all the way below her breasts to reveal an impractical amount of skin for actual combat or for being taken seriously. "How much she zips the costume up seems to depend more on the artist than the actual temperature and weather she's experiencing," Kistler smirks. Often this costume actually shines as if it were made of latex or rubber. The belt has a clear red hourglass on the buckle, a much subtler touch for a spy than some of her spider symbols.

Retrospective

The comic collection *Black Widow: Deadly Origin* (2009–2010) written by Paul Cornell, with art by Tom Raney and John Paul Leon, takes the Widow on flashbacks through all these events of her life, back to her childhood with Ivan and first meeting with Tony Stark. She's been infected with nanites that she's spread to everyone she's touched through her long life so she must go see Hawkeye, Daredevil, Hercules, and all the others while reflecting on their earlier encounters.

As a child in flashbacks she wears a grey military coat to match Ivan's. In training she wears a concealing military uniform, her hair cropped short. She spars with "Uncle" Wolverine in an identical gi. Each time her clothes are modest, masculine and concealing, emphasizing her mirroring of each patriarchal mentor figure.

Chatting with Alexi before their arranged marriage, Natasha wears a military uniform once more, emphasizing duty and matter-of-fact following orders rather than seduction or romance. As Alexi asks about her life, she's caught between parallel stories: She is a ballerina with fake parents on the one side but a Black Widow and spy on the other side … and dating the Winter Soldier. She has two ages—seventeen and twenty-nine, as she's already taken the life-prolonging drugs. As she tells Ivan, the one constant in her life, "I can't tell *what's* true anymore." She's fragmented, split, as shown by her dialog.

The story retcons her appearance, making her dress more modestly through her adventures than actually happened, thus giving the character some dignity. Identity and her personal journey take center stage. As she dates Tony Stark as widow and femme fatale in an elegant black dress, he notes, "I like you a great deal, Natasha, but you don't know who you are." She's a paid contractor messing with superheroes on behalf of others. As Hawkeye attacks Tony out of jealousy, Ivan, her constant companion, asks her, "When will you find someone *whole* to be?"

In the modern scenes, she wears different outfits, blending in as a spy actually should. She has her widow's outfit remade in white to sneak around in the snow. For plain clothes she wears a leather jacket and modest blue turtleneck. She sleeps in a t-shirt (for once). However, her body is beyond her control, as a less empowering trope. The nanites have made her a "poisoned woman" and a tool of others. As she notes, "They made me into my code name. They made me filthy." Promptly, one of the men nearby asks her not to say such a sexist thing about herself, as he plays something of an author stand-in.

As the nanites spread among her friends, she dramatically bursts in on Hawkeye and Bobbi Morse, stopping Bobbi from killing him in nanite-infected rage by kissing her to transfer the antidote. Though the moment is a bit salacious, Widow undercuts it after, noting, "Touching her with my palm would have done it too. Like this." She touches her ex. "But why do we wear these costumes if not for *theater*?" Apparently she sees her black suit as a persona much as her emerald gown once was.

The mastermind is finally revealed as her beloved life companion Ivan, who spent all the intervening years loving her but watching her fall for idiotic young superheroes instead of him. As she tells him sadly in response, "Ivan, I realized years ago, I finally became one whole person only when you left." His expectations throughout her life have pushed her as much as all the men who molded her, until only by casting off this lifelong companion can she choose her own path. She can have an identity, but only without the outfits, chauffeur, and other trappings meant for others.

Conclusion

What's kept Black Widow so popular through 40 years at Marvel? Nathan Edmondson (qtd. in White) has a theory:

> Black Widow is an icon whose identity is so strong and intriguing in a basic, archetypal way that she has transcended multiple eras and speaks to longtime fans and new readers. She is exactly what comics are built on—iconic characters who promise to be continually worthwhile.

Through all her identities, she's retained a charm and sense of purpose, though each era of feminism has her dressing (and undressing!) to seduce and charm as well as imitate the men in her life. Up through the present, Ms. Romanova kicks butt in her black outfit alongside the male heroes. Yet in her there remain echoes of the past, in the seductive outfits that mark her as more femme than fatale.

WORKS CONSULTED

Bendis (w), Brian Michael, and Alex Maleev (i). *Daredevil Vol. 10: The Widow*. New York: Marvel Comics, 2004. Print.

Byrne John, et al. *Iron Man #269, #271–273. Iron Man Epic Collection. Volume 16, 1990–1992: War Games*. New York: Marvel Worldwide Inc., 2014. Print.

Claremont, Chris, and Sal Buscema. *Marvel Team Up #82–85*. New York: Marvel, 1979. Print.

Claremont, Chris (w), and Jim Lee (i). *Uncanny X-Men #268*. New York: Marvel, 1990. Marvel Unlimited. Marvel.com. Accessed 12 July 2015.

Conway, Gerry (w), and Gene Colan (i). *Daredevil #81 (Nov 1971). Black Widow: The Sting of the Widow* . Ed. Jennifer Grunwald. New York: Marvel, 2009. Print.

Conway, Gerry (w), and Gene Colan (i). *Daredevil #87*. New York: Marvel, 1972. Print.

Conway, Gerry (w), and Gene Colan (i). *Daredevil #91*. New York: Marvel, 1972. Print.

Conway, Gerry (w), and George Freeman (i). "The Coldest War" (1992). *Black Widow: Web of Intrigue*. Ed. Jennifer Grunwald. New York: Marvel, 2010. Print.

Cornell, Paul (w), Tom Raney, and John Paul Leon (i). *Black Widow: Deadly Origin*. New York: Marvel Worldwide, 2010. Print.

Englehart, Steve (w), and Don Heck (i). *The Avengers #111*. New York: Marvel, 1973. Marvel Unlimited. Marvel.com. Accessed 12 July 2015.

Englehart, Steve (w), and Don Heck (i). *The Avengers #112*. New York: Marvel, 1973. Marvel Unlimited. Marvel.com. Accessed 12 July 2015.

Gerber, Steve (w), and Bob Brown (i). *Daredevil #109*. New York: Marvel, 1974. Print.

Gerber, Steve (w), and Rich Buckler (i). *Daredevil and the Black Widow #101*. New York: Marvel, 1973. Print.

Isabella, Tony (w), and Bob Brown (i). *Daredevil #120*. New York: Marvel, 1975. Print.

Isabella, Tony, Bill Mantlo (w), and George Tuska (i). *Champions #3*. New York: Marvel, 1976. Marvel Unlimited. Marvel.com. Accessed 12 July 2015.

Kirby, Jack. *Amazing Adventures #1–8 (Aug 1970—Sept 1971). Black Widow: The Sting of the Widow* . Ed. Jennifer Grunwald. New York: Marvel, 2009. Print.

Lee, Stan (w), and Don Heck (i). *The Avengers #29–30. Essential Avengers*. Vol. 2. New York: Marvel Worldwide, 2000. Print.

Lee, Stan (w), and Don Heck (i). *Tales of Suspense* #64. New York: Marvel, 1965. Marvel Unlimited. Marvel.com. Accessed 12 July 2015.

Lee, Stan, N. Korok (w), and Don Heck (i). *Tales of Suspense* #53 (April 1964). *Black Widow: The Sting of the Widow* . Ed. Jennifer Grunwald. New York: Marvel, 2009. Print.

Lee, Stan (w), and John Romita, Sr. (i). *The Amazing Spider-Man* #86 (July 1970). *Black Widow: The Sting of the Widow.* Ed. Jennifer Grunwald. New York: Marvel, 2009. Print.

Lieber, Larry. *Tales of Suspense* #57. New York: Marvel, 1964. Marvel Unlimited. Marvel.com. Accessed 12 July 2015.

Miller, Frank, et al. *Daredevil* #158–161 and 163–167 (1979–1980). *Daredevil Visionaries: Frank Miller, Vol. 1.* New York: Marvel Comics, 2000. Print.

Miller, Frank (w), and Klaus Janson (i). *Daredevil* #187–190 (1982). *Daredevil Visionaries: Frank Miller, Vol. 3.* New York: Marvel Unlimited, 2001. Print.

Nocenti, Ann (w), and Barry Windsor-Smith (i). *Daredevil* #236. New York: Marvel, 1986. Print.

Pérez, George, et al. *Marvel Fanfare* #10–12. (1983–1984). *Black Widow: Web of Intrigue.* Ed. Jennifer Grunwald. New York: Marvel, 2010. Print.

Shooter, Jim, David Michelinie (w), and Sal Buscema (i). *The Avengers* Vol. 1 #173. New York: Marvel, 1978. Print.

Stern, Roger (w), and Al Milgrom (i). *The Avengers* Vol. 1 #239. New York: Marvel, 1984. Print.

Thomas, Roy, and Don Heck. *The Avengers* Vol. 1 #36–37 (1967). *Essential Avengers.* Vol. 2. New York: Marvel Worldwide, 2000. Print.

Thomas, Roy, and George Bell. *The Avengers* Vol. 1 #43 (1967). *Essential Avengers.* Vol. 2. New York: Marvel Worldwide, 2000. Print.

Thomas, Roy, and John Buscema. *The Avengers* Vol. 1 #76. New York: Marvel, 1970. Marvel Unlimited. Marvel.com. Accessed 12 July 2015.

Wein, Len (w), and Gene Colan (i). *Daredevil* #124. New York: Marvel, 1975. Print.

Secondary Sources

Blum, Matt. "Scarlett Johansson on Black Widow's Character Evolution, Solo Movie Chances, and Kicking Ass in The *Winter Soldier." Geek Dad.* 3 April 2014. Accessed 12 July 2015. Print.

Douglas, Susan J. *Enlightened Sexism.* New York: Henry Holt and Co., 2010. Print.

Kistler, Alan. "Agent of S.T.Y.L.E.—Black Widow Keeps It Classy." *The Mary Sue.* The Mary Sue. 16 January 2014. Accessed 12 July 2015.

Madrid, Mike. *The Supergirls: Fashion, Feminism, Fantasy, and the History of Comic Book Heroines.* Exterminating Angel Press, 2009. Print.

Paula. "Women in Marvel." Women in Marvel (tumblr). N. dat., n. pag. Accessed 12 July 2015.

Riviére, Joan. "Womanliness as Masquerade." *Formations of Fantasy.* Eds. Victor Burgin, James Donald, and Cora Kaplan. London: Methuen, 1986. Print.

Roach, David. "Black Widow." *The Superhero Book.* Ed. Gina Misiroglu with David A. Roach. Canton, MI: Visible Ink Press, 2004. 86–87. Print.

Stuller, Jennifer K. *Ink-Stained Amazons and Cinematic Warriors.* New York: I. B. Tauris, 2010. Print.

White, Brett. "Marvel Women of the Seventies: Black Widow." Marvel.com. Marvel. 7 July 2014. Accessed 12 July 2015.

Feminism in American Cinema
The Many Incarnations
of Black Widow

Jillian Coleman Benjamin

The emergence of superhero movies as a recent trend in American cinema is exciting for comic book enthusiasts. However, many feminist fans of such media experience an undercurrent of apprehension, which shrouds the excitement accompanying the new release of even the best-loved characters. I can see the potential for both delight and disaster when I read a newly released comic, see a movie, or even view advertisements containing the characters I enjoy, which creates a splintering of feelings that dilutes my viewing experience. This apprehension stems from representation of female characters as heroes being presented as such a mixed bag. Black Widow is an example of this; her representation is as wildly varying as political opinions are. She is a character who struggles with feminist ideology much as the people in the United States have, with some writers portraying her as intelligent, assertive, and challenging gender norms, while others have treated her more as an object to be saved or as an obstruction or conquest to be defeated. Each generation struggles with its own selection of prejudices and how they are manifested. Black Widow, like many comic book characters, makes for an interesting study in that they have been popular amongst many different generations, and we can see how such prejudices have manifested in the creation and recreation of the same character. This, combined with the fact that modern American cinema is already notorious for its one-dimensional representations of the female gender, causes that ever present veil to thicken.

Exposure to problematic representations of female characters who work more as props than as people—and the ever more disturbing fact that many viewers do not even notice, let alone expect any better—force me to cling to this shroud of apprehension, hoping that I don't have to have a lengthy debate about feminism every time I leave the movie theater or put down a newly released comic book. Along with many other feminists, I am told that "we are never happy" when exposed to a new work, but this criticism is far from fair. What many feminists demand is a higher caliber of writing from our sources of entertainment. We want writers who use their creative forces to create their characters as multi-dimensional beings instead of using a lazier style of writing that falls back on tropes and gender stereotypes to prop up their poorly constructed worlds. I have enough confidence in the power of the human mind and its creative forces to expect more from my media. When *The Avengers* (2012), produced by Joss Whedon, was released I was still smarting from the wound that was *Iron Man 2*. To my surprise, my apprehension dissipated after the first few scenes and I actually enjoyed the movie. I was very impressed with how Whedon had written Black Widow into modern cinema as a powerful character despite some of her previous portrayals.

In media, certain attributes and characteristics are viewed as having intrinsic moral or non-moral values. Sadly, gender is one of these attributes, and certain expectations manifest as a result of a person's gender. Most women and men who break out of their expected gender roles are either viewed as the villain or get punished in some terrible way. For example, the "slut" in horror films is always one of the first to die, and effeminate men are often portrayed as villains with no morals or pride. To be female or effeminate means that being heroic is an impossibility. True heroism is reserved only for male-bodied people who perform their assigned gender roles. Through this type of sexist media representation, traditional gender roles are affirmed, reminding us what our place is and what happens to those who challenge it. As Gilbert and Gubar state, "patriarchal mythology defines women as being created by, from and for men, the children of the male brains, ribs, and ingenuity" (12). Fighting this expectation is in many ways attacking culture itself, which may be one of the many reasons I have seen such a violent reaction against it. Historically a small group of privileged men have been the ones creating most media, which means they have been the ones who have been defining femininity and what it means to be female, with actual women having very little say or representation. This argument can also be applied to racial representation in the media. Such a lack of representation and misrepresentation has been detrimental in the pursuit of equality, since the construction of what it means to be female-bodied is demeaning, often making women caricatures with little depth of purpose beyond depending on and pleasing their male companions. The gender roles that are assigned are unrealistic compared to the actual behavior of individuals and are damaging to the causes of feminism and humanism, which strive to allow all people to be given the same rights and respect regardless of the sex or gender to which they were born or with which they identify.

Since social norms of the masculine have been displayed as morally superior to the feminine, it makes the subject of female superheroes a challenging one for writers to pursue. As Naomi Wolf states in her section on heroines, "A beautiful heroine is a contradiction in terms, since heroism is about individuality, interesting and ever changing, while "beauty" is generic, boring and inert. While culture works out moral dilemmas, "beauty" is amoral" (59). Joss Whedon has created a new model for powerful female characters in *The Avengers* by inverting expected gender roles and allowing these traits to be dissociated from morality and gender and associated with individual behavior. Whedon strips intrinsic moral value from gender and gendered attributes making not only more dynamic characters in *The Avengers* but breaking down the foundation upon which gender roles in media and our culture are built.

One way this is achieved is when Whedon uses stereotypically masculine traits in his female characters and feminine traits in his male characters, challenging gender roles and raising the status of his female characters to that of people, as opposed to objects of desire or scorn. Instead of seeing a male or female character and assuming that their gender defines a large part of how they are to function in the plot or their strengths, weaknesses, or motivations, the viewer is constantly challenged on their gender assumptions. Sherry Ginn points out how this is not only the case with the dialog and plot of *The Avengers* but also in the screen shots of Thor, where we are shown his very muscular physique with no shirt on and oftentimes wet.[1] This also is an inversion of how movie-goers are often presented women's bodies as an object of desire, and not commonly seen with male-bodied heroes. Whedon's writing and character creation do not allow viewers to fall into that comfortable zone of complacency into which so many of us are lulled when watching a film. This is demonstrated in one of the first scenes of *The Avengers*, when we see a woman, who turns out to be Black Widow, in distress and the audience wonders who is going to rescue her. Black Widow is perceived as highly feminine by her enemies and she uses their sexism to her advantage, when in fact, she is not the most effeminate character in the movie. That distinction goes to the delicately-built and robe-clad Loki, another character whose morality is not defined by his gender, though he does possess the basic characteristics and strengths of a typical villain. He is what Black Widow's enemies perceive her to be, only she proves her superiority in her skill set. Loki can be viewed as the typical feminized villain given that his strength lies in manipulation as well as in how he lacks the physical prowess that most virtuous male superheroes possess. However, Black Widow serves as a counter to Loki, and she is considered one of the heroes in the film.

Black Widow's story has already been written in detail, and she has appeared in 2,137 issues of various Marvel comics, the creator of the character Black Widow. A producer of a movie or writer of a new comic needs to be innovative in order to work with her problematic past. Black Widow was first introduced as an antagonist of Iron Man in *Tales of Suspense* #52 which was published in April 1964. One of the major issues with the comic book rendition of Black Widow is that, like most of the female characters in this form of media, her identity and major life events are defined by the men in her life. Her identity is formed by male interaction, whether it is in being rescued by a man, involved in romantic relationships, or seducing men. She is often portrayed as a character used as a tool by others with very little agency and free will of her own. She is constantly being shown as subservient to others, whether it is her love interests, government, or other powerful agency. This prevalent theme can be found in many of her comics. Most of her early history from Marvel's official website has character profiles posted to make her life story more concise. According to the history written in the Marvel Universe's official wiki, she was an orphan born in 1928 in Russia.

> She was rescued by a Russian soldier, Ivan Petrovitch, who saved her from a burning building as a child and kept his eye on her as she grew. In the late 1930's she attracted the attention of Soviet Intelligence, which began [sic] her training. In 1941 she was almost brainwashed into serving the ninja clan The Hand but (again) was saved by Ivan [WSST, Fichera].

Even in early childhood Black Widow is set up as a pitiable creature with no family except the state, and the turning points of her life are when men or other authority figures take an interest in her. Even the wording in this recap makes Natasha seem like a passive party in the events that shape her entire career and future. She doesn't even need to apply for anything or take any initiative; nowhere is there any implication that she strives for or even wants any of this to happen—she just submits. Devin Grayson and Greg Rucka's comic *The Itsy Bitsy Spider* points this out when one of her adversaries states, "You never chose the life of a spy, did you, Natalia? If I recall correctly, it chose you. A husband, the government—various masters pulling at your loyal nature" (48). Her background easily could have been written the way so many of her male counterparts has been: the unwanted orphan earning his way to the top, based on his own talents and ingenuity. But instead this ugly gender expectation arises, and she earns her merits through submission and passively attracting the attention of others. Grayson and Rucka's rendering of Natasha Romanoff is an example of a much more empowered version of Black Widow; she brings to light Black Widow's passivity in her own life and presents it as a problem. In comics by other writers, this submission to the will of her various "masters" is silently accepted and expected. Often they will use this back story to justify many female characters being deemed incapable of making their own decisions, being brainwashed into doing things against their already ten-uous belief systems, and getting rescued yet again by a man who knows better. It seems as if the biggest conflict in Black Widow's back story is between the other men and powers that seek to control her, like being tugged back and forth between children struggling for control of a favorite toy.

The way her first marriage plays out reveals many negative stereotypes about women and marriage that exist blatantly in our society. As her story progresses, her desires and will do not.

> The Soviet state arranged for her to marry Alexi Shostakov, a champion test pilot. After a few years of happy marriage, the KGB faked Shostakov's death in a rocket test; grief for Shostakov's death drives Natasha's resolve deeper and she continued her education with the Red Room Academy, finally being appointed the title of Black Widow [WSST, Fichera].

She is not allowed to choose the man she marries, but that doesn't stop her from being a good, loyal, loving wife to the man the government tells her to love. The first reference to her feelings or opinions at all in Marvel's official biography describes her arranged marriage as "happy," then describes her sorrow when he is taken away from her. His death is the motivation for her wanting to further her education, since clearly she couldn't be expected to do this while married. Even a top notch spy such as the Black Widow is expected to humble herself in the event of a nonconsensual marriage, putting away her career and any desire to cultivate herself further in the pursuit of being an ordinary housewife. As the writers recap her history, "Her masters there arranged a marriage with the hero pilot Alexi Shostakov, and soon with the help of Red Room brainwashing, Natasha became convinced she was an ordinary Russian housewife" (WSST, Fichera).

Many times in her history we see that she has no control over what hap-pens to her body or mind, and she is often violated in this regard in order to turn her into whatever her master's desire is at the time. This does not echo the heroism that we see in many of the male superheroes' back stories, such as Batman who also lost his parents at an early age: who through his own hard work, determination, and love of justice decides to fight crime. As Jeffrey Brown notes in his article "Gender, Sexuality, and Toughness: The Bad Girls of Action Film and Comic Books," "The highly sexualized female body is as capable of being coded as weapon as it is a passive play thing" (65). Black Widow is expected to be both weapon and toy depending on the fancies of those who control her at the time. Many male heroes in the Marvel Universe have wives and lovers, and they continue their careers; they are not only allowed, but expected, to continue to grow and improve in their fields. Often, their newly procured wives and lovers get to play the victim and damsel-in-distress trope for the hero to rescue; clearly this won't do for Black Widow's situation, simply because the genders are reversed.

This is reaffirmed in most of the male character's relationships with their love interests, such as Spiderman's marriage to Mary Jane Watson. Many of the Spiderman comics discuss the burden of his lifestyle taking its toll on her, rather than her husband. Despite the fact that she is not the one in the hero's costume defending the people of the city, it is she who breaks down due to the level of stress it causes to this "delicate little" wife. In much of the comic's depiction of their marriage, she plays the role of devoted wife to Spiderman and places her career second to caring for him. In fact, when a career opportunity arises for her, it creates friction instead of a positive experience in their relationship. As described by the official Marvel Universe Wiki, "Mary Jane was given an opportunity to resume her beloved modeling, for which she was very well paid—a fact which caused Peter some embarrassment" (Fichera). Spiderman is considered the foremost fighter of crime in his world, and Mary Jane faces her own enemies who are, for the most part, crazed stalkers who pursue her because of her extreme beauty. Mary Jane's role as caretaker is foremost in her life, second to being stolen occasionally like a valuable piece of art in need of recovery.

Marvel is not the only publisher whose writers are guilty of this. Gender stereotypes such as these have been around since the written word. Comics are just one of the many sources in which these stereotypes are manifested and reaffirmed. Most comic enthusiasts can name a number of characters from a variety of sources that fit this formula. For example, Superman and his relationship with Lois Lane illustrate a well-known couple who are guilty of the same issues with gender representation; Superman is published by DC Comics. The way their marriage is portrayed provides a common example of sexism in this medium, with women assuming a role of extreme submission, this despite the fact that Superman's wife, Lois, already has a promising career in journalism before she meets him. In one parallel universe, Superman even has two wives, and mocks the two women for their catty rivalry. In the Lois Lane comics, Lois, like Superman, has rivals and enemies; but, unlike Superman, her rivals are not plotting world domination or acts of destruction against the population. Her rivals are other women who aspire for Superman's love and her battles are with these other ambitious women who, other than her all-encompassing desire to make Superman happy, consume her time and concern. Meanwhile Superman is saving the universe from impending doom once again, while Lois is relegated to petty rivalries with other women and humiliated constantly by his lover for her involvement in these antics.

I have frequently heard arguments that since these women are married to superheroes, it only makes sense that their identity gets overshadowed by their husband's great burden. But this was not the case when Black Widow married Shostakov. Later Black Widow enters a relationship with Daredevil, but the images and storyline behind their relationship are hardly what one would consider equal. Most of the art involving these two shows Daredevil positioned above her, and/or Black Widow taking a position of submission while in his presence. In some of the earlier comics, Daredevil has no issue striking his girlfriend when she gets out of line or simply when he feels like it. This gives the reader the impression that Daredevil needs to take a stronger line of action in asserting his dominance over Black Widow, who has strength and a career of her own; Daredevil's female counterpart isn't as virginal and meek as the civilian women that Superman and Spiderman choose for companions. In one of the Daredevil comics that features Black Widow entitled *Cry.... Beetle!,* he slaps her because she is too enthusiastically beating up a man who was mugging an old lady. The supposed reason why she is so overzealous in this beating is because she is emotionally distraught over Daredevil flirting with another woman in the previous issue of the comic. This fear of her boyfriend not loving her anymore causes her emotions to get in the way of her work, and she nearly beats a man to death because of it. This plotline not only advocates violence against one's partner if you don't like their behavior, it also implies that even though Black Widow has the physical strength of a man, she does not have the emotional fortitude of a man to wield it properly and therefore needs a man to keep her in line. Daredevil employs what some have called the "Hank Pym method" by slapping her hard. Of course, historically women were and are still currently labeled with the term "hysterical" when they are being viewed as overly emotional or out of control. As Jane Ussher states in *Women's Madness: Misogyny or Mental Illness?,* this treatment of uncooperative women originates from the Victorian belief that women were unable to control their emotions due to a plethora of strange illnesses that would be laughed at today, such as "the wandering womb which sucked energy from the woman...(and) the theory that women were at the mercy of raging and uncontrolled passions that would ensnare any available man" (92). Though these rationalizations have disappeared, the treatment of women who are out of control or inconvenient remains similar. "If madness is located within the body, the logical conclusion is that the treatment should concentrate on the body.... The belief in the efficacy of a corporal cure was an intrinsic part of the medical monopoly over madness" (106). This is the justification for physical abuse even if the person is not a physical threat and since a good deal of what it means to be "hysteric" is ambiguous at best, and is primarily attributed to women, it puts men in a place of positional authority in relation to women. "Hysteric" is a term that often applies to women who defy gender roles, speak their minds, or refuse to be controlled by others. This practice allows men to physically abuse spouses or lovers whenever they don't see eye to eye.

Daredevil asserts his own masculinity using Black Widow's body. In *And a HYDRA New Year!* (1975) Daredevil is seen slapping her butt hard enough for a seasoned fighter such as her to cry out with an "ow!" while telling her to strip down into an outfit that is, in his words, "barely legal" so he can put her on display for a public event she does not want to attend. She has good reason to not want to be present at this event, since the host is someone who has tried to have her imprisoned on false murder charges, and naturally she is still upset about what he has done to her. Daredevil does not care about her reservations and insists on putting her on display in a dress that he recently purchased for her which doesn't cover much of her perfectly-toned body. He is blind and still insists on putting her within the male gaze of the other party goers and placing her in competition with all of the other women who will be attending. As he slaps her he says, "I want my date to be the most gorgeous thing at the party." The blatant misogynistic nature of her lover referring to her as a "thing" is overt objectification and strips her of what little personhood she has left. What's most concerning is that there is no perceived need on the author or artist's part to even try to mask the objectification of Black Widow in the comic. Sherry Ginn points out that since this comic was written in 1975, when the United States was at the height of the women's movement, some Marvel writers, like many others, responded by contributing to a backlash that resulted from their exposure to feminist ideas that were taking root in the country.[2]

From more recent times in their relationship, the style of sexism is different, but still very much there. In most of the images where they are together, Daredevil is usually seen directly above her and in a position of power while she is literally beneath him. One of the many examples that I can point to would be the December 1998 issue of *Daredevil The Man Without Fear* with Daredevil and Black Widow flying through the air, Daredevil above and in a position of overt dominance, displaying his weaponry and powerful looking physique. Black Widow is underneath him with her body in the typical "S-shaped" pose that is so commonly seen, appearing to be displaying her body more than getting ready to fight evil. Brown has one theory as to why her body is proportioned and displayed as such:

> At least on a symbolic level, the physical extremes that typify the Bad Girl (huge, gravity defying breasts, mile-long legs, perpetually pouty lips and perfectly coifed big hair) amount to an almost hysterical mask of femininity. That these female characters have exaggeratedly feminine bodies is not surprising given the superhero genre's preoccupation with ideal bodies [63].

One scene at the beginning of the comic *Breakdown* shows what looks to be the beginning of a rape scene. A woman wakes up in an unfamiliar apartment and realizes that she no longer looks like herself, but like her rival from the previous issue. Daredevil, a man she doesn't know personally, runs into the room and straight for her. She stands up and tries to kick him away and he grabs her and says, "Sure you want to go another round? I'll take that as a yes." She tries to protest again, speaking Russian, a language that he can't understand, and he grabs her by the nape of her neck while her face is shown contorted with pain. The next scene shows him kissing her while her eyes are widened with fear. The look of the woman's face goes from scared to angry (or perhaps just trying to defend herself despite fear?), to being in pain, and then back to a shocked or scared appearance. With imagery like this, we can again see how it implies that violence against a Bad Girl or a strong woman is justified in order to "keep her in line." This sort of violence is not seen in the domestic relationships between male superheroes who are in their right mind and their domesticated partners. I would have to assume that even most of the desensitized comic book audiences would be uncomfortable if Mary Jane or Lois Lane were the victims of many of the assaults that the men in Black Widow's life commit against her.

Unfortunately, much of Black Widow's storyline is linked to her connection with the various men in her life with whom she has had relationships. The character goes through many relationships throughout the series of comics which eventually lead her to work for S.H.I.E.L.D. As the Marvel synopsis writers explain:

> When she and Hawkeye were captured by General Yuri Brushov, she learned Alexi Shostakov still lived as the Red Guardian; he protested his employers' dishonorable treatment of the Avengers and seemingly sacrificed his life to save them. Unaware Shostakov had again survived, a depressed Natasha retired from action before the Avengers could induct her as a full-fledged member, and she contemplated a marriage proposal from Hawkeye which gained more emotional impact after she briefly believed him dead; however, when Ivan Petrovitch resurfaced in the USA to again serve as her friend and confidant, Natasha's spirits lifted and she broke ties with Hawkeye to pursue a solo vigilante career [WSST, Fichera].

Given this history we can see how significant Whedon's rendition of Natasha is when the relationship between Hawkeye and her remains ambiguous in *The Avengers*, and it shows Black Widow as being able to act independently outside of her attachment to him even though her original motivation is to rescue him. Her actions in both *The Avengers* and *Age of Ultron* show her desire to protect and assist her friend, as opposed to serving him. Black Widow has a chance to show attributes of heroism in relation to her friendship, which is a rare position for women in American media to be placed. We expect her to be handed off from one man to another—which has been the biggest deciding factor in her life, and often determines in which direction her storyline and loyalties will go, whether for good or for evil. *The Age of Ultron*, however, does harken back to more of a traditional subject matter for her, where she establishes a romantic attachment for Bruce Banner, and the storyline around her focuses on her fertility and romantic aspirations. Her rationalizations for the match are also a bit problematic, as she compares her infertility to Banner's transformation into the monstrous Hulk. Such a comparison implies that her infertility is a shameful or monstrous quality that is on level with a man turning into a giant, green, angry monster who can't control his own violent actions.

The movie *Iron Man 2* directly precedes Whedon's *The Avengers* in the Black Widow storyline, and starts off with Black Widow working for Nick Fury and S.H.I.E.L.D. *IM2* is a good example of how the Widow is only viewed as powerful when she is exhibiting masculine traits. When she is not, she is a submissive and hyper-sexualized female. She is in complete subservience to either Nick Fury or Iron Man throughout the film. The twist is that she is doing surveillance on the mental and emotional capacities of Tony Stark/Iron Man the entire time she is in his service. She is the one who is in charge of rating his performance, but she is a passive presence and is completely submissive to his will during her time with him, which includes serving him drinks. Many of the male characters in *The Avengers* have a more contentious attitude to authority, and even though they are in Nick Fury's service, they assert themselves as independent, making their relationship with their superiors more of a negotiation than a traditional employee/boss relationship.

Black Widow (Scarlett Johansson) working undercover as Tony Stark's (Robert Downey, Jr.) assistant Natalie Rushman in *Iron Man 2*. Her sexy outfit is all part of her disguise and designed to keep him from noticing her real intentions (Photofest).

Even when Black Widow shows her physical prowess, it is viewed as more of a novelty. These scenes always take place in the view of another male character that is able to show his awe and approval of her unlikely and exotic skill set, which gives the impression of a pet that can do amazing tricks rather than of a powerful woman. Black Widow's very few speaking parts are neither character building for her place in the movie nor important to the development of the plot.

With Black Widow being used as a character with such a well-documented, often troubled history, I can understand how many avid readers of Black Widow comics might doubt that someone could write her to be authentic to her past representations yet still create a powerful female character with her own agency, without having to rewrite her as a new person entirely. I have heard the argument from some comic fans that it is beyond the power of modern writers to turn a character with a problematic past into someone empowering, since that might require changing fundamental aspects and traits of their prewritten personalities. Whereas I will concede that this sort of shift is challenging, it is certainly not an impossibility and requires writers who are talented and willing to invest their creative energies into this pursuit. Joss Whedon's work on *The Avengers* is proof that this can be done. One method that can be employed is shifting perspective. Change Black Widow from being observed and judged by the male gaze into someone who controls her own narrative, and one can create a character that is authentic to her back story in addition to being portrayed as a person rather than a one dimensional villain, love interest, or object.

In the first scene devoted to Black Widow in *The Avengers*, we see a beautiful young woman tied to a chair with three men bullying her. Two young men, who are the goons of an older man wearing a military uniform, slap her around and threaten her life. No surprise there, our expectations begin to take shape as to the purpose of the scene, and many began to assume that it is written as a way to introduce one of the other Avengers, who will come rescue her and showcase their unique powers. The audience assumes that Black Widow has gotten in over her head and is in a state of vulnerability, since that is what she is displaying to her captors. The older man echoes these thoughts when he looks at her and says "Your outdated information betrays you. The famous Black Widow turns out just to be another pretty face after all." While he is saying this to her he goes back to a small table covered in what looks to be torture tools and picks out a pair of pliers. Her apparent plight is to have her teeth ripped out, but one of the younger men's phone rings. The person who calls demands to speak to "the woman" and informs them that their building is surrounded by armed men and that the person calling could have an F-22 "blow up the block before you even make the lobby" if they do not comply. This threat has the desired effect, and one of the men puts his cell phone to Natasha's face. The caller, whom we later learn to be Phil Coulson, tells her to abort her mission and report for an assignment. To the viewer's surprise, instead of begging for assistance from her powerful friends, she is reluctant, explaining that *she* is in the middle of conducting an interrogation, and that her subject is "giving her everything." What makes this scene so pivotal to Black Widow's position in the movie is the amount of control she has in the situation, and how she uses gender expectations of what people think she is to get what she wants. The assumed damsel-in-distress is now the threat to her "captors," and she tells her associates on the phone to hold while she beats all three of them senseless with no intervention or assistance from her allies. This is shocking to the average audience, since instead of having her associates from S.H.I.E.L.D. come and save her she saves herself, *despite* their interference. Another interesting twist is that her motivation to join the team is because it is her partner who has been compromised. Within a few seconds the supposed female victim is transformed into the hero. Her partner, Hawkeye, has been compromised via Loki's mind control, and, as we already know from Black Widow's history, it is usually she who needs male intervention and guidance in order to regain her morality and position as a hero.

Another important scene that takes place in the movie is when Black Widow speaks with Loki while he is being "held captive" on S.H.I.E.L.D's Helicarrier. Both Nick Fury and Captain America comment that it seems like Loki "let" the Avengers capture him, and it was far too easy. With this suspicion in mind, Black Widow goes to where Loki is being held and starts a discourse with him, making it appear that she thinks Loki is going to win the war, and that her sole purpose in seeing him is to plead for her partner's life. Loki mocks Black Widow for her love for Hawkeye and Black Widow responds "Love is for children, I owe him a debt. I have red in my ledger. I want to wipe it out."[3]

This attitude is extremely deviant from the expected female hero role. As Charlene Tung writes, "She [the heroine] is constructed as masculine only in her ability to handle weapons and physically strike and fight back. She is depicted as both muscular and (hyper) sexualized, while maintaining her emotional vulnerability" (99). This duality is common in the modern day incarnation of the female hero. Sometimes she can fight like a man, but she has a soft heart or intense emotions that don't allow her to mentally handle herself like her male counterparts. Her weakness is in her emotions, and the way to defeat her is straight through her heart. This implies that even if a woman can become a man's equal in physical strength she is still weaker emotionally and may misuse her powers as a result. This is challenged by Whedon when Black Widow is manipulating Loki. She does not appeal to her emotional vulnerability as a woman is expected to. Rather her actions reflect altruism. Altruism is typically portrayed as a masculine type of heroism which derives from an innate "good" and desire to set things right, which is far different from Black Widow being motivated by blind love and loyalty to her male counterpart. This is another way in which Whedon transforms Black Widow into a heroic character. As opposed to appealing to amoral desires or love for a particular person who may or may not be good, she displays a desire for goodness and morality in itself. She shows herself and her motivations to be just as heroic as any of the male characters in her group. Loki ridicules her even further for her desire to pay back her debt, saying, "your ledger is dripping in red, and you think that saving one man's life, who is no better than yourself, is going to make things right?" He proceeds to demean and ridicule her in a soliloquy, while she turns from him, hiding her face and pretending to sob. Loki plays the part of the sexist in this interaction and ultimately he is made to look a fool. He assumes that Black Widow is just another weak-willed woman and that her love for Hawkeye is what motivates her to seek his help, because stereotypically that is what women do for their love interests, regardless of the morality of their methods. Loki attacks her via her emotions because he thinks she is emotionally vulnerable; he insults her morality. The paths he takes would be effective in the case of most women in media, which is why this scene directly challenges those beliefs when he is tricked by them. He is punished for his sexist opinions as opposed to being rewarded. Whedon's Black Widow uses the sexist assumptions that people make about her to humiliate them for their ignorance. While Loki berates and insults her, she tricks him into telling her why he wanted to be captured and his plans for how he intends to attack the Helicarrier, information that others on the team were unable to obtain.

The dialog between Loki and Black Widow also highlights how her image has been constructed in the past. Gilbert and Gubar observe that "the roots of authority tell us, after all, that if woman is man's property then he must have authored her, just as surely as they tell us that if he authored her she must be his property. As a creation 'penned' by man, moreover, woman has been 'penned up' or 'penned in'" (13). This scene clearly shows how men like Loki have "penned up and penned in" women like Black Widow and who take their own insecurities to create her image. Likewise, this explains how Black Widow has been portrayed in the past in other comics and movies. It also explains how her past was defined by the sexists who viewed her as a stereotype and how their own insecurities manifested in their creation of her identity. Much of what Loki is verbally abusing Black Widow for applies to himself and is a throwback to his misbehavior and self-magnified shame, as illustrated in *Thor*. Loki and Black Widow have many strong similarities; yet, the only thing that makes Loki evil is his inability to forgive himself, while

Black Widow is willing to move forward despite the transgressions that she has committed in the past. This indicates that state of mind is far more important to one's morality and character than inborn talents or stereotypical weaknesses within gender.

Another aspect of this scene is how similar it is to our introduction to Black Widow at the beginning of the movie. Both Loki and Black Widow use manipulation to get what they want, and having Black Widow be the one who approaches Loki while he is pulling the exact same stunt that she did earlier is no coincidence. In this showdown—a battle of wits instead of brawn—the two characters who are the most well-known for their ability to manipulate, deceive, and trick others, face-off. Again, Black Widow uses the stereotypes about her gender and reputation in past incarnations to lull her enemies into a false sense of security. This can now be seen as a classic Black Widow tactic, as opposed to a weakness in character as portrayed in previous comics, since these methods are used but in a different light. Either way, Loki falls for it. When Black Widow turns around with tears in her eyes, Loki believes that he has won, that he has broken the will of one of the Avengers; he starts bragging, getting overly confident, and gloating over his perceived victory. Black Widow, being a master at profiling people, knows that Loki is a sore winner, and the best way to get information from him is to make him believe that he is in control; she ends up victorious and is even cheeky enough to thank him for his cooperation. This scene helps show how dynamically her character is written: she gives the impression that she meets the expectations of what is assumed of her, and twists those very expectations to reach her goals. Instead of willfully rejecting everything that has been written of her in the past, she embraces it and uses the misinformed perceptions of others as a part of her strengths without letting gender expectations consume her entire personality, as is often the fate of many other would-be heroines. She is not only outstanding in her ability to destroy her enemies physically, but mentally as well. She repeatedly makes a fool of anyone who underestimates her based on her good looks and perceived gender role, mocking not only the characters she dupes, but the entire social construction of female heroes in media.

In an ideal world, behavior and attributes wouldn't be subjected to such a binary as masculine and feminine, and people's actions would be evaluated in a more comprehensive manner, one that doesn't categorize them into one of two arbitrarily defined groups. An important step to getting to that level of awareness is to take away the moral and gender values ascribed to certain strengths, talents, and attributes of characters in mass media and make the effort to create original personalities whose morality is not determined based on physical attributes or skill sets.

Joss Whedon's *The Avengers* shows how this is possible in cinema, and the excuse that "sex [i.e., sexism] sells" is no longer as convincing an argument given the movie's success at the box office. Not only Whedon's writing, but the reception that his movie has received is a signal to Hollywood and the movie-making industry that destruction of sexist archetypal roles isn't destructive to profit. In addition, it challenges the new era of writers to create a new breed of entertainment that requires originality, one that does not use the crutch of clichéd gender roles to which so many of their predecessors adhered.

NOTES

1. Personal communication 1 July 2015.
2. Personal communication 1 July 2015.
3. Sherry Ginn observes that this scene contradicts the content we later see in *Age of Ultron*. Since Loki is supposed to have learned all of Hawkeye's secrets when he uses the mind control powers of the scepter, he should have known the real nature of Hawkeye's relationship with Black Widow along with the existence and location of Hawkeye's farmhouse and family which are hidden away. Personal communication 1 July 2015.

WORKS CONSULTED

Brown, Jeffrey. "Gender, Sexuality, and Toughness: The Bad Girls of Action Film and Comic Books." *Action Chicks: New Images of Tough Women in Popular Culture.* Ed. Sherrie A. Inness. New York: Palgrave Macmillan, 2004. 47–74. Print.

Cornell, Paul (Writer). *Black Widow: Deadly Origin.* Tom Raney (Pencils), Scott Hanna (Inks), and Matt Milla (Colors). New York: Marvel Worldwide, 2010. Print.

Fichera, Mike. "Watson, Mary Jane." *Marvel Universe Wiki.* Marvel. Accessed 1 July 2015.

Gerber, Steve (Writer). *Daredevil Vol. 1 (# 108): Cry.... Beetle!* Bob Brown (Pencils), John Romita and Paul Gulacy (Ink), and Petra Goldberg (Colors). New York: Marvel Worldwide, 1974. Print.

Gilbert, Sandra M., and Susan Gubar. *The Madwoman in the Attic.* New Haven: Yale University Press, 1979. Print.

Grayson, Devin, and Greg Rucka (Writers). *Black Widow: The Itsy-Bitsy Spider.* J. G. Jones and Scott Hampton (Illustrators). New York: Marvel Worldwide, 1999. Print.

Isabella,Tony (Writer). *Daredevil (#120): And a HYDRA New Year!* Bob Brown (Pencils), Vince Collette (Inks), Petra Goldberg (Colors), and Ray Holloway (Letters). New York: Marvel Worldwide, 1975. Print.

Rucka, Greg, and Devin Grayson (Writers). *Black Widow: Breakdown.* Scott Hampton (Art). New York: Marvel Worldwide, 2001. Print.

Smith, Kevin (Writer). *Daredevil (#2) Guardian Devil Part Two: The Unexamined Life.* Joe Quesada (Penciler), Jimmy Palmiotti (Inker), and Joseph Campbell (Art). Variant Cover Art. New York: Marvel Worldwide, 1998. Print.

Swan, Curt, and George Klein (Cover Artists). *Superman's Girlfriend, Lois Lane (#31): Featuring Lana Lang in The Jealous Lois Lane!* John Forte, and Kurt Schaffenberger (Pencils and Inks). New York: DC Comics, 1958. Print.

Tung, Charlene. *Throwing Down the Gauntlet: Defiant Women, Decadent Men, Objects of Power, and Witchblade.* New York: Palgrave Macmillan, 2004. Print.

Ussher, Jane. *Women's Madness: Misogyny or Mental Illness.* Amherst: University of Massachusetts Press, 1992. Print.

Wolf, Naomi. *The Beauty Myth.* London: Griffin Press Limited, 1990. Print.

WSST [TaXa Wagner], and Mike Fichera. "Black Widow (Natasha Romanova)." *Marvel Universe Wiki.* Marvel. Accessed 1 July 2015.

Red Rooms, Conditioning Chairs and Needles in the Brain

Brainwashing and Mind Control in the Whedon and Marvel Universes

By Sherry Ginn

There's nothing easy about having your brain on display, sir.
—Natasha Romanoff,
Black Widow: Forever Red[1]

The notion that someone can play around with our brains and minds, without our knowledge, is a scary thought. We human beings pride ourselves on our strength of character and ability to resist undue influence. The average person does not understand or acknowledge the various ways in which his or her behavior is manipulated every day. Such manipulations do not just occur in television advertisements via what social psychologists call the "peripheral route" of persuasion. They may also occur during news broadcasts, watching television series or films, listening to the radio, or texting friends. The brain increasingly automates many of the activities in which we engage daily and such automation can be considered brainwashing. However, when the average person hears the word *brainwashing*, he or she thinks of *The Manchurian Candidate* and reports from Korean War veterans of techniques used by the Chinese on American prisoners-of-war, techniques that have been adopted by other countries, including the United States, to program counter-intelligence operatives. Brainwashing is defined as "mak[ing] (someone) adopt radically different beliefs by using systematic and often forcible

Dottie Underwood (Bridget Regan), a graduate of the Red Room Academy. From *Agent Carter* (Photofest).

pressure."² Synonyms include indoctrinate, condition, reeducate, persuade, influence, propagandize, and inculcate. Mind control is a theory that human subjects can be indoctrinated in a way that causes "an impairment of autonomy, an inability to think independently, and a disruption of beliefs and affiliations."³ Synonyms include: brainwashing, reeducation, brainsweeping, coercive persuasion, thought control, or thought reform.

This essay briefly discusses the ways in which "brainwashing" and mind control can occur, specifically in relation to the education and training of the Marvel character Natasha Romanoff, the Black Widow. Additionally, I will consider other Marvel characters, such as Dottie Underwood (*Agent Carter* [2015–2016]) and Bucky Barnes, the Winter Soldier, as well as characters created by Joss Whedon, writer and director of *The Avengers* (2012) and *Avengers: Age of Ultron* (2015), who have been subjected to "brainwashing," including the Dolls (*Dollhouse* [2009–2010]) and River Tam (*Firefly* [2002–2003]). Despite the best efforts of those conditioning these subjects, the conditioning does not destroy all of their memories nor is it permanent.

*"Do you know what it's like to be unmade?"*⁴

At the end of the fifth episode, "The Iron Ceiling," in Season One of *Agent Carter*, we see Dottie Underwood handcuff herself to her bedpost prior to falling asleep. Earlier in the episode, in a flashback sequence, we are given a glimpse of a roomful of little girls, all of whom are handcuffed to their beds; Dottie was one of these girls. The children were part of a Soviet initiative designed to program the girls to be spies. We can speculate that they were taken from their parents at a very early age—when most trainable—and subjected to much conditioning and counterconditioning throughout their childhoods. The handcuffs were used for a number of reasons, but a very practical one was simply to ensure that the children did not try to run away and find their way back to their homes.

We consider the idea of subjecting children to such treatment abhorrent and rightly so; however, what we do not think of is the many ways in which we condition and countercondition children every day or the ways in which we ourselves are conditioned and counterconditioned. The terms suggest a lack of free will and hint at the possibility that we can be made to act in ways contrary to our wishes, desires, and moral principles. These terms also frighten us because they indicate that we are mere puppets and that somewhere—we know not where—is a puppetmaster, pulling our strings, making us dance without awareness of his or her control.

We are given even more evidence of this Soviet training academy in *Avengers: Age of Ultron* in flashbacks of Natasha Romanoff's childhood. From these flashbacks as well as Paul Cornell's *Black Widow: Origins*, we begin to understand her exchange with Hawkeye in Joss Whedon's *The Avengers*:

> HAWKEYE: Have you ever had someone take your brain and play? Pull you out and send something else in? Do you know what it's like to be unmade?
> BLACK WIDOW: You know that I do.

Like the other little girls, Romanoff was trained to do what her Soviet masters desired, and she was very good at what she did until she changed sides, joined S.H.I.E.L.D., and became a member of the Avengers.

Does the Name Pavlov Ring a Bell?[5]

Ivan Pavlov (1849–1936) was a Russian physiologist who won the Nobel Prize for Physiology/Medicine in 1904. One of his greatest contributions to psychology was his recognition that two stimuli could become associated with one another when paired in close temporal contiguity. In his famous experiments, he paired the sound of a metronome ticking (the conditional stimulus) with food powder (the unconditional stimulus). Whereas food powder readily elicits a salivary response in a hungry animal, a ticking metronome does not. However, following repeated presentations of the metronome paired with the food, the dogs began to salivate to the sound of the metronome. This type of conditioning is referred to as classical or Pavlovian conditioning. The response being conditioned is reflexive and thus beyond conscious control. Organisms learn to respond to the so-called conditional stimuli because such stimuli have informational value, that is, the sound of the metronome indicates that food is forthcoming.

Although we might be surprised to think of Dottie's handcuff as a conditional stimulus, it is no different—for her and the other children—than our use of a glass of warm milk, a hot shower, meditation, soothing music, sex, or other stimuli to aid in our transition from waking to sleeping. The children were handcuffed to their beds. More than likely, someone told them to go to sleep and the lights were turned off. The children would have learned that they could not move because the cuffs kept them from doing so and someone was always on watch. Thus, the frightened children learned that resistance was impossible, and they learned that they were helpless, without any control over the circumstances of their lives. But, they might also have learned that they were safe, the handcuff serving as a reminder that they were in a place perhaps safer than where they came from. And, just like we may find it difficult to break a habit, such as wanting to fall asleep to music when a new partner likes quiet, Dottie can no longer sleep without the comforting presence of the handcuff around her wrist.

Edward Thorndike (1874–1949) introduced psychology to the concept of trial-and-error learning and the law of effect. Thorndike's early research involved placing cats in so-called puzzle boxes to see how long it would take the cats to escape the boxes. A puzzle box was a simple wooden box with a lever door activated by a number of devices, such as a paddle or a string. When the cat stepped on the paddle, the door would open and the cat could escape the box whereupon it would be rewarded with food. Thorndike noted that the cats first stumbled upon the solution to the box in a method he called trial-and-error. However, once the cat discovered how to escape, the amount of time it took for the cat to escape decreased as did the number of errors the cat made. Thorndike proposed that escaping from the box and receiving the food produced a "satisfying state" for the cat and thus the cat was motivated to repeat the behavior for what was clearly a reward.

Psychology was dominated by the behaviorist perspective in the first half of the twentieth century. The behaviorists believed that the only subject matter worth studying was observable, objective behavior, hence their name. Thorndike's type of learning was deemed instrumental conditioning, conditioning in which the organisms' actions were instrumental in obtaining the outcome. This type of conditioning was to be distinguished from Pavlov's which was deemed respondent conditioning because the organism was simply responding in a reflexive manner to the conditional stimulus. But in the latter half of the twentieth-century one behaviorist stood head and shoulders above the rest, and his name was B. F. Skinner (1904–1990). Skinner's contributions to psychology include elucidation of various schedules of reinforcement and the partial reinforcement extinction effect as well as the operant chamber, which has applications in business, industry, and education.

Skinner referred to his type of conditioning as operant conditioning because the organism operates on its environment in order to receive an outcome favorable to its survival. Thus feral cats learn which restaurant will put left-over food outside at night's end and which one will not. Cats that cannot discriminate between safety and danger do not survive, but cats that can are rewarded and live a little longer.

Note that instrumental and operant conditioning are virtually identical. In each, the organism must make the correct response, and it will then be rewarded for doing so. If the organism does not make the correct response, it will not receive a reward. As I just mentioned, organisms in their natural environments need to be able to discriminate between safety and danger. They are motivated to search for clues that will provide them with information as to what to do. In psychological parlance, we refer to such clues as discriminative stimuli, or S^D (pronounced "ess-dee"). The stimuli that do not provide clues as to which stimuli signal reward are referred to as S^Δ (pronounced "ess-delta"). Back to the cat example: the cats learn which restaurant will provide food. Perhaps the cook calls the cats or bangs on a pan; such actions become discriminatory stimuli. The staff at the other restaurant does nothing and thus the cats learn they need not attempt to find food at that place.

These stimuli are constantly at work around us. We learn which toilet to use, which food is safe to eat, when to "go" and when to "stop," the difference between flashing blue lights and flashing red lights, which of our parents is the "soft touch," and a whole host of other bits of information. And much of this information works at an unconscious level. The astute reader will understand that the conditional stimulus serves the same function as S^D.

Consider once again the children in the Red Room Academy. They have been separated from their parents. They are lonely and frightened. But they are all lonely and frightened together. They do not know at first what they are supposed to do, but they will learn the skills they need to survive. As in any type of military training they will be told when to wake-up, when to go to sleep, when to eat, and when to urinate and defecate. They will be told whom to like and they will be told whom to hate. They will be told who they are as they slowly unlearn who they were. They will begin to compete for attention, for rewards, for favors. They will bond with their captor-teachers because these are the people who control the rewards and punishers, just like any parents control their children's rewards and punishers. The "skill set" that each child must learn is gradually "stamped" into the child's memory until no conscious thought is required for execution. Actions become automatic, cued by discriminatory stimuli that the children are trained to recognize and respond to automatically. One needs to be able to perceive a threat and respond to it immediately without taking the time to assess the best strategy for dealing with the threat. The time lag between perception and action can make the difference between life and death, hence the need for instantaneous assessment and response. Unfortunately, it can also lead to maladaptive behavior as well.

I am not trying to say that conscious thoughts and decision-making skills are not important elements of cognition. They absolutely are. It takes both automatic and conscious thought processes to help navigate our environments. For example, we have all arrived home with no recollection of actually making the journey; this reflects automatic processors in our brains directing our behavior. However, as we drive home and hear that there is an accident ahead, we can quickly think of an alternate route; this is an example of conscious processors in our brains directing our behavior. Experience helps us gauge whether automatic or conscious processors need to direct our behavior; with experience we can switch more easily between the two and adapt to our environment as circumstances dictate.

"It's kind of hard to trust someone when you don't know who that someone really is"[6]

The Leviathan project's objective was apparently to train spies for use against enemies of the Soviet state. Her history indicates that Natasha Romanoff was one of the children subjected to the project's brainwashing and conditioning programs. This is confirmed in *Ultron* as Romanoff gives Banner glimpses of her history as they talk about their future together.[7] We observe young girls going through physical training exercises. We also watch their handlers teach them that close relationships are forbidden. Dottie Underwood bonds with one of her fellow initiates and then is ordered to kill her, which she does, with no visible emotion. She has learned to follow orders, no questions asked, making no value judgments as to whether or not the action is moral or ethical. She is literally trained to follow orders and she does as she is told.

As I mentioned earlier, the thought that Natasha, Dottie, and the other operatives follow their orders without question terrifies us: what about free will? Can someone really make us act in a way contrary to the "real" us? I submit that none of the girls trained as spies and assassins ever had a free will. They never were "real," or they have not been "real" in so long that they do not remember a time before their entry into the Red Room. They were taken at very young ages, before they had time to fully develop—psychologically, cognitively, emotionally, or physically—and they were then, in effect, brainwashed into being whatever was needed by their handlers. The children never had a choice as to whether they wished to participate in this training; they were simply programmed to do so.

This indoctrination is different from what happens to adults, who must pretty much be "unmade." Adults have a lifetime's—however long their lifetime—worth of memories as the basis for their "self." Those memories, so-called episodic memories, need to be erased and then built again from scratch.[8] Hence, Steve Rogers' best friend Bucky Barnes is believed to have been killed in action in World War II (*Captain America: The First Avenger* [2011]). In actuality, Barnes was rescued by Nazi/HYDRA scientists and subjected to intense brainwashing, after which he served as an assassin, known as the Winter Soldier. He is eventually sent to kill Nick Fury, Director of S.H.I.E.L.D., as well as Captain America in the sequel film, *Captain America: The Winter Soldier* (2014). Cap refuses to kill his friend, not believing that Bucky is "dead." Bucky saves Cap's life, and the film ends with a disguised Winter Soldier standing before an exhibit about Bucky Barnes at the Smithsonian Institution. Although we do not know how the MCU will address the issue of Bucky/Winter Soldier in the next film, it seems certain that one plot will be about Bucky's battle to overcome his programming at the hands of HYDRA. One thing is certain, however: the plotlines involving the Black Widow and the Winter Soldier indicate that one can be *de*programmed as well as programmed.

"Also, I can kill you with my brain"[9]

The term *brainwashing* originated from the Chinese term *xǐ nǎo* which literally means "to wash the brain." As mentioned previously, the term was first used in the United States during the Korean War. United Nations troops captured by the Chinese were subjected to torture and other techniques that we now refer to as brainwashing. Robert Jay Lifton interviewed a number of these former prisoners of war as well as Chinese civilians who defected to the West following the war. Lifton identified ten steps that were involved in the brainwashing process and reported that each step was carried out when the individuals were isolated from their fellow prisoners and under threat of physical harm.[10] In addition, various techniques, such as sleep deprivation and starvation, were used to reduce the prisoners' self-control and ability to think critically.

The first four steps—assault on identity, guilt, self-betrayal, and breaking point—target the individual's "self." The brainwasher attacks a person's identity or ego, and this attack may last for days, weeks, or even months. The point is to exhaust the subjects, disorienting them as to what is real and what is not real about them. Next the subjects are criticized for their beliefs and made to feel increasingly guilty about those beliefs. Once subjects are feeling guilty about their beliefs and values, they are forced to renounce those beliefs and values as well as everyone they know who shares them. Finally subjects reach the breaking point, whereby they have a crisis of identity and experience psychological disturbances, such as uncontrollable crying and depression. They are now ready for conversion to the new belief system.

The next four steps—leniency, compulsion to confess, channeling guilt, and releasing guilt—offer the individual salvation. The brainwasher steps in and offers something to the subject, as the individual experiences various psychological issues. This offer is usually small, but seems quite large to the sufferer and obligates the individual to reciprocate. The brainwasher may suggest that a confession of sins will relieve the individual's sense of guilt and bring about a feeling of relief.[11] At this point, the individual has been living in a state of guilt and pain for a very long time. He or she might be confused and disoriented, not understanding exactly why he or she feels so badly, but realizing that his or her belief system is the reason for feeling shame. As Layton notes, "The old belief system is associated with psychological (and usually physical) agony; and the new belief system is associated with the possibility of escaping that agony."[12] The individual begins to realize that it is not "me" who is bad; rather, it is the old beliefs. If the person being brainwashed will just renounce those old beliefs, then a new identity can be created, one that does not have excess baggage and the burden of sin.

The final steps—progress and harmony and final confession and rebirth—allow the tortured individual to create a new sense of self. Rituals and ceremonies are offered to make the transition complete and some brainwashing victims have claimed that they feel a sense of "rebirth" at this point.

The question of interest to psychologists (and others) is why some people can be brainwashed and others cannot. Further research on the matter reveals that those who are most vulnerable have certain personality traits that make them more susceptible than others. Such traits include self-doubt, a weak sense of personal identity, a tendency toward feelings of guilt, and black-and-white thinking. Those who have a stronger sense of self-identity as well as more self-confidence are less susceptible.

The list of traits that result in susceptibility suggests why young people are more likely to succumb to brainwashing and other mind-control techniques. The majority of those who are indoctrinated into cults are young; however, people of any age can be and are targeted. Those who are experiencing a high level of stress are particularly susceptible to the mind-control techniques used by many cults. It should not be surprising that cults use the same types of indoctrination techniques Lifton identified. It should also come as no surprise that terrorist organizations such as the Islamic State (ISIL,

ISIS) use these tactics to recruit new members and indoctrinate those they capture and enslave.

Regarding the girls and boys being trained at the Red Room Academy, each is young and has been separated from their families. They have no way of getting in touch with their families, no point of reference for their pain and suffering, and probably suffer from "Stockholm Syndrome," or capture-bonding, a form of post-traumatic stress disorder in which hostages and other victims begin to identify, sympathize and empathize with, and eventually defend their captors. In the Marvel-sanctioned novel, *Black Widow: Forever Red*, we learn that Natasha Romanoff was sent to the Red Room Academy when she was 12 years old.[13] Orphaned at a young age, saved by a man who leaves her for others to raise, and then sent to train by Soviet intelligence, the woman we know as Black Widow would have been ripe for indoctrination by someone who controlled her daily life. *Forever Red* gives us more information about Natasha's early education, and the novel also tells us about the training to which another young girl—Ava Orlova, a.k.a. Red Widow—is subjected and to whom Natasha is psychically linked.

If we condemn the Chinese, the Russians, or ISIS for their use of brainwashing and mind-control, we will also have to condemn the U.S. government. After learning of Chinese attempts on captured United Nations service members and its own citizens, the U.S. feared that it was falling behind in this area, establishing its own mind-control programs, such as MKUltra, in the 1950s. This program, developed by the CIA, used drugs (such as LSD), sensory deprivation, physical and sexual abuse, hypnosis, and isolation on test subjects in order to manipulate brain functioning.

The attempt to control brain functioning has a long history. At least at the present time, perhaps one of the most controversial procedures devised to control behavior was the lobotomy. Developed by António Egas Moniz (1874–1955) to help control symptoms of mental disorders, he and other practitioners believed that the personality and behavioral side-effects of the procedure were outweighed by the benefits to the patient and his or her family. Moniz shared the Nobel Prize for Physiology and Medicine in 1949 for his development of the lobotomy, although its usefulness and efficacy have been denied for the last several decades. A frequent staple of horror movie scripts, lobotomies are rarely performed these days.[14]

Joss Whedon's use of mind control and brainwashing through manipulation of the brain occurs in several of his television programs in addition to his *Avengers*' scripts. Whedon's various series have also explored the possibility of mind control and manipulation through the use of psychoactive drugs. It is certainly worth noting that many of Whedon's theories about mind control reflect the CIA's operations during Project MKUltra. He explored mind control in all of his series, from *Buffy, the Vampire Slayer* to

Angel to *Firefly* to *Dollhouse* to *Agents of S.H.I.E.L.D.*; however, I will talk only about *Firefly* and *Dollhouse* here because his exploration of mind control in these two series illustrates ways in which he used it in both *Avengers* and *Ultron* to characterize Black Widow.

Whedon Explores Mind Control[15]

The physically and psychologically fragile River Tam of *Firefly* and its sequel motion picture *Serenity* has been subjected to various types of neurological tampering at the hands of government scientists, although the type of tampering is never made clear. Her brother Simon says that she is a paranoid schizophrenic ("Safe" 1.5), although she displays several characteristics of someone who is hebephrenic.[16] In addition, he states that Alliance scientists treated her mind like a "rutting playground" ("Safe"). Later he will tell Jayne Cobb that those scientists "stripped" her amygdala ("Ariel" 1.9), probably meaning that Alliance scientists destroyed these structures. Simon continues to talk to Jayne, saying,

> You know how you get scared. Or worried or nervous. And you don't want to be scared or worried or nervous, so you push it to the back of your mind. You try not to think about it. The amygdala is what lets you do that—it's like a filter in your brain that keeps your feelings in check. They took the filter out of River. She feels everything. She can't not.

But Simon is wrong. This is not what the amygdala does.

It is true that the amygdalae[17] are involved in emotions by virtue of their location and involvement in the limbic system, a set of subcortical structures comprising an emotional circuit responsive to primitive emotions, such as fear (Kandel, Schwartz, and Jessell). The limbic system lies in a "ring" or border around the brainstem, inferior to the cerebral cortex. Amygdalae connect to the hypothalami, which monitor the internal environment of the body, and also to the peripheral nervous system, the endocrine system, and the autonomic nervous system to effect reactions to the presence of both physical and psychological stressors. Another component of the limbic system is the hippocampus, the gateway to memory. The amygdalae actually sit on the most anterior aspect of the hippocampi. The hippocampi serve as the bridge between short-term, working memory and long term memory, apparently transferring those short-term memories into the long-term stores. It is this part of the brain that is damaged in patients with anterograde amnesia, Alzheimer's disease, and other disorders of memory. It is probably the case that the amygdalae, by virtue of their connections with the hippocampi, contribute the emotional tone to the memories transferred to the long-term memory (LaBar; LeDoux). Patients with temporal lobe damage also frequently experience uncontrollable anger and even rages, presumably because their amygdalae are also damaged, or the connections between the amygdalae and cortical areas mediating rational thought are damaged (LeDoux).

Bradley J. Daniels suggests that River suffers from Post-Traumatic Stress Disorder (PTSD). She has many of the classic symptoms, such as heightened arousal, hypervigilance, and disturbed sleep patterns (DSM-5). Research data suggest a link between the amygdalae and PTSD, with increased activity in the amygdalae being observed in people with PTSD (Shin, Rauch, and Pitman). Daniels notes that if the Alliance had stripped River's amygdala, it would make it more difficult for her to develop PTSD symptoms as the "most integral brain region associated with the experience of fear (central to the development of PTSD) would be destroyed" (138). Further he suggests that if the Alliance wanted to create symptoms similar to the behavior symptoms of PTSD, the Alliance scientists would want to stimulate her amygdalae, not destroy them. But I do not think that was the point. The Alliance scientists *wanted* to destroy her amygdalae so she would not feel fear prior to a mission. The amygdalae are apparently important for reactions to other people's emotions, especially fear. Damage to the amygdalae causes "psychic blindness," or the inability to recognize fear in other people's facial expressions or voices. Such ability would be very important to someone who has to kill people on a mission. In addition amygdalar damage means that River would not feel any remorse afterwards, especially if the links between her amygdalae and her frontal lobes were damaged, and it appears that they were. As Ed Connor states, "River is a frail young girl, but neural manipulation... made her into a homicidal monster" (187–88). In actuality the Alliance was trying to create a super-soldier, a weaponized woman (Marano 46)—in other words, an "Operative."

Whedon also explores the possibility of not just manipulating one part of the brain in order to control behavior and thoughts in the controversial series *Dollhouse*. However, this series explores the ramifications of manipulating memory—the very core of identity—in men and women.[18] Actives exhibit some basic memories although their memories supposedly have been wiped. They answer to their names, albeit their "Active" names. They understand language as evidenced by their ability to talk and understand what is said to them. They also remember basic motor programs. That is, they can all walk and talk and engage in other activities designed to keep their bodies supple (e.g., yoga) and provide them some basic mental stimulation (e.g., painting). Victor's growing love for Sierra is manifested in a "man reaction"; that is, he experiences an erection whenever he sees her naked ("True Believer" 1.5), an example of procedural memory. A more chilling example is Sierra's reaction to Victor's touch in "Man on the Street" (1.6). She screams when he places his hand on her shoulder, a reaction that leads to the discovery that she has been raped by her handler, Hearn. In the episode "Needs" (1.8), Echo notes that she can remember information such as the days of the week and the capital of Nebraska, but nothing about herself. In Season Two, when Victor's contract with Rossum expires and he is re-integrated into the "real" world, vestiges of his Dollhouse imprinting bleed into his life. For example, he cannot sleep in a bed. Instead he takes his pillow and blanket off the bed in his room and sleeps in his bathtub, which physically resembles the sleeping pods in the Dollhouse ("Stop-Loss" 2.9). Examples such as these indicate that the Rossum Corporation is manipulating only the Actives' episodic memories, wiping any memories of the original personality. Although an intriguing idea, completely destroying one type of memory without affecting other types does not appear possible. Even brain-damaged patients continue to have memories of their lives prior to their trauma, even if they can no longer create new explicit memories.

However, in one respect, Whedon and the other writers depicted the reality of the neural basis of memory. As the series progresses through Season One, it becomes increasingly clear that Echo is remembering information from her past imprints, a programming impossibility according to the Rossum Corporation. Theoretically, an Active's true personality is to be wiped "clean," downloaded onto a disk and stored until the Active's contract with Rossum is terminated. During the five-year contracting period, an Active is designed to be imprinted multiple times, usually with a new personality. No "bleed through" is supposed to occur between imprints. Each Active is to be imprinted with the requested personality and then wiped clean after a time period specified by the client. However, Echo clearly shows awareness of those implanted personalities, as well as her original, primary personality.

In the episode "A Spy in the House of Love" (1.9), the suggestion is made that there is a mole in the Dollhouse and that this person has tampered with Echo's program. Episodes prior to this one show that Echo is already remembering bits and pieces of previous imprints; we do not learn the identity of the mole or the mole's true purpose until later in Season Two ("The Hollow Men" 2.12). A complete review of the theoretical basis of Echo's "awakening" is beyond the scope of this essay; however, memories are constructed through association. Memories become associated with each other for a variety of reasons and are stored in vast neural networks. Activating one memory in turn activates a host of other memories associated with that event through an activation of the network. For example, memories of my first car will activate memories of the day my mother drove it home because I could not drive a straight-shift, which will activate the memory of my mother, which will activate memories of a life-time spent with my mother, which will activate other memories of my life-time, et cetera. Thus as Echo remembers one piece of information, she will increasingly remember other pieces, despite the best efforts of Topher and his attempts to wipe and re-implant memories as requested by Echo's clientele.

This is especially evident in the Season Two episode "Vows" (2.1). Although Echo remembers Whiskey when encountering her early in the episode and even talks to her about Whiskey's past ("You were number 1"), it is the blow to the head Echo receives at the hands of her client "husband" Martin Klar that affects her memory. As he repeatedly hits her, Echo begins to see flashes of her previous imprints. Echo tries to reassure him that she is really his wife, but ends up saying, "I will always be Eleanor Penn." Of course, that is the wrong imprint, which Echo realizes as soon as she says it. Later on, when she is back in the Dollhouse, she speaks with her handler, former FBI agent Paul Ballard, about her memories of the imprints. She tells him that she is lost, that she does not know who or what is real.[19] Echo is remembering information from the women she has been with her various clients. That is, episodic memories of these women have been created and stored in her brain. They have not been wiped clean, and the fact that she can access these memories of her "selves" leaves her with a sense of fragmentation. She has no clear memory of a specific self, but rather memories of multiple selves. Her semantic memory, or generalized knowledge, is intact as well. Echo knows that she has been, and is being, programmed repeatedly, but these memories are not personal, or episodic, memories of her self. Indeed she has some problems with the reality of the memories as well. And that is another flaw in the way that memory is presented on *Dollhouse*.

This flaw is the very real inability that we possess of knowing whether our memories are actually accurate. Numerous research studies have demonstrated the fallibility of memory and the ease with which false memories can be created (Loftus). We know that memories are reconstructed with use, which means that any memory may not actually be "real." That is, are the memories that I have of any childhood event real or have I recreated those memories to coincide with what I thought was true or what I believed was true or what I hoped was true? When Echo and the other Actives are imprinted with another person's memories, it is presumed that that person's memories are their actual, "real" memories. Once again, given the ease with which false memories can be created, this assumption may not be true. The episode "Ghost" (1.1) illustrates this fact quite clearly.

"Ghost," the first episode of the series, introduces us to the imprinting procedures used in the Dollhouse. Whenever an Active is requested for an assignment, she or he receives a "treatment" in which the requested personality is imprinted upon her or his brain. It is apparently painful to wipe and insert memories, as witnessed by the facial expressions and vocalizations of the Actives.[20] Memory of the treatment itself is apparently forgotten also, as evidenced by the Actives' question "Did I fall asleep?" after each wipe. We know that Echo is different from the other Actives when we see her walk up the stairs to watch Sierra's programming. Her facial expressions let us know that she is aware that something is happening, even if, at this point, she is unsure of what it is. Wiping an Active's memory is compared to cleaning a slate, as if one were erasing all the information on that slate. As Echo's original personality Caroline notes, however, a slate can never be cleaned ("Ghost"); what has been written prior to the erasure can always be seen. The escaped Active Alpha reinforces this metaphor later. In the Season Two episode "A Love Supreme" (2.8), he notes that a program can never be deleted: "once it's created, it's alive."

Dollhouse's Actives are programmable people; they are "made to order." One reason for *Dollhouse* programmers' ease in imprinting the Actives may have to do with neural plasticity. Plasticity refers to the brain's ability to mold itself over the course of development. Increasingly, research indicates that even "older" brains, that is, brains beyond the age of maturity, which is roughly 25 years, are capable of rewiring and perhaps healing themselves after damage. The fact that the human brain itself is capable of being re-programmed may also underlie the assumptions of *Dollhouse*. Topher states that he is in "neuroplastic heaven" ("A Spy in the House of Love"), and several episodes feature Topher's manipulations of Echo's basic neural processing. For example, in "Ghost" Echo is imprinted with a near-sighted hostage negotiator named Eleanor Penn. For this mission, Echo wears glasses and truly cannot see without them. Topher states that he can mess up the neural connections to her eyesight and change the way that her brain processes information. Indeed, he states that he can make her whatever *he* wants her to be. Later, in "True Believer" Topher operates on Echo, inserting a camera into her visual system. Visual information perceived by her eyes bypasses her cortex—she is in effect rendered blind—but the signals are actually being recorded and broadcast back to the Bureau of Alcohol, Tobacco, Firearms, and Explosives (ATF).

The premise underlying Whedon's *Dollhouse* concerns whether human memory can be manipulated in such a way as to delete previously stored memories, implant new memories, or create artificial memories. Those people who enter the Dollhouses wishing to escape from the pain and suffering in their lives, such as Whiskey and November, could have those painful memories excised and have new, less painful memories created. Other Actives, such as Sierra, who was forced into servitude by a rejected lover ("Belonging" 2.4), would have the memory of her abuse at this man's hands erased, but would have memories of her life prior to her entry into the Dollhouse erased also. Echo, devastated by the death of her lover, volunteers to have the memory of her loss erased; however, given that she was facing imprisonment, she could not actually be said to "volunteer." Although a premise that some might envision as helpful in certain circumstances ("Man on the Street"), many people cannot conceive of the reality of losing their memories nor would they want to. Patients presenting with traumatic brain injuries or diseases such as Alzheimer's, with its concomitant amnesia, serve to illustrate the devastation such memory loss brings to its victims.

Locating River and Echo in Black Widow

Joss Whedon created and produced the series *Firefly* and *Dollhouse*; he also wrote the screenplays for *The Avengers* and *Avengers: Age of Ultron*. It should come as no surprise then that aspects of characters from those series would appear in Black Widow. Whedon certainly played fast and loose with some of Black Widow's canon from the Marvel Universe. There is no mention of the fact that she has taken a serum to prolong her life and no mention of her husband or other lovers, such as Hawkeye. She is only presented as a spy who worked for the Soviet Union before defecting to the United States and becoming a member of S.H.I.E.L.D.

Natasha Romanova entered the Red Room Academy when she was 12 years old. She was conditioned to serve her masters in any way that they deemed necessary. Among her many strengths are the ability to speak multiple languages; to withstand pain; to bear torture and interrogation without succumbing to it; to seduce men—and women if necessary; to kill without remorse; to feel no pity, love, or other "soft" emotions; and to follow orders without question. *Ultron* and *Agent Carter* provide glimpses into the types of lives girls in the Red Room Academy had as does Margaret Stohl's novel, *Forever Red*. It is not a life for the squeamish, and all provide examples of ways in which various methods of brainwashing can be implemented. Interestingly, in *Forever Red*, Natasha finds her brother Alexei alive, but she has no memory of him or their lives before their parents' deaths. Alexei also has no memory of her. Yet, as they interact with one another in an attempt to stop the activation of hundreds of sleeper agents embedded in governments around the globe, they begin to remember bits and pieces of those early years. It is only at the end of the book that we learn that both Natasha and Alexei had their memories wiped, and the wipes were instigated by Natasha in an attempt to keep Alexei safe. Only Phil Coulson and Pepper Potts are aware that Alex Manor is really Alexei Romanov.

To re-arrange the mind, to change the "programs" that we use in our everyday lives, to implant new memories or scramble old ones, to construct new identities, to alter cerebral architecture, to interfere with the activity of the chemicals that direct behavior, thoughts, and emotions—all of these actions have been attempted in the past and continue to be attempted in the present. One can only imagine what techniques will be used in the future to control behavior. Science fiction offers a rich selection of stories and novels in which such attempts have been made, with their resulting consequences. Unfortunately, history offers examples of a large number of such attempts as well and, given the stakes, those who thirst for power are unlikely to deviate from their quest. In the Marvel universes as well as in the Whedonverses, we have champions—heroes—who will keep us safe, who will fight for us, who believe that there is no such thing as making better humans without humanity's consent.

Perhaps she has no superpowers, but Black Widow has what many people need: personal power and agency. She experienced an attempt to recreate her, to make her into something she never wanted to be. Throughout her time in the Marvelverses, Black Widow illustrates that, although brainwashing and mind control are possible, it is also possible to effect change, to remake oneself into the "self" one wants to be. For example, in Ultron we observe a young Natasha befriend a fellow Red Room student whom she is eventually ordered to kill. Natasha does so with no hesitation; the consequences of disobedience are dire. However, the Natasha Romanoff that we have witnessed in four films to date show a woman who is able to develop friendships—witness her relationships with Steve Rogers and Clint Barton and his family—as well as feel strong emotions—witness her tearful eyes and obvious distress when she believes that Director Fury is dead.

The take-home message with respect to Black Widow is that, yes one can be unmade and remade, but one can also beat the programming. In the end, it is the choices and decisions we make that define us. Black Widow was subjected to experiences we cannot imagine. But she has reinvented herself and continues to do so. At the end of *Captain America: The Winter Soldier* she exposes her secrets to the world but refuses to let them be all that defines her. At the end of *Avengers: Age of Ultron* she is working with Steve Rogers to train the new Avengers. She is still writing her story. Let's hope she does so for a very long time.

NOTES

1. Natasha Romanoff, in Margaret Stohl, *Black Widow: Forever Red*, 181. This essay contains spoilers.

2. Google definitions. Accessed 20 Feb. 2016.

3. *Wikipedia* definitions. Accessed 20 Feb. 2016.

4. Hawkeye, Marvel's *The Avengers*.

5. The material in this section summarizes the information one would receive in a chapter on "Learning" in a standard introductory psychology class at any college or university. More in-depth references can be found in any textbook for such a course. I have used many in my twenty-something-years teaching experience. In addition, many of the classic texts can be found at Christopher D. Green's website, Classics in the History of Psychology: http://psychclassics.yorku.ca/.

6. Steve Rogers to Black Widow, *Captain America: The Winter Soldier*.

7. Like many Black Widow fans, I was distressed (to put it mildly) about this

story line. Whereas I know that she has a history with various men (such as Daredevil, Hawkeye, and the Winter Soldier), I worry that her agency will be reduced by having her engage in romantic relationships, especially with any of her colleagues.

8. Episodic memory is one type of declarative memory. It is composed of events that happened to a person or in their presence, hence it is autobiographical memory. This type of memory requires conscious effort for recall. One way we distinguish episodic memories from the other type of declarative memory—semantic or conceptual memory—is that we "remember" episodic memories.

9. River Tam, "Trash," *Firefly*, Season One, Episode 11.

10. An excellent summary of these can be found in Layton.

11. Removing an *aversive* stimulus is beneficial to the organism, and we refer to this as negative reinforcement. Reinforcement is always good for the subject.

12. Layton, n. p.

13. This does not contradict the information on Marvel's website about Natasha Romanova.

14. Jeffrey Dahmer (1960–94) performed crude lobotomies on his victims in an attempt to turn them into his "sex slaves."

15. Material about *Firefly* and *Dollhouse* was published in *Power and Control in the Television Worlds of Joss Whedon* © 2012 Sherry Ginn by permission of McFarland & Company, Inc., Box 611, Jefferson NC 28640.

16. Apparently some of the research subjects participating in the CIA's MKUltra project became increasingly psychotic, displaying symptoms one would classify as schizophrenic. Because of their experiences many of them might have suffered from PTSD as some have claimed for River. Some of the symptoms presented by hebephrenic schizophrenics are: active, but in an aimless and not constructive way; bizarre and inappropriate emotional responses; false, fixed beliefs (delusions); inability to feel pleasure; inappropriate grinning and grimacing; lack of emotion and motivation; seeing or hearing things that aren't there (hallucinations); and silly behavior. Some of these symptoms are also observed in other types of schizophrenia. The main difference is erratic behavior, with speech that is not grammatical or is randomly ordered. A colleague pointed out that this is characteristic of River, but I think that River's speech makes perfect sense when one realizes that the seeming randomness of her speech actually presages future events on the series.

17. The word *amygdala* is singular; the plural is *amygdalae*. There are two amygdalae and two hippocampi located in each cerebral hemisphere.

18. Project MKUltra supposedly used men, women, and children as sexual slaves according to sources whose credibility is not clear (such is the nature of conspiracies). However, Dalia Daudelin has written the novel *Monarch Mind* (Midnight Climax Publishing, 2013) which states, "Monarch mind control was an offshoot of the MK ULTRA experiments. The women exposed to these experiments were turned into *sex slaves*, dolls that would do anything for their handler. If they were told to have sex with someone, they did. If they were told to kill someone... they did." Note the use of the terms "dolls" and "handler."

19. Ava Orlova has been psychically linked with Natasha Romanoff by the sadistic and brutal head of the Red Room Academy, Ivan Somodorov. Orlova is confused as to how she can know Alex Manor before she meets him and why she knows certain things, like how to fight and use weapons. She will learn the truth about her upbringing when Somodorov begins his master plan: activating the sleeper agents who are embedded all over the globe.

20. Given that the brain has no pain receptors, there should be no pain in the

process. Note that the Winter Soldier is also placed in a conditioning chair. Rogers realizes that the Solider is his longtime friend, Bucky Barnes, when the Soldier loses his face mask during a fight. Rogers calls him by name and Barnes leaves. Later, when he asks his handlers who he is and indicates that he is remembering his past, he is placed in the chair for reprogramming. He places a bite bar in his mouth and, once the process starts, he contorts in pain. Despite this round of conditioning his memories of Rogers and their friendship continue to surface and compromise his ability to complete his mission—which is to kill Steve Rogers.

WORKS CONSULTED

American Psychiatric Association. *Diagnostic and Statistical Manual of Mental Disorders.* 5th ed. Washington, DC: APA, 2013. Print.

Condon, Richard. *The Manchurian Candidate.* New York: McGraw-Hill, 1959. Print.

Connor, Ed. "Psychology Bad." Ed. Joy Davidson. *The Psychology of Joss Whedon.* Dallas: BenBella, 2007, 185–95. Print.

Cornell, Paul (writer), Tom Raney (pencils), Scott Hanna (inks), Matt Milla (colors). *Black Widow: Deadly Origin.* New York: Marvel, 2010. Print.

Daniels, Bradley J. "'Stripping' River Tam's Amygdala." Ed. Joy Davidson. *The Psychology of Joss Whedon.* Dallas: BenBella, 2007, 131–40. Print.

Darowski, Joseph J. *The Ages of the Avengers: Essays on the Earth's Mightiest Heroes in Changing Times.* Jefferson, NC: McFarland, 2014. Print.

Ginn, Sherry. *Power and Control in the Television Worlds of Joss Whedon.* Jefferson, NC: McFarland, 2012. Print.

Kandel, Eric, James H. Schwartz, and Thomas M. Jessell. *Principles of Neural Science.* 4th ed. New York: McGraw-Hill, 2000. Print.

LaBar, Kevin S. "Beyond Fear: Emotional Memory Mechanisms in the Human Brain." *Current Directions in Psychological Science* 16.4 (Aug. 2007): 173–77. Print.

Layton, Julia. "How Brainwashing Works." *How Stuff Works.* InfoSpace, 10 May 2006. Accessed 8 Feb. 2016.

LeDoux, Joseph. *The Emotional Brain: The Mysterious Underpinnings of Emotional Life.* New York: Touchstone, 1996. Print.

Lifton, Robert Jay. *Thought Reform and the Psychology of Totalism: A Study of Brainwashing in China.* Chapel Hill: University of North Carolina Press, 1989 [W. W. Norton, 1961]. Print.

Loftus, Elizabeth F. "Creating False Memories." *Scientific American* 277.3 (1977): 70–75. Accessed 22 Feb. 2016.

Marano, Michael. "River Tam and the Weaponized Women of the Whedonverse." Ed. Jane Espenson. *Serenity Found: More Unauthorized Essays on Joss Whedon's Firefly Universe.* Dallas: BenBella, 2007, 37–48. Print.

Marks, John D. *The Search for the "Manchurian Candidate": The CIA and Mind Control.* New York: W. W. Norton, 1991. Print.

Mashour, George A., Erin E. Walker, and Robert L. Martuza. "Psychosurgery: Past, Present, and Future." *Brain Research Reviews* 48 (2005): 409–19. Print.

Myers, David G. *Exploring Social Psychology.* 7th ed. New York: McGraw-Hill, 2015. Print.

Shin, Lisa M., Scott L. Rauch, and Roger K. Pitman. "Amygdala, Medial Prefrontal Cortex, and Hippocampal Function in PTSD." *Annals of the New York Academy of Sciences* 1071 (July 2006): 67–79. Print.

Stohl, Margaret. *Black Widow: Forever Red.* Los Angeles: Marvel, 2015. Print.

Joss Whedon's Radical Icon of Third Wave Feminism

LEWIS CALL

Joss Whedon's *Buffy the Vampire Slayer* is often read as an artifact of American feminism's third wave (Karras, Byers, Pender, Levine). The strong, sexy, feminine Slayers embody third wave "girlie" feminism. Yet Whedon's *Avengers* seems anti-feminist. Critics accuse Whedon of tokenism, since the initial six-person Avengers team features just one woman: Natasha Romanoff, the Black Widow. I argue, however, that Black Widow is no token. She is an integral part of the Avengers, and a legitimate heir to *Buffy*'s third wave agenda. Like real-world girlie feminists, the Widow makes tactical use of her beauty and her sexuality. Her commitment to teamwork represents third wave forms of collective action which include both men and women (Karras).

Furthermore, I argue that Whedon's Widow is a radical third wave figure who goes beyond *Buffy*'s limited feminist representations. Black Widow embodies the crucial third wave theory of intersectionality, which analyzes interlocking identities such as gender, sexuality and ethnicity (Dicker and Piepmeier). Black Widow brings intersectional diversity to the Avengers. While *Buffy* lacked ethnic diversity until its final season, the Russian Romanoff fulfills the third wave's promise to promote multiethnic feminism. Scarlett Johansson, a Russophone actress of Belarusian descent, convincingly conveys Romanoff's Slavic ethnicity. And while Buffy often hesitated to invoke her sexual power, Black Widow readily invokes hers. As she does so, the Widow evokes the alternative sexuality known as dominance and submission (DS). The Widow is not merely a "do-gooder who dresses like a dominatrix," as Anthony Lane has argued (57). She uses DS strategically, to advance her agenda and that of her team. In *Avengers: Age of Ultron* she devel-

106

ops a consensual, erotic DS relationship with Bruce Banner/Hulk; this relationship benefits both of them.

"Nothing so only *about being female*"
The Widow Before Whedon

The Black Widow was born into American feminism's second wave. She first appeared in 1964, a year after Betty Friedan's *Feminine Mystique*. Before she defected from the Soviet Union, Natasha Romanoff lived in an arranged marriage with test pilot Alexei Shostakov, who became the Soviet agent known as Red Guardian. Believing Shostakov to be dead, Romanoff defected to the United States and began a new life as the single, childless, independent Black Widow. By 1970 she had a new costume: a sleek, sexy black jumpsuit, "more in keeping with the swingy Seventies! ... and with the modern image of the new Black Widow" (*Amazing Spiderman* 86 in Lee et al. 26). The Widow's fashion choice may have been influenced by that other jumpsuited Avenger of the 60s, Emma Peel (Diana Rigg). Black Widow resembled the image of liberated womanhood, which American women were seeing in the pages of Helen Gurley Brown's *Cosmopolitan* and, from 1972, Gloria Steinem's *Ms.* magazine. Writer Gerry Conway made this resemblance explicit when he had a group of fictional female fans declare that Black Widow was "*definitely* the Gloria Steinem of the jump-suit set!" (*Daredevil* 91, quoted in Howe 129).

The Widow always projected a confident sexuality. Conway suggests that the version of Black Widow which he developed with artist Gene Colan was "comics' first empowered sexy babe" (quoted in Howe 115). Mike Madrid reads the Widow in the context of the sexual revolution of the late 60s, noting her penchant for jetting off to Switzerland with playboys (254). Here the Widow's values challenged what Jane Gerhard has called "the second wave's foundational premise ... that sexuality was the universal source of women's oppression" (49). By the late 70s, cultural feminists and lesbian feminists were emphasizing the "failures of sexual liberalism" (Gerhard 152). The Widow's assertive heterosexuality would not sit well with *these* second wavers.

In some ways, the Black Widow of the 70s foreshadowed the third wave feminism that would develop two decades later. When an overconfident thug declares that she's "only a female," the Widow replies that "there's nothing so *only* about being female, fellas. You ought to *try* it some time" (*Amazing Adventures* 5 in Lee et al. 92). Like a third waver *avant la lettre*, the Widow suggests that a female gender identity is available to men, and that men might benefit from performing such an identity. While the second wave was moving towards the gender essentialism which found its most famous expression in the cultural feminism of the late 70s (Gerhard, chapter 5), Black Widow was moving in the opposite direction. She had to wonder if there was "really a *place* for her in a world such as this?" (*Amazing Adventures* 1 in Lee et al. 49). Perhaps there was no place for her in the world of second wave feminism. But the idea that female identities were available to men as well as women would find a home in the world of the third wave.

Jon Favreau's disappointing *Iron Man 2* introduced Black Widow to American moviegoers in 2010. Favreau presented a flat, two dimensional Black Widow, completely lacking in emotional complexity. Johansson was undeniably alluring in her skintight jumpsuit; throughout the film, she invites the male gaze and even insists upon it. We can go further, and say that this sexually objectified Widow is actually a *product* of the male gaze. "The determining male gaze projects its fantasy onto the female figure, which is styled accordingly," as Laura Mulvey has it (19). The cold beauty of Favreau's Widow is the crystalized form of heterosexual male desire. Even here, of course, the fantasy image of the objectified Natasha Romanoff is already a strategy: the Widow wields this image deliberately, to distract Tony Stark from her espionage activities. But Favreau remains unable to explore the feminist potential of this strategy. Favreau's Widow is a caricature, not a character, and hers is an empty beauty: this Widow is eye candy for the fanboys. The only saving grace of Favreau's Black Widow is that she provides a dramatic contrast with Joss Whedon's complex, nuanced interpretation of the character.

"Never a damsel in distress"

Whedon's Widow has far more feminist potential than Favreau's did, but this potential is hard to see at first. The American superhero film is such a thoroughly masculine genre that it resists *any* representations of superheroic women. Even when a superhero film does feature a female superhero, the film's marketing will often render her invisible. The cover of *The Avengers* DVD is divided into six roughly triangular segments; this cover attempts to showcase the individual members of the team by featuring one Avenger in each segment, but Black Widow must share her section with Hawkeye, and she is missing entirely from the Blu-Ray cover (Graves 9). By the time *Age of Ultron* arrived, Disney's cynical refusal to market Black Widow merchandise had become so egregious that outraged feminist fans began organizing online, using a change.org petition and social media tags such as #WheresNatasha.

This is a serious political problem for a feminist filmmaker like Joss Whedon. While Whedon emphasizes that he is not in control of the merchandising, he also notes that he has a daughter who identifies with the female characters in his films (Hawkes). Whedon says,

[M]y daughter watched *The Avengers* and was like, "My favorite characters were the Black Widow and Maria Hill," and I thought, Yeah, of course they were. I read a beautiful thing Junot Diaz wrote: "If you want to make a human being into a monster, deny them, at the cultural level, any reflection of themselves" [quoted in Pascale 375].

Whedon is concerned about the impact that his films' gender representations will have on the girls and women in his audience, including his daughter. He clearly wants to provide those girls and women with significant positive reflections of themselves, in the form of strong, authentic female heroes. This is undoubtedly what motivated him to include Scarlet Witch in *Ultron*. "We count," Whedon said just before the domestic release of *Ultron*. "When you get enough [women] so that you can stop counting, then we've accomplished something" (quoted in Clark). While making *The Avengers*, Whedon struggled to get Marvel Studios to count as high as *one*. He actually had to fight to keep Black Widow in the film. While Marvel found her character superfluous, Whedon argued successfully that without her, the S.H.I.E.L.D. Helicarrier would feel like a "gay cruise" (Rogers). Even then, it was clear that Black Widow would be the film's only female superhero, and that she would be surrounded by men.

In *The Avengers*, the Widow is what Katha Pollitt would call a Smurfette: "a lone female, stereotypically defined," who exists within "a group of male buddies." Pollitt accurately identifies the political problem inherent in the Smurfette trope: it implies that girls and women exist only in relation to boys and men. This leaves women few available roles (and no desirable ones): they can be sidekicks, or sexy decorations (Sarkeesian). Favreau's *Iron Man 2* offered Pepper Potts the first role and Black Widow the second: as Megan Kearns notes, even in a film with multiple female characters, the women often orbit the men. The Smurfette trope hinges on its appeal to stereotype. In the American superhero film, women characters depart from stereotype rarely (albeit considerably more frequently in the works of Joss Whedon). When they do leave stereotype behind, however, they challenge the relational system of representation which defines women strictly by what they do for men: nurturing, seducing, assisting. As Kearns observes, in *The Avengers* Black Widow is neither sidekick nor sexy ornament; she is neither shoved aside nor reduced to a man's love interest.

Smurfettes can easily be spotted by applying the Bechdel Test. Alison Bechdel's well-known test for cinematic representations of women requires a film to feature at least two women, both with names, who have a conversation about something other than men (Bechdel). Britt Hayes contends that *The Avengers* meets every criteria but the last, "as both Black Widow (real name: Natasha Romanoff) and Agent Hill have names." But Hayes's language is telling: Hill only has a partial name. Many moviegoers will not know her first name (Maria). For many in the audience, her first name (as Tony Stark says of Phil Coulson) is "Agent." In any case, Romanoff and Hill have no significant interactions in the movie, even though, as Stephanie Graves points out, this dialog-heavy film has plenty of opportunities for such interactions (5). *Ultron* adds another woman to the Avengers' roster: Wanda Maximoff, the Scarlet Witch. Yet the film still fails the Bechdel Test; Maximoff and Romanoff have no significant interaction.

While the Bechdel Test does tell us important things about a film's gender representations, however, the fact that *The Avengers* and *Ultron* fail the test does not necessarily mean that the films' representations are conservative. As Hayes points out, even though Hill and Romanoff don't speak to each other in the first film, "both women are still positively represented" as "sensible, intelligent, and strong—physically *and* mentally." In *Ultron,* Whedon certainly portrays Maximoff as strong; indeed, she immediately becomes one of the most powerful members of a team that includes an indestructible green monster and a Norse god. Actress Elizabeth Olsen, who plays Maximoff, certainly understands what is at stake in her portrayal of the second female Avenger: "I can imagine myself during recess or before school on the playground being like, 'I'm Scarlet Witch! Pow!' To think of little girls being like, 'I'm powerful and strong and tough!'—that's really cool," says Olsen (quoted in Clark). As for Natasha Romanoff, she's all about the *work*. True, her coworkers are all men. But that says more about her chosen profession than it does about her (or about Whedon's representation of her). Romanoff is a strong woman holding her own in a male-dominated profession, and that is a feminist representation. While a second wave feminist might insist upon gender equality in the workplace, Romanoff simply assumes that she is entitled to such equality, as do her male colleagues. As Scott Mendelson argues, *The Avengers* is progressive and feminist to the considerable extent that it normalizes Black Widow's equality on the team. The male Avengers treat her as an equal, and "this is simply accepted as just the way things are" (Mendelson). This confirms the film's third wave orientation.

Although Whedon's Black Widow is a positive and indeed feminist representation, film critics have nonetheless charged Whedon with tokenism. *New York Times* critic A. O. Scott describes *The Avengers* as "a superhero frat party with Scarlett Johansson upholding the "'yeah, but it's not all guys' clause." Rick Groen of the Toronto *Globe and Mail* argues that "in the token sexy female department, Scarlett was a pale pink at best." Whedon's Widow, however, is anything but a token (Pascale 374). Although Whedon is constrained by the conservative gender dynamics of the superhero genre, he does everything he can to subvert those constraints. *The Avengers* ends up promoting a feminism as radical as one could possibly find in a corporate (Marvel/Disney) film. Black Widow has the third most screen time of any Avenger, as she does again in *Age of Ultron* (Mulhauser and Shafer, Lockett). In *The*

Avengers, she has more unbroken dialog than any of her male colleagues (Mulhauser and Shafer). As Jess d'Arbonne has argued, Whedon's Widow is a "fully-realized, multi-dimensional character with complete personal agency." Daniel Snyder argues persuasively "in accordance with Whedon's M. O., this version of the Black Widow is more than a token female team mate in constant need of rescuing." In fact, this is what attracted Scarlett Johansson to the character: "I love that she's never a damsel in distress," says Johansson (quoted in Surrell 70).

If anyone is a damsel in distress, it is Black Widow's colleague Clint Barton/Hawkeye (Kickpuncher). By positioning Black Widow as the rescuer and Hawkeye as the rescuee in *The Avengers*, Whedon reverses the standard gender logic of the superhero genre, much as Buffy reversed the gender logic of the horror genre. Whedon further subverts gender expectations by consistently refusing standard action movie clichés about relations between men and women. As d'Arbonne notes, "not once does Black Widow fall prey to being the token girl in the boy's club simply so that she can be wooed": she has a purely platonic friendship with Hawkeye, something which is extremely rare in superhero and action films. As Stephanie Graves points out, however, Romanoff's character is still defined in relation to a man; her main motivation throughout the film is to save Hawkeye (6). Again in *Age of Ultron* her char-

Black Widow (Scarlett Johansson) holding a gun. From *Avengers: Age of Ultron* (Photofest).

acter is defined largely in relation to a man, this time through her controversial relationship with Bruce Banner/Hulk. Even Joss Whedon cannot infinitely expand the representational limits of the American superhero film. Yet Black Widow's subversion of the superhero movie's gender stereotypes is certainly sufficient for us to call her a feminist superhero. Indeed, I argue below for a feminist reading of the Romanoff/Banner relationship; this reading is based upon a recognition that their relationship is largely structured by dominance and submission.

Third Wave Dominance via Girlie Submission

Like Buffy, Whedon's Widow embodies the "girlie" feminism that was such an important part of the early third wave. During the 90s, third wave magazines like BUST described "a new breed of feminists who were determined to embrace … everything that was traditionally girlie, and therefore just as traditionally marginalized" (Karp and Stoller 46). Baumgardner and Richards have shown how the Girlies rebelled against the assumption of female asexuality, and against the idea that girls and power don't mix (137). Like Buffy, Black Widow uses her power and her sexuality tactically, to advance the causes she believes in. But while Buffy often used her sexuality in a tentative or uncertain way, Natasha Romanoff has a refreshing sexual confidence. Stephanie Graves is quite right to suggest that "Romanoff isn't sexualized, apart from the way she sexualizes herself—her femme fatale persona is deliberately performative on her part" (7). Romanoff *chooses* to deploy an active, powerful female sexuality. *The Avengers* and *Age of Ultron* present this choice as an empowering one. Black Widow is a successful spy and superhero, and she owes much of that success to her performance of sexuality. In *Ultron* she uses her sexual power to pursue a consensual, ethical relationship of dominance/submission with Banner/Hulk.

As Elana Levine has observed, third wavers embrace a contradictory notion of femininity, simultaneously girlie and tough (177). Black Widow nicely embodies this contradiction: tough enough to trounce a gang of Russian gunrunners without breaking a sweat, girlie enough to pick up her sexy high heels on the way out. Levine notes that Buffy's third wave style combines traditional markers of girlish femininity with those of masculinity, such as a no-nonsense fighting style (178). Here Black Widow may be even more of a girlie than Buffy: the Widow's Wushu fighting style is graceful, fluid and feminine (Surrell 168). And while Buffy may have been a girlie "hot chick with superpowers," Black Widow is something more radical: a sexy non-super hero. The male Avengers Thor, Hulk, and Captain America need superpowers to be superheroes. Most male Avengers rely upon powerful prostheses: Iron

Man's suit, Thor's hammer, Cap's shield, Hawkeye's bow. Black Widow has nothing more than her wits, her Wushu, and some small arms. (She can easily do without the guns.) "Black Widow, though just a human amongst gods, is just as skilled and powerful as her comrades," observes Andy Park, the concept artist who designed Black Widow's look for every film except (interestingly) Favreau's *Iron Man 2* (Johnston 40, 244). "What do you need to be in order to keep up with Iron Man, Hulk, Captain America and Thor?" asks Karrin Anderson. "A woman." Although Stephanie Graves is right to point out the limitations of *The Avengers'* gender representations, I must disagree with her claim that "the film does little to push the dominant cultural ideologies regarding gender" (9). The suggestion that a woman with no extraordinary powers or prostheses could be equal in power and status to any superpowered man certainly represents a challenge to the dominant, sexist gender ideology of the American superhero film.

Elana Levine has demonstrated that third wave girlie feminism "explicitly recognizes the element of 'masquerade'" inherent in feminine accouterments such as lipstick and high heels (177). As Jess d'Arbonne quite rightly argues, the masquerade is Black Widow's primary tactic. Twice in *The Avengers*, Black Widow encourages her enemies to underestimate her by masquerading as a weak, vulnerable woman (d'Arbonne). She does this in her confrontation with the Russian gunrunners, and again in her interrogation of Loki. I expand d'Arbonne's analysis by emphasizing that whenever Black Widow employs this tactic, she simultaneously evokes the alternative sexual practice known as dominance and submission (DS). She performs submission from a position of invisible dominance. This is one of Black Widow's secret superpowers.

Natasha Romanoff is in bondage when the audience first meets her. She is tied to a chair, apparently helpless. The scene takes place in a grimy industrial warehouse, replete with hooks and heavy chains. The Russian gang boss, Luchkov, has an extensive collection of torture tools, which he plays with as he interrogates Romanoff. The *mise en scène* encourages the audience to read this encounter according to the logic of DS. By that logic, Romanoff appears to be completely submissive. Luchkov mocks her femininity, which he associates with weakness: "the famous Black Widow, and she turns out to be simply another pretty face." Romanoff parodies this weakness even as she performs it for Luchkov. "Do you really think I'm pretty?" This performance is deeply informed by her girlie feminism. Since she is, in fact, strong and secure in her womanhood, her prettiness is actually a source of power for her. Luchkov completely misunderstands Romanoff's prettiness, and this misunderstanding proves disastrous for him. Blinded by patriarchal assumptions about a woman's beauty and her presumed insecurities regarding that beauty, Luchkov is entirely vulnerable to Black Widow's girlie feminism.

When she receives her phone summons from Coulson, Romanoff immediately switches to the dominant role. She escapes her bondage and gives the Russian gang a sound thrashing. She wraps a heavy chain around Luchkov's leg and leaves him dangling in the air. She has completely reversed the power relations which obtained when the scene began. Romanoff is now thoroughly dominant, and Luchkov is in the submissive role. Whedon points out that this scene is his career in a microcosm: the "helpless" female who turns out to be stronger than anyone around her (Whedon, "Commentary").

Black Widow also switches from submission to dominance during her interrogation of Loki. This is Whedon's favorite scene from *The Avengers*; he loves the power struggle (Whedon, "Commentary"). At first the Widow allows herself to appear uncertain. She admits that she made a name for herself as a spy and assassin before joining S.H.I.E.L.D. "I have a very specific skill set. I didn't care who I used it for. Or on." Like Luchkov, Loki is fascinated by her apparent emotional weakness. He tries to exploit this weakness, recounting failures from her past. Then he pounds his fist against the thick glass wall of his cell and tells her that he will make Hawkeye kill her, slowly, intimately, in every way that he knows she fears. Romanoff lets herself appear devastated. She turns away. Her shoulders are hunched. We hear her sobbing. She appears to offer Loki her submission. "You're a monster," she says, her voice quivering. This is the moment when Loki gives her what she was after all along: information. "Oh, no. You brought the monster." She straightens up, resuming her normal, confident posture. She turns to face Loki, calm, centered, completely in control. The tears are gone. Her voice is steady. "So. Banner. That's your play." She immediately undermines Loki's (illusory) dominance, simply by revoking her (equally illusory) submission. "Thank you for your cooperation," she says smoothly. Once again she has used submission tactically, in the service of her dominance.

"I adore you…. But I need the other guy"

Like *Avengers, Age of Ultron* is centrally concerned with Black Widow's use of dominance and submission. Some feminists have criticized the representation of Black Widow in *Ultron*. For example, Shaun Huston views Romanoff's reaction to her forced sterilization and her somewhat awkward attempts to develop a relationship with Banner/Hulk as evidence that *Ultron* takes "a strong turn towards conventional gender roles." I argue, however, that both of these elements may reasonably be read as feminist, provided that we take the crucial step of reading Romanoff/Widow as a dominant woman, and her relationship with Banner/Hulk as a DS relationship.

In an open letter to Whedon, Sara Stewart expresses her disappointment with *Ultron*'s treatment of Black Widow, citing her "mini-breakdown" over her inability to have children. Meredith Woerner and Katharine Trendacosta argue that *Ultron*'s message is that the Widow "can't ever have babies, so her life is ruined." But this reading oversimplifies Romanoff's emotional reaction to her inability to have children, and misrepresents the politics behind that reaction. Shaun Huston points out that this story simply reveals the "lack of options" for a writer/director who wants to explore what it means to be a female superhero—especially if that writer/director is working in the Marvel Cinematic Universe (MCU), and not Marvel's comic book or television universes, both of which feature diverse and interesting casts of female characters. Alyssa Rosenberg makes a similar point, arguing persuasively that Whedon's attempt to explore "what it means to be both a woman and an action hero … is a worthy entry in the oeuvre that made Whedon a feminist icon in the first place."

Natasha Romanoff's forced sterilization does indeed represent a powerful woman's disturbing loss of agency, but *Age of Ultron* is clearly a feminist *critique* of this loss. Libby Hill is quite right to argue that it is "dismissive" to reduce Romanoff's sterilization story to baby lust: "it's about being stripped of things before you even have a chance to decide whether you want them," and is therefore linked to the fight for reproductive rights. Read in this light, Whedon's sterilization story can be seen as a bold denunciation of the forced removal of a woman's reproductive agency, and thus part of a tradition of activist-representational feminism that stretches back at least as far as the second wave feminism of *Roe v. Wade*. Romanoff's forced sterilization is indeed "a form of state-perpetrated violence against the female body" (Adams), and we may read Whedon's film as a critique of that violence: a comfortable (if somewhat traditional) feminist position. However, since the film argues for a form of female agency broad enough to include the right to choose gender roles usually deemed traditional (e.g., motherhood), its politics are actually more third wave than second. The third wave tends to define agency in this broader way. Criticism has focused on Romanoff's assertion that forced sterilization made her a "monster," but as Amanda Marcotte quite rightly observes, the world does often tell women who want an independent existence that they are monsters. (Following the logic that Whedon borrowed from Junot Diaz, pop culture tells independent women the same thing by denying them any cultural reflection of themselves.) A crucial indicator of the film's gender politics (and one often overlooked by critics) is the fact that Natasha Romanoff readily recognizes the possibility of a meaningful, satisfying, non-reproductive relationship with Banner. As Marcotte argues, her willingness to depart from social expectations of what the good life should look like is "pretty feminist."

The sterilization story allows Romanoff to offer DS as the basis for a non-reproductive erotic relationship. Her relationship with Banner/Hulk is not precisely sexual and certainly not reproductive (since neither of them can conceive children). But it is deeply erotic, and it conforms to the erotics of DS. The relationship allows Romanoff to transform the DS she used non-consensually against the villains Luchkov and Loki in the first film. In *Ultron,* she deploys her dominance in the service of a consensual, erotic and loving relationship with Banner, one which clearly benefits both of them. Krystal Clark and Tara Bennett have argued that "this superhero version of Beauty and the Beast ... neuters a once fierce heroine." But Natasha Romanoff is different from Beauty in at least one crucial way: she has all the power. She can use that power to tame the beast or summon him (and she does both in *Ultron*). But the choice—rage-filled monster or awkward, nebbishy scientist—is hers, because she is the dominant party in the relationship. "Not only does the film put her in an unnecessary romance but they actually make her a damsel in distress," lament Clark and Bennett. In fact neither claim is true. The relationship is necessary in that it allows the couple to explore the potential benefits of DS, something they both need desperately. And Black Widow is *never* a damsel in distress in *Ultron,* any more than she was in the first film. Captured by Ultron, she cobbles together a transmitter to alert her teammates to her location. When Banner arrives to rescue her, she refuses. "I'm here to get you to safety," Banner declares. "Job's not finished," she replies. Disney may refuse to market or merchandise the Black Widow character because they assume that their Disney Princess characters have already given them a lock on the "girl market" (Vincent), but at least Whedon gives us a rescue-*rejecting* "princess."

Far from throwing away her agency by pursuing a relationship with Banner, as Clark and Bennett assert, Romanoff uses that relationship to lay claim to an extremely powerful type of agency: that of the dominant woman. As Andrea Towers observes, in *Ultron,* Black Widow is growing, learning and (perhaps most importantly) "taking control of her life." As Towers plausibly argues, "that's a *great* way to further her character." Scarlett Johansson seems to agree. "Oh, *of course* these characters are together," she thought as she started to work with Mark Ruffalo, who plays Banner/Hulk (quoted in Clark). "Because it's not just beauty and the beast." Johansson points out that the two characters have an important shared experience: trauma. Ruffalo understands that his character's relationship with Johansson's does not compromise the Widow's agency or diminish her strength in any way: "I don't think it makes her any weaker ... if anything, Black Widow is much stronger than Banner. She protects him" (quoted in Cox).

She does this especially through the mechanism of the lullaby, her unique method of pacifying the Hulk. This method also represents the centerpiece of her DS relationship with Hulk/Banner. Banner is justifiably terrified of his uncontrollable Hulkish powers. He therefore makes the rational, ethical decision to grant Romanoff control over his body and its powers. Here he resembles a submissive man surrendering control of his body to a dominant woman. Whedon has been here before: in his *Astonishing X-Men*, Scott Summers submits to the dominant Emma Frost in order to bring his powers under control (Call). Like Frost, Romanoff uses her power responsibly, to meet her partner's needs. It is also important that Romanoff/Widow develops a relationship not only with Banner, but also with the Hulk. This means that the relationship meets her needs, too: like Buffy before her, Romanoff needs a little monster in her man. Indeed, as Rosenberg quite rightly argues, Romanoff "would rather bring out her lover's dark side than contain it." Romanoff does not merely tolerate the Hulk's darkness, rage and monstrosity. She seeks it out and celebrates it. She has no fear of it. "You're not a threat to me," she observes. Indeed he is not, for she is always in charge.

The lullaby is clearly a seduction. The Widow performs this seduction after *Ultron*'s opening battle scene. "Hey, big guy," she purrs. She offers Hulk pouty lips, bedroom eyes, and gentle touches along the fingers, hand and upper arm. Her movements are precise and deliberate. She is clearly deploying a form of physical discipline. This practice (like much erotic discipline) is designed to create a particular emotional state in the submissive. The only difference between this and a real-life DS scene is that the evidence of the dominant's success is more obvious. Romanoff turns her head and allows herself a half-smile when she sees that the lullaby has succeeded. Hulk reverts to Banner. Critics have argued that the lullaby infantilizes Hulk and points the Widow, once again, towards a problematic maternalism. For Woerner and Trendacosta, the film's message is "Black Widow don't be sad—you have a baby Hulk." Reading the Widow/Hulk relationship in terms of DS gives us another option, however. In a DS context, Widow's infantilization of Hulk looks a lot like "age play," a form of roleplaying in which the submissive partner takes on the role of a child, while the dominant acts as an adult (and often a parent). This form of play can be satisfying, meaningful and in some cases therapeutic—as indeed it is for Hulk. As for the Widow, she seems to have no trouble eroticizing her maternal role with respect to Hulk; in fact, she seems to enjoy the power it gives her over him. Like any DS play, the lullaby requires trust to succeed in the long run. "How long before you trust me?" Romanoff demands as she and Banner discuss the effectiveness of the lullaby. Banner may not completely trust Romanoff, but he clearly trusts her enough to submit to her. During the Avengers' initial fight with Ultron, Banner lands on top of Romanoff behind the bar. Here he is physically dominant but psychologically submissive. "Don't turn green!" Romanoff commands, and he obeys.

Crucially, the film also offers us a model of the "anti-lullaby." Late in the film, the Avengers need the Hulk, but Banner is reluctant to transform. "You're not gonna turn green?" Romanoff demands. "I've got a compelling reason not to lose my cool," Banner replies. Here he reveals the risk inherent in Romanoff's dominance strategy. If he submits too thoroughly to her, he runs the risk of losing his Hulk-self altogether. But Romanoff won't let that happen. "I adore you," she says. The two share a passionate kiss, which confirms that she desires Banner as well as Hulk. Then she pushes him into a pit, forcing his transformation. "But I need the other guy," she explains, to herself and to the audience. Banner transforms into Hulk and jumps free of the pit. "Let's finish the job," Romanoff says. Once again, she has used her dominance to create a particular emotional state in her submissive—in this case, rage. And once again, she has used DS tactically, in the service of her mission. But in this case, she simultaneously uses DS in the service of a loving, erotic relationship. This makes her dominance over Banner ethically superior to the dominance she deployed in the first film. While her cynical use of Luchkov and Loki was sanctioned by their status as villains, the dominance she exerts over Banner is much more than mere manipulation: it is the sign of a mutually satisfying DS relationship.

Like the best dominants, the Widow orders her submissive to take actions which she believes will allow him to become his authentic self: "Now go be a hero." This strategy also allows the Widow to pursue authenticity herself. Rosenberg has it just right: surrounded by men, Romanoff deliberately chooses the one who responds to the darkness in her. That is the right choice for her, because it allows her to harness her darkness and Banner's via DS, and thus allows them both a safe, ethical and satisfying way to express their darknesses. Darren Franich agrees that "there's an angle where Black Widow loves Bruce Banner *because*, not despite, the Hulk: where Widow recognizes that all the other Avengers are nice guys at their core, whereas Bruce Banner's core is dark and weird and Freudian." However, Franich is too quick to conclude that this is *not* the movie's angle. If we read Widow/Hulk as a DS relationship rather than a more conventional vanilla one, then we can see that the Widow *does* love the Hulk, and also loves her power over him. To tame a raging green monster like the Hulk is surely the ultimate triumph for a dominant woman like Black Widow.

And tame him she does. As the Battle of Sokovia winds down, the Widow tries to give Hulk a lullaby. He starts to respond, but Ultron strafes them, and the Widow is wounded. Whedon gives the couple a touchingly intimate moment: Hulk lays the injured Widow gently on the deck of the Helicarrier, the perfect image of a concerned submissive caring for his dominant. Hulk then steals a plane and sets off for parts unknown. The Widow tries to give him a lullaby via video phone. "Hey, big guy," she begins. This seems to be the lullaby's standard opening line. She tells Hulk the job's finished, tells him to turn the plane around. But he ignores her, and hangs up.

The lullaby fails here because of the physical distance between the two. The lullaby is a form of physical discipline, and it requires bodily contact. Romanoff ends the film thinking that she may have lost Banner, but Nick Fury (and the audience) suspects that he will be back. He needs her dominance as much as she needs his submission.

"I'm Russian—or I was"

Whedon's Widow promotes a multiethnic, multilingual feminism. In this respect, the Widow does more to advance a third wave agenda than Buffy did. Michele Byers finds Buffy's failure to incorporate ethnic difference to be one of the show's most problematic aspects (180). Patricia Pender has shown that Buffy's final season did address the crucial third wave issue of cultural diversity, but almost as an afterthought (231). The show's belated international expansion of the Slayer line can be dismissed as—you guessed it—tokenism (Pender 233). Yet Pender has demonstrated that a generous reading can see a narrative of transnational feminist activism in the extension of the Slayer's powers to young girls across the globe (233). We can easily identify similar narratives around Black Widow, even without such a generous reading.

When we first meet Romanoff in *The Avengers*, she is speaking to Luchkov in her native Russian tongue. Scarlett Johansson delivers this Russian dialog with confidence and conviction. Johansson is the descendent of Belarusian Jews; she once "had a Russian language teacher" and she learned the language "phonetically" (Tchesnokova). Joss Whedon also studied Russian in school (Whedon, "Commentary"). This crucial introductory scene foregrounds Romanoff's Russian ethnicity and ensures that the audience will recognize her as a figure of multifaceted difference: a female, Slavic Russophone. By the time the Avengers finally assemble, the team includes four English-speaking white American men, an Asgardian who looks Scandinavian and speaks like an Englishman ("Shakespeare in the park," as Tony Stark puts it)—and Natasha Romanoff. Romanoff recruits the white male American Bruce Banner. The team may be largely composed of white American men, but it is important that the invitation to assemble comes from a Russian woman (acting on behalf of an African-American man, Samuel L. Jackson's Director Nick Fury). John McDowell acknowledges that the early scenes in *The Avengers* with Romanoff in Russia and India are meant to provide "a sense of the global"; however, McDowell denies the progressive potential of these scenes, arguing that Romanoff is immediately drawn back to the United States to do her heroic business (40). Of course, it makes sense that Romanoff would work in the U.S., and for the predominately American S.H.I.E.L.D. After all, she suffered unspeakable trauma at the hands of the United States'

Soviet enemy during the Cold War. The unfortunate symbolic effect of this sensible narrative choice, however, is to suggest that Romanoff is easily subsumed into an essentially white American superhero culture. But we must not mistake setting and political allegiance for cultural identity. Romanoff may do much of her superhero work in the United States. She may even act on behalf of U.S. officials or organizations. But at no time during *The Avengers* is she actually an American.

Romanoff invokes her ethnicity again later in the film, during her interrogation of Loki. "Regimes fall every day. I tend not to weep over that. I'm Russian—or I was." Here she associates her Russian identity with a certain kind of pragmatic cynicism regarding changes in government. This is understandable, given that Romanoff has lived through the collapse of the Soviet Union and the uncertainties of the Putin regime. Of course, the politically cynical Russian is a bit of a cliché. But we must remember that Romanoff is playing Loki here. She stereotypes her own ethnic identity in order to convince Loki that she has no particular loyalty to the World Security Council which governs S.H.I.E.L.D. Her skillful manipulation of ethnic clichés intersects smoothly with her equally nimble use of gender clichés. A very specific skill set, indeed! It is also interesting that Romanoff regards ethnic identity as something that she can leave behind (she *was* Russian). It is something that she can pick up again whenever it suits her purposes, as she does in this scene. For her, ethnicity is not fixed or absolute; it is a tool that she can use as she sees fit—a very third wave perspective.

Age of Ultron is even more preoccupied with the desire to represent a multi-ethnic, global society than *Avengers* was. Much of *Ultron* takes place outside the U.S., in South Africa, Oslo, Seoul, and the fictional East European nation of Sokovia. As David Betancourt observes in *The Washington Post*, "'Age of Ultron' gives all the feeling of being a global event." But perhaps *Ultron* tries too hard to attain a global perspective. *The Atlantic*'s Christopher Orr points out that "an *awful lot* of the final act revolves around the rescue of nameless, line-less, interchangeable Sokovians." The film clearly craves a global feel, but it has trouble imagining convincing non–American *characters*. This means that *Ultron* runs the risk of "eating the Other," as bell hooks would say (21): the film adds non–American locales and non-white characters (often "extras" without speaking roles), perhaps in an attempt to add exotic "spice" to what would otherwise be a strikingly white superhero film.

The introduction of Wanda Maximoff/Scarlet Witch does not help the film's efforts to promote ethnic diversity. Like Romanoff, Maximoff is meant to be a Slavic Eastern European: Maximoff hails from Sokovia. But critics find Elizabeth Olsen's portrayal of Slavic ethnicity unconvincing. Unlike Scarlett Johansson, Olsen is no Russophone. Richard Lawson calls Olsen's Scarlet Witch "shakily accented," while Orr calls Olsen's Sokovian accent "tongue-y."

It is also unfortunate that the Avengers' second female member has the same Slavic ethnicity as its first. While there is clearly a space for intersectional diversity in the Avengers, that space is defined in strangely narrow terms. Slavic women provide the team's only images of diversity, and the only counterweight to its roster of white, mostly American men.

The good news is that this unfortunate representational choice only further underscores the crucial symbolic significance of Black Widow. In *Ultron*, the Widow continues to provide an authentic model of intersectional identity. While Elizabeth Olsen's Wanda Maximoff might read like a caricature of a Slavic woman, Scarlett Johansson's Natasha Romanoff remains plausibly, convincingly Slavic. In *Ultron*, she models the experience of an Eastern European immigrant who gradually assimilates into her adopted American culture. Like many immigrants, she has ambiguous feelings about her Old World name. On the one hand she wants to pass it on, in this case to Clint and Laura Barton's unborn child (who turns out to be "Nathanial" instead). On the other hand, she encourages her friends to Americanize her name. "Natasha" is a diminutive form of Natalia. The name Natalia could become "Nata" in Russian, but it could only become "Nat" in American English. Nat gets behind the bar, mixes drinks, and talks about the man who done her wrong, like a femme fatale in an American film noir. She hones her knowledge of American culture, and learns to deploy that culture to great comedic effect, offering a pitch-perfect rendition of the Warner Brothers cartoon Roadrunner's "beep beep" in the midst of a massive motorcycle chase. In *Ultron*, she is well on her way to becoming a Russian-American. But the audience will remember, from the first film, that she can pick up and deploy her original Russian ethnicity whenever she wants to do so. This is the power of her third wave understanding of identity: for her, ethnicity, like gender and sexuality, is performance.

"We got this"

Whedon's Widow also models third-wave forms of collective feminist action. Irene Karras has suggested that the cooperation of women with men in the struggle against evil is a "distinctly third wave" phenomenon. Black Widow's commitment to teamwork definitely includes men. For example, in *The Avengers*, she works closely with Bruce Banner to help him control his rage and violence. Here she resembles real-world third wave activists who work with men to oppose violence against women. Black Widow tries to help Banner stay calm, so he will not transform into the Hulk. She fails, probably because at this point in the narrative, she hasn't yet developed the DS relationship with Hulk/Banner that will enable her to perform the lullaby in

Ultron. The enraged green monster chases her through the corridors of the Helicarrier. This scene reads like an attempted sexual assault. The Hulk is the very image of uncontrolled, testosterone-fueled male aggression. As Daniel Snyder observes, Hulk is "the perfect embodiment of the unchecked male rage that so often victimizes women." Romanoff is afraid of this rage, but she is never a helpless victim. She manages to protect herself from an assailant far more physically powerful than she is. Here Whedon gives Natasha Romanoff what Snyder has called "the most human moment in 'The Avengers.'" Having narrowly escaped the Hulk's assault, she sits on the deck, wounded and visibly shaken. But when she hears that Hawkeye is on board, she instantly suppresses her own fear and comes to the aid of her brainwashed comrade. So she has another secret superpower: courage (Mulhauser and Schafer). She uses that courage in the service of collective action.

Romanoff's commitment to teamwork remains clear as she helps Hawkeye recover from Loki's brainwashing. "You're gonna be all right," she assures him. Her first thought, as always, is for the health and safety of her comrade. Barton tells her that Loki will make his play soon. "We gotta stop him," Romanoff insists. Her use of the first person plural is important. She understands that individual heroism will not be enough to stop Loki; teamwork will be required. Barton is skeptical: "Who's 'we?'" Romanoff reveals her pragmatic side: "I don't know. Whoever's left."

During the Battle of New York, Romanoff works closely with her teammates to save civilians. Captain America is not sure he should leave Romanoff and Barton to defend the civilian population against Loki's army. "We got this," Romanoff assures him. Again she invokes the first person plural. This "we" gives her the cool confidence she displays in this scene. Cap gets the message. A few minutes later the team re-assembles and prepares to attack Loki and his minions. "How do we do this?" Romanoff asks. "As a team," Cap replies. Clearly he has learned Black Widow's lesson: that no individual hero stands a chance against this rogue Asgardian god, but a team like the Avengers might. This endorsement of collective action is one of the film's central themes. Ensley Guffey has convincingly categorized *The Avengers* as a classic combat movie; as Guffey notes, "the partial surrendering of individual agency for the good of the whole" is an important characteristic of this genre (288). Whedon's *Avengers* perfectly models this central generic feature of the classic war movie, a genre which was quite important to Whedon's mentor, Wesleyan film studies professor Jeanine Basinger (Guffey 281). Thanks in large part to Black Widow, the members of the Avengers eventually discover that by sacrificing the most dangerous elements of their individualism, they not only stand a better chance of survival and victory; they also have a unique opportunity to create what the military calls "unit cohesion," and finally come together as an effective team.

Bloodied but unbowed, Natasha Romanoff hatches the plan to close the portal which carries Loki's armies to Earth. Captain America reveals the limits of individual heroism: "Our biggest guns couldn't touch it." The "big guns" are the cocky, superpowered male Avengers, who often act on their own initiative, and frequently forget to coordinate their efforts with their teammates. "Well, maybe it's not about guns," Romanoff replies drily. As always, she rejects a strategy which relies on individual "guns" in favor of one which will draw upon the strengths of the team. Romanoff doesn't hesitate to ask for help from her teammates as she makes her way to the portal. She lets Cap give her a boost up to her "ride." As she maneuvers the captured alien flyer through the streets of Manhattan, she calls on Hawkeye for assistance. "Uh, a little help?" When she lands on the roof of Stark Tower, she works with Dr. Selvig to figure out how to close the portal. And once she is sure she can close it, she notifies her teammates that she can do so and waits for their reply. This gives Iron Man time to push the nuclear cruise missile up through the portal and fall back to Earth before the portal closes. Romanoff's commitment to teamwork saves Tony Stark and the entire population of Manhattan. Then she gets to have shwarma with the boys.

By the time *Age of Ultron* arrives, most of the Avengers have accepted and internalized the Widow's message about the importance of collective action. Crucially, Captain America is especially convinced of the value of teamwork. Cap is the team's undisputed moral center; when he endorses the Widow's collectivist message, he speaks with a moral authority no other Avenger could muster.

This becomes particularly clear when Cap and his teammates confront Tony Stark, the Avenger who is least committed to collective action. Scarlet Witch's mind games inspire Stark to pursue the Ultron project with exceptional zeal, but as always, the Witch plays on existing psychological weaknesses: ultimately Ultron comes into existence and nearly destroys the world because of Stark's pathological inability to work with a team. He hides the reckless research that produces Ultron from everyone but Banner. He continues to keep the team in the dark about the project, even when Banner points out that this is a bad idea. When his teammates realize just how dangerous Stark's hubris and egotism are, they challenge him. Traumatized by the Battle of New York (and by the apocalyptic version of it that Scarlet Witch has placed in his mind), Stark invokes the specter of Loki's invading alien army. "That up there, that's the endgame. How were you guys planning on beating that?" By now Cap can answer with conviction: "Together." Stark still refuses to accept teamwork as an option: "We'll lose." But Cap refuses to cede any ground on this point. "Then we'll do that together, too." The toxic nature of Stark's narcissistic individualism is now so clear that Cap is willing to risk defeat rather than subscribe to Stark's ideology. Cap makes an impressive moral stand in favor of collective action, but it was the Black Widow who brought him to the place where he could do so. The film consistently endorses Black Widow's position. Laura Barton tells her husband Clint that he needs "to be sure that this team is really a team." The Vision exhorts the Avengers to take collective action against Ultron, arguing that "not one of us can do it without the others." By the end of the film, even Stark gets it. "How can you possibly hope to stop me?" demands Ultron. "Like the old man said… together," says Stark, quoting Cap's formulation of Black Widow's argument.

At the end of the film, Romanoff contemplates the possible loss of her lover, Banner/Hulk. Whedon frames the Widow standing alone in a large, open, empty office space of cold steel and glass. "You want to keep staring at the wall, or you want to go to work?" Captain America demands. "I mean, it's a pretty interesting wall." The Widow quickly sets her personal problems aside, and marches out with Cap to assemble the Avengers. As they walk, the two heroes assess their new group. "They're not a team," Cap observes, knowing that the Widow will understand better than anyone why that's a problem. "Let's beat 'em into shape," she replies. This suggestion captures both her dominance and her commitment to collective action: if the new Avengers are not yet a team, she will help Captain America *make them one*. By doing so she will model effective teamwork, specifically team teaching. If Cap and Widow are successful—as the audience has every reason to suspect they will be—then they will also pass Natasha Romanoff's values of teamwork and cooperation on to the next generation of superheroes.

Conclusion

Whedon's Widow fulfills a promise *Buffy* made, but didn't really keep: the promise to promote a truly radical third wave feminism. Black Widow's flexible Slavic ethnicity intersects with her equally flexible girlie gender to produce a truly diverse model of identity. Her easy use of dominance and submission suggests that this diversity extends to sexuality as well. She models forms of collective action which operate across gender lines. The Widow thus achieves several major objectives of the third wave. And perhaps she points to something beyond the third wave: not a fourth wave, but rather a recognition that all these waves are finally eroding fixed concepts of identity, sexual norms, and all forms of single-gender politics. The Widow may transcend the third wave agenda even as she fulfills it: a very specific skill set, to be sure.

Works Consulted

Adams, Sam. "Age of Ultron's 'Black Widow Problem' Isn't a Problem: It's What the Movie Is About." *CriticWire*. 5 May 2015. Accessed 6 June 2015.
Anderson, Karrin Vasby. "Why 'The Avengers' is a Feminist Film." *The New Agenda*. 9 May 2012. Accessed 20 Feb. 2015.

Baumgardner, Jennifer, and Amy Richards. *Manifesta: Young Women, Feminism, and the Future*. New York: Farrar, Straus and Giroux, 2000. Print.

Bechdel, Alison. "The Rule." *Dykes to Watch Out For*. 1985. Accessed 10 June 2015.

Betancourt, David. "'Avengers: Age of Ultron': A Fanboy's 11-point Breakdown of the Masterful Sequel." *The Washington Post*. 1 May 2015. Accessed 6 June 2015.

Byers, Michele. "*Buffy the Vampire Slayer*: The Next Generation of Television." *Catching a Wave: Reclaiming Feminism for the 21st Century*. Ed. Rory Dicker and Alison Piepmeier. Boston: Northeastern University Press, 2003. 171–187. Print.

Call, Lewis. "'That Weird, Unbearable Delight': Representations of Alternative Sexualities in Joss Whedon's *Astonishing X-Men* Comics." *Slayage: The Journal of the Whedon Studies Association* 12.2/13.1 (Winter 2014/Spring 2015): n. pag. Accessed 6 June 2015.

Clark, Krystal, and Tara Bennett. "How Avengers: Age of Ultron dropped the ball with Black Widow." *Blastr*. 4 May 2015. Accessed 6 June 2015.

Clark, Noelene. "'Avengers: Age of Ultron': Scarlett Johansson on Black Widow's journey." *Hero Complex*. 9 May 2015. Accessed 6 June 2015.

Cox, Carolyn. "*Age of Ultron* Stars Talk Joss Whedon, Lack of Black Widow Merch, and Female Representation in the MCU." *The Mary Sue*. 6 May 2015. Accessed 6 June 2015.

d'Arbonne, Jess. "The Women of 'The Avengers': Breaking Down Stereotypes." *Examiner*. 12 May 2012. Accessed 13 Nov. 2012.

Dicker, Rory, and Alison Piepmeier. "Introduction." *Catching a Wave: Reclaiming Feminism for the 21st Century*. Ed. Rory Dicker and Alison Piepmeier. Boston: Northeastern University Press, 2003. 3–28. Print.

Franich, Darren. "Entertainment Geekly: The Black Widow Conundrum." *Entertainment Weekly*. 1 May 2015. Accessed 6 June 2015.

Gerhard, Jane. *Desiring Revolution: Second-Wave Feminism and the Rewriting of American Sexual Thought 1920 to 1982*. New York: Columbia University Press, 2001. Print.

Graves, Stephanie. "'You Really Think I'm Pretty?': The Problem of Gender Representation in *The Avengers*." Sixth Slayage Conference on the Whedonverses. California State University, Sacramento. June 2014. Conference presentation.

Groen, Rick. "The Avengers is both a Marvel and Not." *The Globe and Mail*. 2 May 2012. Accessed 13 Nov. 2012.

Guffey, Ensley F. "Joss Whedon Throws His Mighty Shield: Marvel's The Avengers as War Movie." *Reading Joss Whedon*. Ed. Rhonda V. Wilcox, Tanya R. Cochran, Cynthea Masson and David Lavery. Syracuse: Syracuse University Press, 2014. 280–293. Print.

Hawkes, Rebecca. "Joss Whedon: 'I Think of Myself as Ultron in 'Avengers: Age of Ultron': 7 Burning Questions." *The Telegraph*. 6 June 2015. Accessed 28 June 2015.

Hayes, Britt. "Reel Women: Has 'The Avengers' Smashed the Bechdel Test?" *Screen Crush*. 3 May 2012. Accessed 20 Feb. 2015.

Hill, Libby. "What 'Avengers' got right about Black Widow: Infertility is Devastating—Even for Superheroes." *Salon*. 7 May 2015. Accessed 6 June 2015.

hooks, bell. *Black Looks: Race and Representation*. Boston: South End Press, 1992. Print.

Howe, Sean. *Marvel Comics: the Untold Story*. New York: Harper, 2012. Print.

Huston, Shaun. "Black Widow and the Burden of Being the Female Avenger." *PopMatters*. 20 May 2015. Accessed 6 June 2015.

Johnston, Jacob. *The Art of Marvel's Avengers: Age of Ultron*. New York: Marvel, 2015. Print.

Karp, Marcelle, and Debbie Stoller. *The BUST Guide to the New Girl Order*. New York: Penguin, 1999. Print.

Karras, Irene. "The Third Wave's Final Girl: *Buffy the Vampire Slayer*." *Thirdspace: A Journal of Feminist Theory & Culture* 1.2 (March 2002): n. pag. Accessed 13 Nov. 2012.

Kearns, Megan. "'The Avengers,' Strong Female Characters and Failing the Bechdel Test." *Bitch Flicks*. 9 May 2012. Accessed 20 Feb. 2015.

Kickpuncher. "Why Do People Hate Black Widow?" *FemPop*. 7 June 2012. Accessed 13 Nov. 2012.

Lane, Anthony. "Her Again: The Unstoppable Scarlett Johansson." *The New Yorker*. 24 March 2014. 56–63. Print.

Lawson, Richard. "*Avengers: Age of Ultron* Entertains, but Strains to Surprise." *Vanity Fair*. 21 April 2015. Accessed 6 June 2015.

Lee, Stan, et al. *Black Widow: The Sting of the Widow*. New York: Marvel, 2009. Print.

Levine, Elana. "*Buffy* and the 'New Girl Order': Defining Feminism and Femininity." *Undead TV: Essays on Buffy the Vampire Slayer*. Ed. Elana Levine and Lisa Parks. Durham: Duke University Press, 2007. 168–189. Print.

Lockett, Dee. "*Age of Ultron*: How Much Screen Time Does Each Avenger Get?" *Vulture*. 4 May 2015. Accessed 20 June 2015.

Madrid, Mike. *The Supergirls: Fashion, Feminism, Fantasy, and the History of Comic Book Heroines*. Exterminating Angel Press, 2009. n. pag. Print.

Marcotte, Amanda. "In Defense of Black Widow in Age of Ultron." *Raw Story*. 11 May 2015. Accessed 6 June 2015.

McDowell, John. *The Politics of Big Fantasy: The Ideologies of Star Wars, The Matrix and The Avengers*. Jefferson, NC: McFarland, 2014. ProQuest e-book. Accessed 22 Feb. 2015.

Mendelson, Scott. "Why *The Avengers* May Be This Summer's Most Progressively-Feminist Blockbuster." *Huffington Post*. 16 May 2012. Accessed 20 Feb. 2015.

Mulhauser, Paul, and Daniel Schafer. "Avengendering." *Women and Language*. Accessed 12 Nov. 2013.

Mulvey, Laura. "Visual Pleasure and Narrative Cinema." *Visual and Other Pleasures*, 2d ed. Basingstoke: Palgrave Macmillan, 2009. 14–27. Print.

Orr, Christopher. "*Avengers: Age of Ultron* Is Too Much of a Good Thing." *The Atlantic*. 1 May 2015. Accessed 6 June 2015.

Pascale, Amy. *Joss Whedon: The Biography*. Chicago: Chicago Review Press, 2014. Print.

Pender, Patricia. "'Kicking Ass is Comfort Food': Buffy as Third Wave Feminist Icon." *Third Wave Feminism: A Critical Exploration*, 2d ed. Ed. Stacy Gillis, Gillian Howe and Rebecca Munford. Basingstoke: Palgrave Macmillan, 2007. 224–236. Print.

Pollitt, Katha. "Hers: The Smurfette Principle." *New York Times*. 7 April 1991. Accessed 20 Feb. 2015.

Rogers, Adam. "With *The Avengers*, Joss Whedon Masters the Marvel Universe." *Wired*. May 2012. Accessed 6 June 2015.

Rosenberg, Alyssa. "The Strong Feminism Behind Black Widow, and Why the Critiques Don't Stand Up." *The Washington Post*. 5 May 2015. Accessed 6 June 2015.

Sarkeesian, Anita. "Tropes vs. Women: #3 The Smurfette Principle." *Feminist Frequency*. 21 April 2011. Accessed 20 Feb. 2015.

Scott, A. O. "Topsy-Turvey." *New York Times Magazine*. 9 Dec. 2012. Accessed 12 Nov. 2013.

Snyder, Daniel D. "Scarlett Johansson Has the Most Human Moment in 'The Avengers.'" *The Atlantic.* May 2012. Accessed 12 Nov. 2012.

Stewart, Sara. "An Open Letter to Joss Whedon from a Disappointed Feminist Fan After Watching 'Age of Ultron.'" *Women and Hollywood.* 30 April 2015. Accessed 6 June 2015.

Surrell, Jason. *The Art of the Avengers.* New York: Marvel, 2012. Print.

Tchesnokova, Yekaterina. "Scarlett Johansson hopes to star as Russian spy again." *RIA Novosti.* 17 April 2012. Accessed 6 June 2015.

Towers, Andrea. "Dissecting the Black Widow/Hulk relationship in *Age of Ultron.*" *Entertainment Weekly.* 1 May 2015. Accessed 6 June 2015.

Vincent, Alice. "Is Disney Ignoring Marvel's Female Fans?" *The Telegraph.* 24 April 2015. Accessed 6 June 2015.

Woerner, Meredith, and Katharine Trendacosta. "Black Widow: This Is Why We Can't Have Nice Things." *i09.* 5 May 2015. Accessed 6 June 2015.

Athena's Daughter
Black Widow's Impact Aesthetic

DAVID KOCIEMBA

"There's a chance you're in the wrong business."
—Captain America to Black Widow

Some cinema studies scholars have dismissed action movies as "mass culture at its most crudely capitalistic" (Arroyo ix), as merely products of a misogynist cultural backlash of the 1980s, or as obvious, dialog-light spectacles produced by an industry that lost its mind in pursuit of global markets and video game tie-ins. "Most critics simply take [action cinema] for granted and therefore approach it too imprecisely" (Lichtenfeld 6). Other scholars have a more sympathetic understanding of the aesthetics of action. Richard Dyer describes these movies' persistent and detailed attention to the exerting body in almost sensual terms, calling them spectacles of extreme sensation (18). Yvonne Tasker described the central appeal of images of physical power is in their counterpoint to a world defined by restrictive limits (127). The hero's body too is in a continual state of becoming that renegotiates the limits imposed upon it by real-world physics or narrative descriptions of super-powers. The superhero's Action Body is particularly American in its redefinition of limits and, increasingly, provides a freedom and power available to women in film and television action narratives.

The Black Widow of the Marvel Cinematic Universe franchise is part of a long line of armed maidens of righteousness whose roots in visual mass media go back at least as far as *The Perils of Pauline* and who achieved media prominence as 1980s warrior women and 1990s highly feminine superpow-ered women, which includes Joss Whedon's vampire slayer, Buffy Summers (Early and Kennedy 4–6). Like Captain America, Black Widow plays a central role in establishing the ground rules of the impact aesthetic of the superhero action movie's intensified continuity style for audiences of *The Avengers*. She plays the Everywoman Superhero, used as the figure of the viewer in the text along with the Everyfan figure of Agent Coulson, an extraordinary ordinary archetype frequently found in Whedon's works (Kociemba). Black Widow presents a rare bi-gendered fighting style for women, whose choreography features both graceful moves and brutal brawling, in a manner most reminiscent of Faith in *Angel* among Joss Whedon's prior works.

"No, we could use a little worse": Understanding the Action Genre

Action movies mean more than you might think. Narratives tell us about the cultures in which they're produced and consumed. Genre theory has a foundational assumption that members of a mass-mediated society develop and participate in complex systems of relatively unexamined beliefs. Generic entertainment at its most basic and its finest is a myth-making process in which the studios/networks and the mass audience reciprocally participate. The demands of the marketplace, and the perception of those demands by executives and creatives, shape the cultural and formal conventions in ways that are most pronounced in genre works. Audience response grants the audience an active but still indirect and secondary participation in the product's creation, especially in franchises, serial narratives, and genre works. Corporate entertainments exploit the structures of mythic rituals in the pursuit of monetary gain even as audiences use them for their own cultural profit.

Hollywood is a myth factory as much as it is a Dream Factory. Genres are defined by the cluster of worries that categorizes them for Thomas Schatz. This definition provides a reason why only certain forms have been refined into genres, why others become exhausted or end (e.g., safari genre), or are transformed (e.g., with *Death Wish*, the inner city became the western's frontier in the 1970s vigilante genre). Formal conventions serve to shape these worries. Michael Wood observes:

> All movies mirror reality in some way or other. There are no escapes, even in the most escapist pictures.... Movies bring out our worries without forcing us to look at them too closely.... It seems to be enough for us if a movie simply dramatizes our semi-secret concerns and contradictions in a story, allows them their brief, thinly disguised parade.... Entertainment is not, as we often think, a full-scale flight from our problems, not a means of forgetting them completely, but rather a rearrangement of our problems into shapes which tame them, which disperse them to the margins of our attention [16–18].

Genre film has a ritualistic and socially functional character which Thomas Sobchak describes in this way: "The cathartic potentials of the genre film can be seen in the way in which the tensions of cultural and social paradoxes inherent in human experience can be resolved" (128). Ritual is, in John G. Cawelti's words: "a means of affirming certain basic cultural values, resolving tension, and establishing a sense of continuity between present and past" (32, cited in Schatz 113). A ritualized form, religious or secular, is a myth. The function of myth is practical and social. Myths promote feelings of unity and harmony between members of society and the world. The narrative structures, iconography, and art history of genres are a textual system with a set of rules of construction used to accomplish specific communicative functions. The purpose of myth is to provide a model for overcoming contradiction, transforming certain cultural contradictions and conflicts into a unique conceptual structure that is familiar, accessible, and non-threatening. The mythic ritual of the folktale, or the media in an industrial/digital society, "is a society collectively speaking to itself, confronting basic human issues in a familiar context" (Schatz 116). Genres ritualize collective ideals by arousing anxiety about conflicting cultural demands then celebrating temporarily resolved social and cultural conflicts, all while concealing disturbing cultural conflicts behind a guise of entertainment. With action movies, the explosions make the ideology go down more smoothly.

So, what does the action genre tell us? The action genre goes back to the oldest stories known, such as *Gilgamesh*. In cinema, it's one of the oldest genres, dating back to films like *The Great Train Robbery* and Buster Keaton's physical comedies of cause and effect. Yet, this genre has not received the sustained critical attention in media studies that the western or noir have, despite the genre's age and box office appeal.

There are many reasons the action genre remains difficult to theorize. It's an unstable category. It's always incorporated tropes from other genres: westerns, swashbucklers, war films, disaster movies, and many science fiction narratives. In genre terms, action can be a noun or an adjective, a standalone genre form or one that influences the primary genre, like romance, comedy, and melodrama. Indeed, this multiplicity is a problem with genre theory in general. *Birth of Nation* is a silent film, a plantation epic, a romantic melodrama, an anti-war film, racist propaganda, a blockbuster, and an action film. Janet Staiger argues that all films contain multiple genres as a means of broadening their audience, such as the romance B-plot. Genre, meant in part to simplify through its categories, ends up complicating due to the industry's intertextual practices.

Scholars react poorly to action movies today because their rise has paralleled cinema's fall. The one virtue of the genre was that its focus on action and motion made it particularly suited for motion pictures from a medium-specificity perspective. Action has become less specifically cinematic recently, depending on digital technologies for its audiences and aesthetics in ways unnecessary for classic cinema. As their big images require big screens, action movies were once unique to theaters and thus countered the VCR threat to cinemas in the way that 3D does now with video-on-demand streaming technologies. But in the last decade, home theaters made action pleasurable enough through the sharp resolution provided by blu-rays while the comparatively larger images on flat screen televisions permitted viewer immersion in the spectacle, undermining the one virtue of the genre for cineastes. While *The Avengers* earned $1.5 billion world-wide in theaters (*Box Office Mojo*), it earned $227 million in domestic sales of DVD/Blu-rays, which was roughly 1/3 of the domestic box office (*The Numbers*). Superhero action movies particularly rely on digital technologies. Pre-CGI superhero films either look quaint (Donner's *Superman*), campy (the 1960s *Batman* series), or unable to effectively pull off the effects (e.g., 1977's *Spider-Man* or CBS' late 1970s superhero series *Wonder Woman*). Action movies are easily reformatted for video games, an even lower cultural medium paired with a low culture genre. Worse, for these critics, action aesthetics have come to be influenced by video game play (Purse 4), such as the doctors and Joker's sequence of *The Dark Knight*, which looks like a video game's level tutorial.

Another problem is that action is literal and physical, not abstracted. Plot and dialog mean much less than spectacular images and bodies, making it more difficult to build critical readings from the cultural studies approach. Linda Williams observes that such body genres as horror, melodrama, pornography, and action tend to be undertheorized as "low" genres. Action provides a direct sensory experience whose meanings are felt in the body and the gut rather than through appeals to intellectual distance.

Not that much cool critical distance would be required. The common understanding of action movies, and especially superhero action movies save for perhaps *The Dark Knight* and *The Matrix*, is that they are dialog-light spectacles mass-produced for global markets (Purse 4). To appeal to global audiences, the stories must necessarily be simple and with lessened cultural specificity. Grunts, car chases, and explosions need no translation. Superhero movies, which could be more culturally specific, have that meaning drained out of them, as they require huge budgets for CGI for which only global distribution can pay. Thus, these narratives must feature primal fantasies about dominating others, free from societal constraints, a power fantasy easy to understand. Yet, much the same used to be said of melodramatic theater, which also was critiqued by cultural elites as the mob's theater, arousing and justifying blood lust, according to Christine Gledhill (14–20).

"I've been compromised"

What might Black Widow's meaning be within traditional action movie ideology? Black Widow's opening scene in *The Avengers* is an inversion on one of the traditional covert pleasures of the action genre: the masochism of torture scenes. Torture scenes and beatings allow men to consume hurt-comfort narratives, which feature a character tormented physically or emotionally but who is then cared for by another character. Audiences can safely sample the pleasures of passivity due to the genre's promise of the return to active agency.[1] Black Widow, of course, is fully in control of her torture by the corrupt Russian military official. She puts on a masquerade of helpless femininity to gain power, in place of the action hero's traditional transformation into greater physical power through their masochistic ability to take punishment like a man. She asks General Georgi Luchkov as she's being interrogated, "You really think I'm pretty?" She's been extracting information from "this moron" before beating him and his men largely while still tied to a chair. Later, when Loki seemingly turns the tables on Black Widow's interrogation of him, she fakes tears at Loki's promised destruction of Barton to use Loki's monstrous ego against him, luring him into a confession of his plan to use Banner to create chaos on the Helicarrier. In this scene, Black Widow demonstrates the genre-savvy of the Marvel fan in the audience. What drives supervillains to act is their wound, according to Peter Coogan (83–88). Their wound derives from mistreatment in childhood, creating a superiority complex to make up for feelings of inferiority and inadequacy. Loki's grandiosity arises from his sense of victimhood from being adopted and living in the shadow of his brother, Thor. To get Loki to monologue and give away his plan, Black Widow plays on Loki's need for superiority, which means attention to him. The pleasures of passivity and agency are intertwined in Black Widow's interrogation scenes.

In comics, these scenes would be called character showcasing. In martial arts movies, characters grow from a setback by learning a new move that evokes their growth, such as the crane stance in *The Karate Kid*. But that doesn't typically happen in the action movie or in the superhero comics; characters get the opportunity to showcase what makes them extraordinary after they recover from a setback. Other examples of character showcasing include Hulk revealing that he's always angry, Hawkeye's vision, and Captain America's visible leadership winning the peace after the battle is over. Black Widow's two interrogation scenes establish her as sufficiently badass to be an action heroine and cunning enough to trick the god of mischief, and thus a superhero.

Most war combat films like *The Avengers* have a death that unifies the troops; this is Agent Coulson for Captain America and Tony Stark (Guffey 289). Having spent five films gathering the Avengers, Coulson fits an early World War II archetype described by Whedon mentor Jeanine Basinger as "the dead father figure ... who originally rounds up the group of volunteers for an important mission" (48). However, that motivating figure can also be a maternal or nurturing "beautiful soul" needing male protection who embodies why the heroes fight, such as Laura Barton (Early and Kennedy 1). Challenging gendered expectations in this genre, Hawkeye fills this function for Black Widow in an archetypal hurt-comfort scene after she knocks him out. He calls her Tasha, not Natasha or Black Widow, which she mirrors when she calls him Clint. This re-personalizes them to each other, as Black Widow calls other characters by their title, like Captain, or last name, like Banner. She comforts Barton in his despair at what he had done while controlled by Loki, saying, "Don't. Don't do this to yourself, Clint. This is Loki. This is monsters and magic and nothing we were ever trained for." She gives him permission here to move on by saying he hasn't failed them. She shows she trusts him by removing his bonds. She rhetorically includes him in the group by saying that "we gotta stop him," which allows him to reclaim the agency taken from him by promising violence against Loki. Her nod to Captain America makes her faith in him public, rather than private between the two of them. Her language personalizes, consoles, re-integrates, and empowers. She makes Clint Hawkeye again.

In other films, her emotional nurturing of Clint's embattled masculinity would be the end of her work in the film. But Clint's brutalization by Loki is a mind-rape that personifies why she should fight, as its effect is similar to her Red Room training. Clint's presence on the Helicarrier brought her back from her traumatized reaction to facing The Hulk. Clint notes that she doesn't sound like herself, as she's "a spy, not a soldier. Now you want to wade into a war." He uses her full first name, Natasha, to ask her to articulate her feelings. She responds with her rote language of professional obligation, "I've been compromised. I've got red in my ledger. I'd like to wipe it out." These words are more telling than they appear. She owes Clint nothing; their ledgers are balanced. Each saved the other by making a call in the field to ignore an order in favor of helping the other. During her interrogation of Loki, she doesn't use the term "compromised' while she does use the other two sentences. But she rejects Clint's suggestion that Loki did something to compromise her. The only other use of the term is by Agent Coulson to describe Clint's capture and brainwashing. She feels compromised because Clint's violation makes her want to be a superhero, not the spy she is. She is becoming an armed maiden of righteousness. In both cases, "compromised' signals a radical transformation of consciousness, good and evil. Like Clint and other hurt heroes comforted to the point of fierce resolve in this genre, Natasha must take the field to protect others and pay back the hurt to the villain to complete the warrior's healing process. Being nurturing doesn't disqualify her from a heroic action role.

In doing so, Natasha is not only becoming a different Black Widow, but also joining a tradition of just female warriors that speak to gender-integrated audiences about power and responsibility. Frances Early quotes Jean Elshtain's observation that being an "armed maiden of righteousness … is an identity in extremis, not an expectation…. As representation, the Ferocious Few are routinely eclipsed by the enormous shadow cast as the Noncombatant Many step into the light" (57). Early and Kennedy trace art history, mythology, and history to uncover the meanings of the Western woman warrior tradition (1–6). These temporary transgressors are women like Celtic Queen Boudicca, Joan of Arc, Amazons, or the many female pirates. Steve Neale finds precedents in two-reel westerns of the 1910s, 1920s adventure films like *Flaming Barriers*, 1930s aviation films like *Women in the Wind*, and rodeos, Wild West shows, and dime novels prior to cinema (57). The major discourse of action movies is about what makes a warrior just, a hero. The just warrior is the responsible citizen. Their mastery over themselves and willingness to shed blood for the common good gives them the right to violate the state's monopoly on just violence. They are bound by at least two principles, according to Todd McGowan. They must not kill, or be forced to do so only in extreme situations to protect others. This leaves the ultimate sanction to the state, protecting the core of its monopoly of sanctioned violence. Heroes must also react in response to crises, as it is villains who actively initiate change (Coogan 112–114). As a result, action movies tend to be conservative, engaging repeatedly in quests to save the status quo. This passive-then-active structure finesses the agency panic of male audiences in a time when the middle classes are defined by staid office work, not physical prowess. To have agency is to be ready, to hear the call. As women entered the workforce in increasing numbers after second wave feminism, they too began to experience agency panic. Film and television forged a new tradition, albeit painfully, slowly, and with deeply flawed attempts at translating narratives to shore up masculinity within female and male audiences simultaneously.

The female characters who helped women fantasize about physically escaping a world defined by limits began to form a tradition of their own in the 1980s. There are, of course, important precursors like girl detectives inspired by the Nancy Drew franchise or the Final Girl archetype of horror films, but these figures have a different sort of empowerment, speak to related issues in distinct ways, tend towards female-only or male-dominated audiences rather than integrated ones, and either lack physical violence or have different aesthetics shaping its interpretation. Lisa Purse argues that the warrior women of 1980s and 1990s films (from *Red Sonja*, *Aliens*, and *Terminator 2* to *GI Jane* and *Courage Under Fire*) were different from past representations by foregrounding the musculature of physically capable bodies (77–79). The training necessary for these bodies was laid bare, shown to be not natural to masculinity but rather the result of skillful labor (Purse 77). These films countered this new image with narrative containment that sought to show why they were not men in drag (Tasker 149). Purse lays out the containment strategies (Purse 77–78). They were driven to it. Their instinctive maternal drive explained it, e.g., Ripley's saving of the cat and Newt early in the *Alien* franchise. They were damaged, pathological, irrational, hysterical, or lesbians who were exceptions to the norm, especially if they were villains. Or they were reassuringly heterosexual through romance plots. Television in the 1990s and later progressively removed many of these containment strategies. The next wave of action heroines (*Xena: Warrior Princess, Alias, Dark Angel, La Femme Nikita*, and, of course, *Buffy the Vampire Slayer, Dollhouse*, and *Serenity*) are highly feminine superpowered women that don't waste much time explaining it to a presumed skeptical audience (78). Serial narrative made the prior containment strategies difficult: heterosexual closure was always deferred or contingent on the next season, while irrational or damaged representations undermined the ongoing identification necessary in a series (78). Overtly femme display was all that remained: erotic, but also active, capable, and physical (78). This representation cycled back into film franchises like *The Mummy, X-Men, Kill Bill, Resident Evil, Tomb Raider*, and *Underworld* (79). Other containment strategies remaining include the use of broad comedy to undermine action (e.g., *Charlie's Angels*) and restricting this tradition to the white middle classes or in fantastical settings (79–85). By the end of the 2000s, more naturalistic portrayals of violence and the number of credible, physically potent women increased, with examples like *Mr and Mrs Smith, The Kingdom*, and the *Resident Evil* franchise (91). Powerful femininity defines the representation of Black Widow in the Marvel Cinematic Universe, although her action scenes show a more complicated fighting style than strictly femme display of cunning, kicks, and dexterity.

Feminists have been concerned with women's inclusion in this action movie trend (Early and Kennedy 2–6). Must women become visually and narratively identical to men to be considered just female warriors? The sadistic appeals of violence, dominance, and revenge are concerning across all these periods. Audiences become prisoners of the fantasy of liberating violence, even if it is turned upside down with women as action icons rather than damsels in distress (2). Feminists can regard these developments in the action genre, however, as opportunities to redesign expectations of heroism to include female agency (3). Writers for female action stars, especially on television, tended to undercut the inevitability of violence with occasional nonlethal plot resolutions, such as empathy for the monstrous Other (Early 61–2). The action movie's critique of authorities and bureaucracies as smothering, corrupt, and interfering fits well with feminist criticisms of institutionalized patriarchy and hierarchy. The new variety in fight choreography might teach audiences to appreciate female empowerment as pleasurable and possible. Finally, the very newness of the physical action heroine might permit critical distance from action ideology, albeit only until female action scenes become a new norm.

While the Marvel Cinematic Universe franchise is not feminist in the sense of depicting women (and men) working together to solve gender-based problems through political activism, the representations of S.H.I.E.L.D. and Black Widow provide pleasures to audiences with that political persuasion. Certainly, *The Avengers* is not feminist in its appeals to violence, dominance, and sadism, as Loki is humiliated charmingly by several heroes. There are several women, however, who make the franchise palatable to female audiences, who were 40% of the audience for *The Avengers* (Ryan). While Agent Hill shows no sign of being anything other than a company woman, Melinda May's mentoring of Skye and general status as queen of the action sequence in *Agents of S.H.I.E.L.D.* provides alternatives. Skye's superpower plays a role in her final fight with her mother, but her best fight scenes in season two are straight from the tactical training she received from Agent May. In *Age of Ultron*, Scarlet Witch's thrown energy and telekinesis presents a new fighting style mixing elements from Hulk's shredding of opponents and Iron Man's lasers. In the films, Black Widow has a vastly different visual, interpersonal, and fighting style from the male agents, showing that women do not have to be men to be action heroes. Black Widow solves nonlethally all three problems the narrative gives her in recruiting Dr. Banner, saving Hawkeye, and closing the dimensional portal. Yet, she can be a credible physical threat, shown to be quite capable, brutal, and imaginative in her fight choreography. She operates without orders at the end of *The Avengers*, stepping outside her role as merely an agent of S.H.I.E.L.D., like Captain America. S.H.I.E.L.D. is the epitome of the kind of hierarchical organization rejected by feminists and, indeed, many action movies. With S.H.I.E.L.D., the franchise offers a complicated representation, full of disappointments, for this thinly-disguised NSA. S.H.I.E.L.D. is embraced in the Phase One films when it plays a largely peripheral role, because they recruit the superheroes of the new Marvel Cinematic Universe. But this secretive, manipulative agency is also sidelined by the end of *The Avengers*, useless in its alien invasion, then infiltrated by HYDRA in *The Winter Soldier*. The organization is thoroughly problematized in the television series *Agents of S.H.I.E.L.D.* through Director Fury's machinations reviving Agent Coulson, HYDRA's takeover, and even a second S.H.I.E.L.D. organization critiquing Coulson's decision-making as Director. Since S.H.I.E.L.D.'s role in the television series' first two seasons is frequently to suppress and contain super-powered characters, the organization thwarts audience desires for more superhero action and the universe-spanning changes that would result. S.H.I.E.L.D. is trying to prevent the audience from seeing things to marvel at.

Action movies want to astonish audiences with the spectacular. Their central visual rhetoric deals with the limits of what can be represented on screen by making the impossible visible. Neale defines the action movie not just by its themes, but by its narrative and technological elements, as these movies feature "a propensity for spectacular physical action, a narrative structure involving fights, chases, and explosions, and in addition to the deployment of state-of-the-art special effects, an emphasis in performance on athletic feats and stunts" (52). David Bordwell defines action by its visual and aural style, calling it intensified continuity, although this craft practice can be found in most American mass-audience films to some degree (120–121). This aesthetic features percussive bursts of speed, extreme use of space, and a louder soundtrack. Speed is not just depicted in the frame, but also conveyed with rapid editing, cuts on bursts of light, rapid shifts in focus, whiplash pans, and other techniques. Captain America and Thor fighting aliens on the street of New York provides an example of speed ramping—in which time slows to allow the audience to marvel at their virtuosity when a bit of slow motion is sandwiched between regular speed imagery in the same shot. Whedon returns to speed ramping in *Age of Ultron* with the team charging all in one shot in the opening at the HYDRA base and to make comprehensible a final mass combat with nine superheroes and dozens of Ultrons. Space also expands and contracts wildly in these sequences through wide-ranging camera movement, extreme lens lengths used in the same sequence, and slamming between close-up and extreme long shot framing. When Black Widow rides the alien flying chariot, it leads into a flowing CGI process shot featuring every Avenger in action, the cinematic equivalent of a splash page in a comic book. Black Widow's ironic commentary at the spectacle of the alien troop carrier chasing Iron Man, "I don't see how that's a party," not only serves as a reaction shot but also showcases the massive difference in scale between the Avengers and this enemy. She grounds the spectacle. The action sequence soundtrack tends to be louder: lines are shouted, environmental sound is foregrounded, and even larger gun sounds are dubbed onto smaller guns, such as Black Widow's handguns, which would otherwise feel absurd in such a battle. Composer Alan Silvestri's theme to *The Avengers* builds up throughout the film, mixing in bits and pieces of it and *Captain America*'s theme, so as to burst onto the audience during the battle of New York, according to Kristen Romanelli, managing editor of *Film Score Monthly*.

For *The Avengers*, Joss Whedon called Silvestri to request an identifiable cue for Black Widow, which resulted in the Eastern European-influenced motif that accompanies her two interrogation scenes and her ride through the skies of New York City to the top of the Stark Building (Silvestri and Burden). Romanelli describes how Silvestri uses her motif, "It begins with Natasha's theme, recalling back to when she 'interrogates' Russian thugs at the start of the film. The music is hushed as Loki works to manipulate her, but just as we hear the two melodies play counterpoint to each other, Natasha is playing against Loki. After the Black Widow wins her bluff, Loki's manipulation continues—her counterpoint disappears and he weaves beneath the increasingly heated conversation of the Avengers." Sonically, this is Captain America's film, as he's the only one with a full-fledged theme. But Black Widow's motif elevates her to Loki's level, who is the only other character with a motif.

Black Widow plays a similarly important secondary role in the resolution of the plot. José Arroyo describes the narrative structure of the action movie as "Equilibrium, disruption, a quest for resolution against deadline interspersed with set pieces, the restoration of equilibrium and the impression of closure" (viii). Generally, there will be a second deadline complicating the first one, requiring improvisation as a distinctively American form of excellence (c.f. *Raiders of the Lost Ark*). In *The Avengers*, Iron Man resolves the second complication of the incoming nuclear missile, as he "knows just where to put it," in one of the most nakedly sexual military metaphors since *Star Wars*.[2] Having delivered his payload, Iron Man is seemingly set to become a martyr, as his beloved technology fails him twice over: he cannot reach Pepper Potts by phone and his suit does not provide air to breathe in outer space. Richard Slotkin, who taught Joss Whedon in Wesleyan University's film studies program, observed that "the core of the mythic narrative that traverses the mythic landscape is a tale of personal and social "regeneration through violence"" (352). Yvonne Tasker also linked such moments of regenerative violence to mythologies and religions in which "martyrdom and sacrifice are central" (39). This act fits the action genre's ethos of manly suffering and sacrifice, as masochism is as central as dominance in the definition of masculinity. Iron Man's symbolic death and emotional abandonment proves him a hero to Captain America, the audience, and himself. While Black Widow does not symbolically sacrifice herself like Iron Man, she is the one who remembers that the ultimate goal of the Battle of New York is to shut down the Tesseract.

The action genre relishes these kinds of exchanges. By asking Captain America to lead them through the Battle of New York, Iron Man shows that he appreciates what makes Captain America a superhero: leadership, not the serum that made him physically mighty. Captain America curses mildly in wonder at Iron Man's sacrifice and return from the abyss. The central appeal of the appreciation of individual merit is what makes the action genre particularly American. When Black Widow showcases what makes her special in her two interrogation scenes, none of the other superheroes witness her prowess. Only the audience knows her worth for a while. That changes when Captain America gives her a boost so that she can catch a ride on the alien flying chariot. The audacity of her plan stuns Captain America enough to ask her if she's sure; after all, a simple fall from that height would kill her. As she flies off dangling from the chariot by one hand, Captain America pauses and smiles in astonishment and admiration. She is confirmed as an Avenger and a superhero, rather than a S.H.I.E.L.D. spy, in this moment of recognition within the text. This gaze of appreciation is as central to the genre as the controlling male gaze and the camera's stare at the homoerotic spectacle of male musculature.

The limits matter, paradoxically, in action movies. Yvonne Tasker argues that images of physical power function as a counterpoint to a world defined by restrictive limits (127). These movies are spectacles of cause and effect. The films establish the characters' physical limits to facilitate the audience's immersion in the world. Heroes then press up against and push slightly past those limits. Heroes are not just defined by their physical capacity, but also by their potential. The hero's body is in continual state of becoming that renegotiates limits. Black Widow becomes a superhero the moment she pushes past her limits as an ordinary skillful human to become extraordinary.

Black Widow's Fighting Style

Such postures and gestures of mastery are a core part of the performing style of acting within the action genre. The central conflict between performing martial arts and acting is that martial artists hide fear and anger, while acting brings guarded emotions to the surface. This contradiction is finessed through pose and martial choreography. Action scenes often feature postures of mastery just prior to intense confrontations or in a pause in the midst of one (Purse 66–67). These poses with weapons cocked, fists readied, or a determined expression can be found in the very earliest action one-reelers of the silent film era (66). Such still moments declare the potential of the action body just before unleashing its powers with what Purse calls "gestures of mastery" (67). These poses and actions show a body poised between loss of control and mastery (67).

Jonathan Eusebio's choreography for Black Widow's first extended fight scene in *Iron Man 2* has her make use of postures of mastery after dispatching each contingent of guards. While most of the poses have her standing at the ready with fists clenched, the most well-known is her pose with one knee on the ground and her left leg straight out, glaring. These pauses draw attention to the intense speeds at which she fights, while also showcasing the role of calculation in her fighting style and her mastery of the situation. Her fight choreography uses circular shapes, whirling mobility, surprise, and gadgets. Black Widow rushes her opponents, slides past two guards, and does two leaping, flipping kicks—one off a cart and another off a stunned combat-

Black Widow (Scarlett Johansson) in one of her classic poses. From _Iron Man 2_ (Photofest).

ant—to disable two more. She electrocutes the first guard, uses flash-bangs to temporarily blind two more, then uses a garotte to disarm then strangle a guard while fighting another two. The gymnastic choreography (taking advantage of veteran stuntwoman Heidi Moneymaker's beginnings in that sport) culminates with flying circling takedown. She ends that fight stalking through the smoke towards her objective, not even pausing while she casually maces a last opponent.

Black Widow's choreography changed for _The Avengers_, adding brutal punishing maneuvers to her graceful gymnastic fighting style. Fight choreographer Jonathan Eusebio (qtd. in Wilding) describes the change, saying, "We wanted to make Black Widow very fluid and acrobatic. Wushu, a Chinese fighting style, works well for her body mechanics. It's very graceful but requires a lot of strength and flexibility. You are also going to see Black Widow executing more sacrifice throws and using a variety of weapons. The game has changed and so has her skill set." Her first fight with the Russian military smugglers occurs in a confined area with Black Widow strapped to a chair for most of it. (This set-up has precedents in _Highlander, Killer Elite, Charlie's Angels_, and _NCIS_.) She does two head butts and flips to land her chair on a prone opponent. There are continuities with _Iron Man 2_, as she uses surprise, a gymnastic kip-up from prone, and another charging scissor-kick take-down. The victims' screams in the sound design are louder, however, emphasizing the brutality. Her sweat and grimaces signal her strength and physical exertion rather than her prior effortlessness.

Such a shift in representation is significant. Fight choreography is gendered (Purse 81). Men typically show effort through red faces, veins popped, bloodied and sweating bodies, and facial contortion. Action sequences persistently downplay the physical consequences of women's action, such as pain, injury, swelling, and dirty or bloodied faces. Women tended not to take punishment in their fluid, flowing martial arts choreography until very recently (81). Partially, this is middle class decorum, as "really" hitting a girl would undermine audience pleasure at equal opportunity brawls. The beauty culture of stardom plays a role too, as actresses must not only be active subjects in these sequences, but also sexualized objects with perfectly made-up faces. There's precedent for this shift in Whedon's work, as Buffy gradually began to show the bruises and cuts in the last two seasons of *Buffy the Vampire Slayer* whereas in the first two seasons they were only described as hidden with makeup. After Black Widow's flight from the Hulk on the Helicarrier, she sweats, pants, shudders in shock, and clutches her side in pain. In all of the rest of her fights, the exertion shows.

Moreover, Black Widow's sound design in the initial interrogation scene is masculine, then changes in later scenes. Like male action stars, she's rarely heard breathing heavily fighting the Russian smugglers, with only a few tiny grunts of exertion heard over the score. Heroines, on the other hand, are typically much louder and varied, with grunts, gasps, ragged breathing, and angry shouts (Purse 74). In her later scene fleeing the Hulk, however, her gasps and ragged breathing are foregrounded.

Her fight with Hawkeye is basically an extended violent embrace, exhibiting the sexual tension in their friendship far more than their dialog scenes together. E. D. Walker argues on her blog that their personal relationship informs everything about this fight. Their professional intimacy is shown through the foreknowledge implicit in the intricate move-countermove choreography. They face one another and Hawkeye tries to win the fight with an arm lock. Her plan to capture Hawkeye is suggested through her ambush and her kneeling pose after she kicks him unexpectedly. She courageously takes on this tactical disadvantage despite Loki having just threatened her with having Hawkeye kill her and the profoundly upsetting experience of her powerlessness against the Hulk. This fight is about their relationship more than about Black Widow as an individual. It ends with Hawkeye calling her Tasha, then she puts him down.

In her fights on the streets of New York, Black Widow's fighting style mixes elements coded both extremely masculine and feminine. She twice grapples a Chitauri soldier by riding its shoulders. She uses her comman-deered alien laser rifle as much as an axe as a ranged weapon, but when she does, she twirls gracefully on one knee. She punches through the back of the neck of one soldier to shock him (and herself) before shooting him. She gri-maces in pain throughout, with blood oozing from her hairline, a split lip, and cement dust all over her Black Widow uniform. She pants and slouches in fatigue. We are far from the effortless feminine fighting style seen in *Iron Man 2*.

Black Widow's choreography for *The Winter Soldier* and *Age of Ultron* remains much the same. When Black Widow secures the engine room in her first fight scene in *The Winter Soldier*, James Young's choreography quotes her prior work. She rides the shoulders of one combatant to electrocute him, head butts an assailant behind her, trips and circle kicks, and throws an enemy to the ground. She tries to ride the shoulders of the Winter Soldier and garotte him, but Bucky Barnes uses the wire to flip her into a car. Her final fight is similar. She surprises Alexander Pierce by looking like a familiar, middle-aged female politician. She throws a gun to knock out one agent and throws two more agents to the ground. The character growth is all in the buddy film chemistry she develops with Captain America and her decision to go public, not the fight choreography. James Grogan's fight choreography in *Age of Ultron* elaborates on prior work as well. Her flying circling takedown returns, this time taking down two soldiers when she starts one with a kick as she vaults to ride the other, then tackling one with her legs and the stunned one with her arms. Her fights go fully aerial more frequently, with a flying punch down a hill, a leaping kick from a jeep, and aerial vehicle stunts. Her electricity theme continues with a new costume design and electrified escrima sticks. The buddy film chemistry developed in the prior film leads to sharing Captain America's shield in her fight choreography here, which happens only with Thor otherwise.

Action movies give a persistent and detailed attention to exerting bodies. Richard Dyer describes them as spectacles of extreme sensation "experienced … in the body's contact with the world, its rush, its expansiveness, its physical stress and challenges" (18). The goal is to intensify the spectator's engagement with the depicted bodies, give them a contact high and an adrenaline rush through assaults on their senses. Viewers flesh out what happens on screen: hold their breath, recoil, and tense up. Action offers a lively encounter within a passive experience. Dyer explains this contradiction at the heart of action films, which promote "an active engagement with the world, going out into it, doing to the environment; yet enjoyment of them means allowing them to come to you, take you over … we may identify with [action heroes], imag-ine the rush of excitement as we brace ourselves against, and master, the world; but we're also letting ourselves be carried along, going with the flow

Black Widow (Scarlett Johansson) holding a really big gun. From *Captain America: The Winter Soldier* (Photofest).

of the movie, ecstatically manipulated" (21). Action is considered a low spectacle precisely because it is embodied rather than intellectual. Critics fear body genre audiences do not have sufficient critical distance and have become too close emotionally with melodrama or sadistically with action or horror (Williams 4–5).

With action, mirror neurons in the brain respond in the same way whether watching or performing action (Purse 44; citing Rizzolatti et al. and Cisek and Kalaska). The mental rehearsal of action produces synaesthesia: sight produces bodily feeling. Watching Black Widow move through the air, we experience proprioception, the intuitive sense we have of our bodies in space. The internal consistency of real world physics and physiology permits this rehearsal. The limits of action matter here too, as our embodied response is conditioned on recognition as much as imagination. As the comparatively normal superheroes, Captain America and Black Widow make the limits and potential of spectacular action recognizable in ways that a Norse God or a green rage monster can't. Just as Whedon's prior film, *Cabin in the Woods*, had two Final Girls (male and female), Captain America and Black Widow are the everyman and everywoman of *The Avengers*. What Black Widow does, we witness and rehearse. She's closest to our level. We directly experience Black Widow's choreography as both feminine and masculine, graceful and strong, gymnastic and brawling, requiring the toughness to endure pain and recover from trauma. Male and female audiences are integrated through Black Widow.

Did Black Widow Lose All of this Progress in Age of Ultron?

Critics from the blogosphere like Sara Stewart, Meredith Woerner and Katherine Trendacosta, and Jen Yamato felt Black Widow's character development sidelined her character culturally, although others disagreed. The major areas of debate centered in industrial practices around product tie-ins, gendered themes, and textual analysis. All sides agreed that waiting 19 movies for the first Marvel Expanded Universe film headlined by a woman was part of the problem, especially since Scarlett Johansson's ability to headline a Black Widow film was demonstrated when her *Lucy* grossed $458 million (Yamato). That Chris Evans and Jeremy Renner jokingly referred to the character as a whore and a slut, which Renner did a second time after previously apologizing, did not help. What also fanned the flames was that just three of 60 licensed Disney/Marvel products featured Black Widow (Yamato) because, according to a former Marvel executive, "that's not why Disney bought us. They already have the girl's market on lockdown" (Mouse). These factors hold back Black Widow from entering the global mythology like other female just warriors and from promoting her example generationally through toys that spark children's imaginations. The epicenter of the dispute in textual analysis was in the implications of her confession to Banner: "You know what my final test was in the Red Room? They sterilized me, said it was one less thing to worry about. You think you're the only monster on the team?" Had Whedon reduced Black Widow to "a shell of a superheroine who can never be a complete woman" (Yamato)? Woerner and Trendacosta noted that her motherhood became a running theme, with her lullaby calming the Hulk and saying as she retrieves Captain America's lost shield, "I'm always picking up after you boys." The essentialism that all women want babies, from this view, is furthered in *Agent Carter* when another Red Room agent, Dottie, plays with a carriage.

Yet difference from masculine models of heroism may present important alternatives rather than deficiencies. While Black Widow may joke about picking up a superboy's toys, it's in the context of the first film to truly explore her skills in vehicle stunt scenes, one of three in *Age of Ultron*. It's a quip that showcases the ease with which she accomplishes the amazing. Sharing Captain America's shield in this and other battles showcases a partnership continued from *The Winter Soldier* and highlights a different model from the exclusively individualistic Hammer of Thor. As with *The Avengers*, Black

Widow plays a central role in building the team, from her gentle kidding of an injured Hawkeye to nurturing the haunted Banner to her daring problem-solving in the field. Promoting unity in the face of the incessant alpha male posturing of the Thor, Iron Man, and Captain America triangle shows how teams are better forged, an alternative type of leadership that will balance the inspirational field model of Captain America in their next film together, *Civil War*. Black Widow's ability to calm the Hulk after battle through soft touches and behavioral programming is a feminist application of her "very specific skill set" by defusing violence rather than improving it. Her "lullaby" is an extension of her charisma, previously used to manipulate Loki and the Russian mafia. After Simon's use of a safe word on his sister River in *Serenity*, Romanoff's ability to calm the Hulk is only the second positive representation of mental conditioning in Whedon's work, with the Rossum Corporation in *Dollhouse*, the First Evil in *Buffy the Vampire Slayer*, and the Alliance in *Firefly* controlling minds rather than restoring reason.[3] Black Widow's calming of the angry Hulk is a potentially progessive turn on the otherwise retrograde trope of the Beauty and the Beast, as skill rather than blind love is the woman's solution to masculine agression run amok.

Similarly, the film engages with this myth through genre inversion, as the Hulk will be pursued by Black Widow, even as the reticent Banner is actively courted by Natasha. Notably, the concern over having a family is initiated by Banner in this scene, after watching her be an honorary aunt in Barton's family. It's an ongoing concern for Banner, who's unable to have sex in *The Incredible Hulk* and says to Natasha, "We don't always get what we want," as he idly rocks a cradle in their first meeting in *The Avengers*. A man whose superpower is the ultimate expression of masculine strength mourns his emasculation and sterility, as gamma radiation may lead to genetic defects (Lynch) and his rage makes him an unsafe father and lover. Referencing past television series as an important context for *Age of Ultron*, Todd VanDerWerff writes,

> Whedon's feminist storytelling is, thus, placed within the idea of institutionalized, patriarchal sexism that ultimately must be destroyed if women will finally get everything they deserve.... In this context, the Black Widow storyline becomes not about her mourning for the children she can't have, but about her creation by a system that cared nothing for her as a human being and everything for her as a game piece it could move around on the board. Her reproductive rights were violated in the most heinous way possible and her freedom of choice stolen from her.

Alyssa Rosenberg seconds that reading, writing, "The tragedy of Natasha's character isn't that she's been felled from her mission by her love for babies. It's that her mentor (Julie Delpy) took something away from Natasha that didn't have to be removed for her to be a hero." The additional context of Red Room girls handcuffed to their beds in *Agent Carter* and the requirement to murder a peer in Black Widow's flashback provides additional weight to this reading. As Sam Adams notes, Banner and Natasha's discussion of reproduction is part of a broader theme of the Avengers team as an evolutionary dead end, the result of monstrous tampering with the human heart (Iron Man), body (Captain America), and emotions (the Hulk), along with Banner and Stark usurping the roles of god and women through the creation of artificial life (Ultron). Tony Stark observes that the Avengers' goal is their own obsolescence as a team, so that the Earth will no longer need them. Yet Steve Rogers ends the film accepting that he is more at home in the Avengers as Captain America than as Steve Rogers, confessing, "I don't know, family, stability. The guy who wanted all that went in the ice seventy-five years ago. I think someone else came out." Signficantly, he seeks out Natasha to share that new home and seeks her help in passing on the Avengers' legacy to the next generation.

In *The Avengers*, Black Widow becomes a superhero. She's no longer limited to dealing with ordinary guards and criminals after her verbal duel with Loki and her battles with the Chitauri. Black Widow's masculine and feminine fighting style, whose choreography features both graceful aerial gymnastics and brutal brawling, speaks to all audiences. She is deadly, yet capable of finding nonlethal solutions to problems. She leaves behind the undercover outfits which were her prior uniform. Her black leather costume changes the meaning of her code name from a femme fatale spy's false masquerade of femininity to reference the lethal surprise of the tiny black widow spider. She joins a recent line of armed maidens of righteousness with deepest roots in the recent highly feminine superpowered women in visual mass media. Black Widow becomes the Everywoman Superhero, used as the figure of the viewer in the text, one of us, only more clever, graceful, and gutsy. In *The Avengers*, she develops a prosocial, selfless, other-directed mission through Clint's suffering after Loki's mind control. *The Winter Soldier* shows her to be the responsible citizen a just warrior must be, taking up arms against institutionalized oppression from any source. In *Age of Ultron*, she showcases an alternative leadership style, demonstrates newly amazing skills that increase her ability to solve problems without violence, and deepens her connection to Steve Rogers professionally and Bruce personally. Through these films, it becomes clear that Black Widow truly is in the wrong business, no longer following orders as an Agent, but possessing the agency of a superhero. She is the latest armed maiden of righteousness, truly Athena's daughter, confirmed as an Avenger, no matter how badly Disney's tie-ins and Marvel's Creative Committee might fail her.

Notes

1. Think of how many battles Superman or the X-Men lose before their final triumph, or the extended torture scenes in *Lethal Weapon*. Action narratives always feature a major setback before the final triumph.

2. Specifically, it is an anal sex metaphor, as Iron Man inserts the nuclear phallus into the hole in the sky that has been dropping enormous turd-shaped Leviathans. The fact that Iron Man is saved by his hulked-out bro-mance partner after having been emotionally abandoned by his heterosexual partner completes Whedon's naughty joke.

3. See Sherry Ginn, this volume, for more on this topic.

WORKS CONSULTED

Adams, Sam. "*Age of Ultron*'s 'Black Widow Problem' Isn't a Problem: It's What the Film Is About." *Indiewire*. Accessed 13 September 2015.

Arroyo, José, ed. *Action/Spectacle Cinema: A Sight and Sound Reader*. London: British Film Institute, 2000. Print.

Basinger, Jeanine. *The World War II Combat Film: Anatomy of a Genre*. Middletown, CT: Wesleyan University Press, 2003. Print.

Bordwell, David. *The Way Hollywood Tells It: Story and Style in Modern Movies*. Berkeley: University of California Press, 2006. Print.

Box Office Mojo. "*Marvel's The Avengers*." Accessed 13 September 2015.

Cisek, Paul, and John F. Kalaska. "Neural Correlates of Mental Rehearsal in Dorsal Premotor Cortex." *Nature* 431 (2004): 993–6. Print.

Coogan, Peter. *Superhero: The Secret Origin of a Genre*. Austin: Monkeybrain, 2006. Print.

Dyer, Richard. "Action!" *Sight and Sound* 4.10 (October 1994): n. pag. Reprinted in Arroyo, José, ed., *Action/Spectacle Cinema: A Sight and Sound Reader*. London: British Film Institute, 2000. Print.

Early, Frances H. "The Female Just Warrior Reimagined: From Boudicca to Buffy." *Athena's Daughters: Television's New Women Warriors*. Syracuse: Syracuse University Press, 2003. 55–65. Print.

Early, Frances H., and Kathleen Kennedy. *Athena's Daughters: Television's New Women Warriors*. Syracuse: Syracuse University Press, 2003. Print.

Elshtain, Jean Bethke. *Women and War*. New York: Basic, 1987. Print.

Gledhill, Christine. "The Melodramatic Field: An Investigation." *Home Is Where the Heart Is: Studies in Melodrama and the Woman's Film*. Ed. Christine Gledhill. London: British Film Institute, 1992. 5–39. Print.

Guffey, Ensley F. "Joss Whedon Throws His Mighty Shield: Marvel's *The Avengers* as War Movie." *Reading Joss Whedon*. Eds. Rhonda V. Wilcox, Tanya R. Cochran, Cynthea Masson, and David Lavery. Syracuse: Syracuse University Press, 2014. 280–293. Print.

King, Geoff. "Maximum Impact: Action Films." *Spectacular Narratives: Hollywood in the Age of the Blockbuster*. London: I. B. Tauris, 2000. 91–116. Print.

Kociemba, David. "Why Xander Matters: The Extraordinary Ordinary in *Buffy the Vampire Slayer*." *Supernatural Youth: The Rise of the Teen Hero in Literature and Popular Culture*. Ed. Jes Battis. Lanham, MD: Lexington, 2011. 80–101. Print.

Lichtenfeld, Eric. *Action Speaks Louder: Violence, Spectacle, and the American Action Movie*. Westport, CT: Praeger, 2004. Print.

Lynch, Ashley. "The First Unicorn—Why Everyone Is Misinterpreting *Age of Ultron*." *Medium*. Accessed 13 September 2015.

McGowan, Todd. "The Exceptional Darkness of *The Dark Knight*." *Jump Cut: A Review of Contemporary Media* 51 (Spring 2009): n. pag. Accessed 13 September 2015.

Mouse, Annie N. "Invisible Women: Why Marvel's Gamora & Black Widow Were

Missing from Merchandise, and What We Can Do About It." *The Mary Sue.* Accessed 13 September 2015.

Neale, Steve. *Genre and Hollywood.* London: Routledge, 2001. Print.

The Numbers. "The Avengers (2012)." Accessed 13 September 2015.

Purse, Lisa. *Contemporary Action Cinema.* Edinburgh: Edinburgh University Press, 2011. Print.

Rizzolatti, Giacomo, Luciano Fadiga, Vittorio Gallese, and Leonardo Fogassi. "Mental Representations of Motor Acts." *Cognitive Brain Research* 3.2 (1996): 131–141. Print.

Romanelli, Kristen. Conversation. *Film Score Monthly.* 26 April 2015. Accessed 13 September 2015.

_____. "Six Cues from the Whedonverse." *The Official Blog of Tracksounds: The Film Music Experience.* 25 September 2013. Accessed 26 April 2015.

Rosenberg, Alyssa. "The Strong Feminism behind Black Widow, and Why the Critiques Don't Stand Up." *The Washington Post.* Accessed 13 September 2015.

Ryan, Joal. "Five Reasons *The Avengers* Was the Biggest-Opening Movie Ever." *EOnline.* Accessed 13 September 2015.

Schatz, Thomas. "The Structural Influence." *Film Genre Reader IV.* Ed. Barry Keith Grant. Austin: University of Texas Press, 2012. 110–120. Print.

Silvestri, Alan. Interview by Tim Burden. "Silvestri Assembles: Alan Scores One of the Biggest Box-office Smashes of All-time." *Film Score Monthly.* 17.5 (May 2012): n. pag. Accessed 26 April 2015.

Slotkin, Richard. *Gunfighter Nation: The Myth of the Frontier in Twetieth-Century America.* New York: Atheneum Press, 1992. Print.

Sobchack, Thomas. "Genre Film: A Classical Experience." *Film Genre Reader IV.* Ed. Barry Keith Grant. Austin: University of Texas Press, 2012. 121–132. Print.

Staiger, Janet. "Hybrid or Inbred: The Purity Hypothesis and Hollywood Genre History," *Film Genre Reader IV.* Ed. Barry Keith Grant. Austin: University of Texas Press, 2012. 185–199. Print.

Stewart, Sara. "An Open Letter to Joss Whedon from a Disappointed Feminist Fan After Watching *Age of Ultron.*" *Indiewire.* Accessed 13 September 2015.

Tasker, Yvonne. *Spectacular Bodies: Gender, Genre and the Action Cinema.* London: Routledge, 1993. Print.

VanDerWerff, Todd. "A Guide to the Growing Controversy over Joss Whedon's Avengers and Marvel's Gender Problem." *Vox.* Accessed 13 September 2015.

Walker, E. D. "Dissecting Fight Scenes [Black Widow vs. Hawkeye]." *E. D. Walker: Official Website for Fantasy & Romance Author E. D. Walker.* 19 January 2015. Accessed 26 April 2015.

Wilding, Josh. "Scarlett Johansson and More Discuss Training for Black Widow's Fight Scenes." ComicBookMovie.com. Accessed 26 April 2015.

Williams, Linda. "Film Bodies: Gender, Genre, and Excess." *Film Genre Reader I.* Ed. Barry Keith Grant. Austin: University of Texas Press, 1986. 140–158. Print.

Woerner, Michelle, and Katherine Trendacosta. "Black Widow: This Is Why We Can't Have Nice Things." *IO9.* Accessed 13 September 2015.

Wood, Michael. *America in the Movies.* New York: Columbia University Press, 1975. Print.

Yamato, Jen. "The Avengers' Black Widow Problem: How Marvel Slut-Shamed Their Most Badass Superheroine." *The Daily Beast.* Accessed 13 September 2015.

The Elusive
Black Widow Film
Fan-Made Texts
as Social Desire Paths

Tanya R. Cochran

Over the last several years, "We want Widow!" has been the consistent cry of a large number of Marvel enthusiasts and Scarlett Johansson admirers. Science fiction and fantasy fans and entertainment critics have multiple reasons such a film should exist: Johansson has earned it, the character deserves it, and the film would be a feminist statement. All of this buzz is important in schooling Marvel—if they will be schooled—about what some audience members need and want to see and see as soon as possible. At the same time, unlike their television counterparts, film writers, directors, and producers are not as intimately engaged with their audiences; the nature of filmmaking does not allow or invite the kind of input television showrunners now take into account by communicating, sometimes directly, with viewers through social media platforms such as Twitter and Tumblr. Yet Marvel is listening to some degree because executives continue to communicate that they have a "master" plan of twenty-plus films, that they must be trusted, that they have good reasons—both narrative and financial—to *not* make a Black Widow film or, at least, to not make it now.

In the face of these explanations (or protestations) from Marvel, fans in this technological era are not waiting on the so-called "powers that be," though. They are exercising their own agency, satisfying their own desires. Using self-made opening credits and recut film trailers shared via YouTube and other social media platforms, among other tactics, they are blazing their own trails toward the Black Widow film they anticipate. On the surface, these texts merely represent one of many ways mediaphiles demonstrate that we

149

live in a digital participatory culture. Upon deeper inspection, however, these texts speak to the more complex questions of why these fan-fashioned opening credits and trailers matter and who cares or should care about what message the texts convey. To explore those questions, I first present several specimens of unofficial Black Widow-centric texts. I then introduce two concepts—one from landscape architecture, one from applied sociology—to aid in understanding the significance of those unsanctioned texts. Finally, I consider the nature of the fan-producer relationship within the context of film as a medium and argue for a more dialogic one, a relationship that would honor a more diverse and complex Marvel Cinematic Universe (MCU).

Fan-Made Opening Credits and Trailers

In May 2015, Black Widow admirer Christopher Haley received online media attention when he posted to his YouTube channel an original work titled "Black Widow Title Sequence." According to Jill Pantozzi of *The Mary Sue*, Haley submitted the sequence as his capstone project for a course in Adobe After Effects, software designed for creating motion graphics and visual effects. In addition to displaying his technical skill with the software, Haley thoughtfully constructed a plot for the imagined film:

> Cut off one head, two more shall take [its] place.... [Yelena] Belova believes herself to be the superior Black Widow, and in some ways she is right. Swift and ruthless, Belova is the most talented assassin to graduate from the Red Room—and now she is Hydra's most deadly weapon. At Belova's side is a super-soldier of her own, Alexi Shostakov—the Red Guardian, who also happens to be Natasha's former lover. When the new heads of Hydra make a play for the power of the infinity stones, it is up to S.H.I.E.L.D.'s top agent to stop them.

Additionally, Haley cast the film and assigned writing, directing, and producing roles. Rosamund Pike plays Yelena Belova, and Samuli Edelmann portrays Alexi Shostakov. Clark Gregg and Ming-Na Wen make appearances as their *Agents of S.H.I.E.L.D.* (2013–) characters Phil Coulson and Melinda May. As *A. V. Club*'s Alex McCown notes, "Michael Giacchino, the Oscar-winning composer of everything from Pixar films to *Lost* [(2004–2010)] will be supplying the music. And it looks like someone was a fan of *Mission: Impossible—Ghost Protocol* [(2011)] and *The Incredibles* [(2004)] because Brad Bird is writing and directing. That means no scenes of alien worms devouring stupid scientists, co-writer Damon Lindelof." Other credits include Casting Director Sarah Finn, Stunt Supervisor James Young, Visual Effects Supervisor Ray McMaster, Director of Photography Robert Elswit, Producer Kevin Feige, and Executive Producers, J. J. Abrams, Victoria Alonso, Louis D'Esposito, and Stan Lee. Scarlett Johansson, of course, reprises the lead role as Natasha Romanoff.

Haley scored the title sequence with Portishead's "Sour Times" and deliberately gave the credits a James Bondesque look and feel. *Tech Time's* Robin Burks argues that the allusion is fitting "given that Natasha Romanova is less of a superhero and more of a spy." (Of course, that depends on one's definition of *superhero*.) Reporting for */Film*, Ethan Anderton adds, "While this may not be the best plot for a Black Widow movie, it seems Haley has done more to make this movie happen than Marvel has." And Pantozzi declares, "Christopher Haley just shared something magical with us…. It is everything we've always wanted. Well, except for the movie being real." Many fans and critics agree. Gavia Baker-Whitelaw of *The Daily Dot* states that it is likely a solo film for the character will never be made, "which makes … fanmade [opening credits and] trailers all the more tantalizing." Less than a year later, as this book goes to press, Haley's video has been viewed nearly 290,000 times on YouTube. Whereas Haley has received more media attention than most who turn their talents into fan-art, there are plenty of other notable examples of this now-common fan practice. In fact, Baker-Whiteclaw points readers to two "incredible" trailers by popular fanvidders Elinor X and Alex Luthor.[1]

Summarizing the plot of her hoped-for film *Black Widow: The Origin*, Elinor X teases, "When S.H.I.E.L.D. Agent Clint Barton was ordered to terminate the infamous Black Widow, Natalia Romanova, he made [an] unexpected choice, and that choice had its consequences…." The trailer, like its sister texts, capably weaves together scenes from MCU films featuring Romanoff as Black Widow as well as other films starring Johansson, including a favorite of fan-artists, Luc Besson's science fiction action-thriller *Lucy* (2014). With over 103,000 notes on Tumblr and close to 240,000 views on YouTube, the trailer for *Black Widow: The Origin* makes the interest in a standalone Black Widow film clear, especially considering how many times other fan-crafted trailers have been viewed.

Alex Luthor, another YouTuber, added his video to the mix around the same time as Elinor X, a movie preview that offers similar visuals and voiceovers borrowed from MCU films. Only, Luthor captures the plot of his offering in one simple sentence, "It is the origins story of the hottest Avenger!" Views for Luthor's trailer have reached nearly 175,000 as of the spring of 2016, a number placing this example in the middle of a range that goes as high as 915,000 for a fan-fashioned trailer posted to the YouTube channel Top New Movies and as low as several thousand for others. Some two dozen similar artifacts exist on YouTube alone.

These numbers might seem insignificant considering how many viewers the MCU films themselves have garnered. After all, the audience represents a massive global following. As mentioned above, fan-made title sequences and movie trailers admittedly represent only one type of activity. That, however, is part of the point. There are myriad ways devotees have expressed and continue to express their discontent with Marvel's overarching plan and their desire for a Black Widow feature film—from forming online fan clubs to posting open letters to Marvel and *Avengers* director Joss Whedon, from organizing world-wide cosplay flash mobs to taking to Twitter with #WeWantWidow.[2] Taken together, these various and recurring efforts demonstrate attempts to instruct Marvel in what many film-goers need and want, and what they need and want is inextricable from a larger socio-political conversation about what gender one needs to belong to in order to be a "real" science fiction and fantasy fan and what female audience members want to see on the silver screen.

In his May 16, 2015, blog post "How the Extended Marvel Universe (and Other Superhero Stories) Can Enable Political Debates," Henry Jenkins notes that whereas comic books themselves have not been selling well lately, the genre and its heroes have consistently been holding the top profit slots in the film and television industries. Thus, "the genre's commercial success," argues Jenkins, "has contributed to its high visibility within contemporary popular culture." In turn, popular culture texts have become sites of struggle and conversation about many important public issues. Jenkins continues,

> Witness the ways that [*Avengers: Age of Ultron* (2015)] has become the focal point for debates about gender in American media, especially centering around the figure of the Black Widow, who was slut-shamed by several cast members, critiqued and defended by various feminist critics, and used on *Saturday Night Live* [*SNL*] to parody the industry's tendency to write women's experiences primarily through the rom-com genre.

Burks predicts that the *SNL* skit, featuring Johansson, is likely to be "the closest thing we'll ever see to a solo Black Widow outing." *The Daily Dot*'s Aja Romano adds a deeper insight, suggesting that *SNL*'s choice to write such a sketch is the direct result of fans' fierce advocacy. Romano notes, "*Saturday Night Live* recently skewered Marvel's unwillingness to deliver [a fan-desired Black Widow feature film] by making a parody that envisioned the film as a cliché-filled chick flick"—as if a romantic comedy is the only type of film Marvel thinks female fans could possibly want to see.

In the sketch (currently still available on *SNL*'s YouTube channel), the trailer's disembodied narrator asks why a Black Widow film has not been made when audiences all over the world have loved the many other iterations of Thor, Captain America, Hulk, and Iron Man movies. "Does Marvel not know how to make a girl superhero movie," queries the narrator. "Chill," the narrator continues. "Marvel gets women." At this point, the music and visuals of the sketch shift from a high-octane score and powerful images of Black Widow from previous MCU films to a light-hearted tune and shots of a cityscape and Natasha Romanoff (portrayed by *SNL* guest star Scarlett Johansson) walking along a busy street in floral-printed pumps and her black leather gear topped with a bright pink cardigan. The rest of the sketch requires no summary as it follows the stereotypical plot of a so-called "chick flick," including her platonic group of male friends (Thor and company), her new job at a fashion magazine, and her search for love—which, of course, promises to vacillate between success and failure for the entire 97 minutes of the feature. The sketch ends with the promise that the movie will hit theaters on Valentine's Day 2016. Whereas this example does not fit the technical definition of a fan-made text, it certainly counts as unofficial and unsanctioned as well as speaks to the very real struggle waged among Black Widow admirers. With nearly 7,000,000 views on YouTube, the skit adds credence to fan voices exercised through their own media artifacts. As Romano observes of Christopher Haley's title sequence, "Between this and a stellar fan-made Black Widow trailer," Marvel's work "has practically been done for [them]." Romano concludes, "At least fans like Haley help make up for Marvel's wasted opportunity.... A little." Evident from listening to both film audiences and media commentators is the language of "lost opportunity," and in an industry that is largely if not ultimately about profit, it is at least puzzling and at most stupefying why Marvel refuses to go down the fan-cut path of film centered on this female Avenger. To understand what I mean by "fan-cut path," I next turn to a discussion of desires lines and how they provide insight regarding the significance of texts like the ones described in this section.

Desire Lines and Social Desire Paths

The phrase *desire lines* (or *desire paths*) probably does not sound immediately familiar, but we humans are actually quite familiar with and perhaps even guilty of creating such lines. Those grassless paths in city parks that we make with foot traffic or bicycles? The shortcut everyone at work takes from the parking lot to the office building or college students take between their dormitories and their campus cafeteria? Yes, those. Desire lines or paths—colloquially called cow paths, goat tracks, pig trails—visibly emerge when over time enough pedestrians, cyclists, or others deviate from a paved, graveled, or otherwise designated route to erode the natural terrain. Donald A. Norman notes that these "trails are social signifiers, a clear indication that people's desires do not match the vision of the planners" (126). And according to urban planners and landscape architects, these unsanctioned trails develop for many reasons and represent a variety of human wishes.

Several reasons seem fairly benign—at least, to those cutting the paths. An obvious and typical motive is efficiency. The shortest distance between two points, after all, is a straight line—something most if not all of us learned in grade school. The demands of contemporary life, especially in highly populated areas, mean that we are usually in a hurry. If we can get somewhere faster, we will. In fact, we will take the faster route even if that means ignoring signs that remind us, "Grass grows by inches, but dies by feet."[3] Perhaps less common but understandable reasons we cut such paths are curiosity, pleasure, or playfulness. We want to see something "off the beaten path" or explore a direction no one else seems to be going or simply have a little fun. The explorer or trailblazer within gets the best of us, and we just cannot resist taking the "road less traveled." Matthew Tiessen summarizes these reasons this way: "Desire lines can express … [a] need for speed, for they efficiently cut corners; but they are also, at times, expressions of playfulness, perhaps meandering to and fro amidst flowers or trees. The desire line's creator, when s/he blazes through newly fallen snow, is, quite literally, a trail blazer in whose steps others will follow." I will return to Tiessen's final thought—"in whose steps others will follow"—in a moment. For now, let us examine two less benign desires we express with our shoes or with various types of wheels.

We sometimes use our bodies or vehicles to draw lines along forbidden paths out of defiance or desperation. On the one hand, we might live in a culture that suggests we constantly find ways to "stick it to the man," to solely live for and satisfy ourselves. "I'll go the route I damn well please," we screech with raised fist. "Oh, you're telling me I can't go that way? Watch me!" We can be quite disagreeable when we wish to be, regardless of the logic of a request to avoid going a certain way. Drivers who use the shoulder of a road to pass stalled or slow-moving traffic fall into this category. Psychologists call this kind of response *reactance*, a theory that describes how we are motivated to act when we experience negative emotions such as stress and anxiety as the result of freedoms being revoked or perceived threats being issued. In other words, if we feel coerced, we will react by trying to restore our freedom or safety. We resent being restrained; therefore, we defy whatever is holding us down or back or is making us feel threatened ("What Is Reactance Theory?").[4] On the other hand, desire paths may arise out of sheer necessity, a reason I have observed first-hand but have not discovered in the scholarship on the subject. For example, years ago when I lived inside the perimeter of Atlanta, Georgia, an area populated by immigrants living in rows of apartment complexes, residents made heavy use of MARTA, the city's public transportation system—most often, buses that connected with subway stations. To access MARTA bus stops and because there were no sidewalks, workers, parents with strollers, and retirees cut narrow dirt trails alongside the five-lane highway they lived on, less than two feet between themselves and speeding cars. Though these paths were dangerous to travel, people who required transit were forced to make their own way. The city delayed well over a decade before finally laying sidewalks along the major thoroughfare.

Whether a line is cut for efficiency, curiosity, pleasure, defiance, or desperation, an obvious subsequent question concerns how those in authority address desire paths. In general, these figures or entities respond in two ways: they attempt to block the paths *or* they study them to understand what the lines mean and make adjustments accordingly. One response is authority-centered or top-down, the other user-centered or bottom-up. Of course, it cannot be said that all attempts to block a path or deter pedestrians, cyclists, and others are sinister and involve the power-hungry. There are legitimate reasons to block or close a path. For instance, blockades or closings may be the result of potential or confirmed dangers, such as hiking trails that cannot be used due to heavy snow or rains or construction areas that are fenced off because of falling debris. Certain portions of national parks may be off limits to pedestrians or vehicles to preserve wildlife or protect endangered habitats. These are reasonable situations in which to deny or alter access. At the same time, authorities do sometimes use road blocks and other strategies to control the population in what appear to be unreasonable ways. It is at these times that we might choose to cut a path out of defiance. As a result, setting up orange cones in a parking lot or putting up chains on bike paths is not always the best way to respond to human desire lines. As Norman declares, "Wise urban planners should listen to the message underlying these desire lines. When a desire line destroys the pristine plan, it is a sign that the design did not meet human needs" (126). Thus, planners and landscape architects are often employed to examine such lines and determine what has led to their emergence. What needs are not being met by the current design? These experts are especially helpful when opportunities arise to create a new public space or renovate an existing one. Attentive planners and architects, for example, might study an unpaved green space, one open to the public, *before* paving to first observe what needs or uses the naturally-forming paths express. In this way, those with the power and resources to shape the space work *with* human desires rather than against them. That approach sounds ideal, does it not? What a considerate, human-centered approach! Unfortunately, working *with* human desires rarely happens, according to Norman, because the practical constraints of time, budgets, and the physical messiness of waiting long enough to "read" human desire lines before installing sidewalks and other formal pathways thwarts that approach (126, 128).

At this point, the concept of desire lines and their relation to how fan-made texts express anticipation of and for a Black Widow film should be coming into focus. When Norman says that unsanctioned paths are "social signifiers, a clear indication that people's desires do not match the vision of the planners" and that "wise urban planners should listen to the message underlying these desire lines" (126), it is not a mental stretch to understand Marvel Studios and executives such as Kevin Feige and Louis D'Esposito as the film industry's version of urban planners. Feige and D'Esposito, president and co-president of the company, respectively, are the key players responsible for crafting the MCU. As such, they are directly and/or indirectly concerned with timing the films well, budgeting for them wisely, putting writers and directors at the helm of the movies, and even keeping an eye on casting, among other tasks. At the same time, they are responsible for responding to the desires of the audience—that is, if we understand each installment in the franchise as a product or commodity and think in terms of supply and demand and customer service (i.e., an economic metaphor). More on metaphors later. Upon first glance, box office numbers alone might suggest that the MCU *is* meeting the desires of its global audience. But ticket sales are deceiving because the numbers do not tell a nuanced story. Even those moviegoers who are disgruntled (e.g., with the way Black Widow was portrayed in *Avengers: Age of Ultron*) or who are creating opening credits and trailers for a film that does not yet exist are counted with everyone else purchasing tickets. The profits do not speak to the fact that not every audience member is falling in step behind the next person on the sanctioned path that is the MCU. To repurpose Norman, fan-made texts are the desire lines cutting *away* from Marvel's "pristine plan"; they are "a sign that the design [is not meeting] human needs" for every person sitting in a theater seat.

The scholar to first draw a connection between desire lines and fan-fashioned texts is Kathleen Amy Williams, who fleshes out the concept in her journal article "Fake and Fan Film Trailers as Incarnations of Audience Anticipation and Desire." Williams defines "recut trailers" as texts created by fans skillfully splicing together "source footage from one or more texts and [recutting] it, either to displace [a] film's original genre or to create a new film that will never exist" (para. 2.2). In general, these types of texts resemble the art of vidding, a tradition that "involve[s] uncovering a slash story line, giving a trailer a new soundtrack, or ... creating trailers for a film before the official trailer has been disseminated to demonstrate the fans' anticipation for the film" (para. 2.4). By *anticipation*, Williams means the most basic definitions of the term: the acts of (1) looking forward to and (2) predicting. The examples of fan-produced texts I describe above all represent fans looking forward to and predicting what having an official Black Widow film might feel like as well as what the content, style, and look of such a film may or could be. For instance, Christopher Haley uses his opening credits not only to express anticipation, but also to argue that a James Bondesque spy-action-thriller is a suitable genre for a character who herself was inculcated as a spy. Williams notes that she uses "anticipation to demonstrate the ways in which audiences, as producers, consumers, and sometimes fans, build, enact, and perform their interest in a feature film" (para. 3.4). In other words, anticipatory texts created by fans represent a type of desire line.

Williams also distinguishes between the "fan trailer" and the "fake trailer." As she describes them, fan trailers are those texts that usually appear *before* the release of an official trailer but *after* an official announcement that a film will in fact exist. She uses the case of *Twilight* fans producing their own trailers for forthcoming movies in the series based on their familiarity with the novels as well as earlier installments of the big screen adaptations. In contrast, the fake trailer represents a film that will never be made or viewed: "The end point of a fake trailer's desire line is not to bypass or speed up the typical path of film production [which are sometimes the goals of fan trailers]. Instead, as there is no actual film, fake trailers suggest films that can never exist. Their creators wish only to revel in anticipation of what can never be obtained" (para. 4.2). The Black Widow trailers, however, do not necessarily fall into either of these categories. They neither anticipate a film that is sure to be made nor anticipate a film that "can never exist." The use of the word *can* is important here. The truth is that a Black Widow film *can* exist if Marvel choses to make it. Thus, in this particular case, Williams' work is somewhat helpful in understanding the expression of fans' desires but not entirely helpful. Turning to the perspective of applied sociologist Laura Nichols offers still deeper insight into the making and distributing of these novice and novel artifacts.

Through her innovative use of the concept, Nichols suggests that her discipline adopt the concept of desire lines or paths from urban planning and landscape architecture as a metaphor to better identify, understand, and address the needs and wants of the people they work with in applied sociology settings. "In the applied context," asserts Nichols, "social desire path analysis provides a means to uncover the interests of stakeholders in ways that illuminate both the limitations of existing structures and point the way toward potential solutions" ("Social Desire Paths: An Applied Sociology of Interests" 166). Rather than addressing in depth the various reasons people cut physical desire lines—efficiency, felicity, defiance, necessity—Nichols succinctly states that such paths emerge because an existing, sanctioned route does not provide people with what they need or want so they seek an alternate route (166). The sanctioned paths simply do not work. These physical lines are not unlike their social counterparts.

As Nichols defines them, "social desire paths" emerge when individual interests or desires accumulate over time, at some point expressing collective interests or desires even as these "imprints on the social landscape" occur independently of one another ("Social Desire Paths: An Applied Sociology of Interests" 167). She offers the example of parents who take their children out of local public schools (perhaps opting for private school or homeschool instead) or personnel who seek ways around office rules. As Tiessen explains, the first person to step into freshly fallen snow is "quite literally, a trail blazer in whose steps others will follow." That is, if others follow. A desire line cannot be formed by a one-time, off-trail excursion made by a solo explorer. Unbeknownst to the original trailblazer, others must follow in the same path for a line to develop—whether physically or socially. Both types of paths begin "without explicit contemplation" and without a conscious wish to enact change (Nichols, "Social Desire Paths: An Applied Sociology of Interests" 168); rather, they begin by one person and then another person and then another individually trying to meet a need or desire. In other words, social desire paths slowly, visibly make evident the results of multiple individuals separately but similarly not getting what they need or want from "formal social structures"; thus, when the individuals react to the structures in parallel ways, social desire paths eventually appear and become obvious—to the individuals themselves and to those responsible for the formal social structures. In the case of social desire paths, Nichols explains that when *enough* parents remove their children from a public school or *enough* employees work around office regulations, these paths "may indeed reflect ... collective interests.... [and] capture instances of agentic adaption to better meet interests or to re-imagine existing structures" (168). Put another way, social desire paths represent a person's agency as well as point to better ways of doing things. In terms of the conversation about Marvel and Black Widow, fan-made artifacts do not represent an organized, mass movement. In that sense, the opening credits and trailers do not technically denote fan activism—which is not to say they cannot *become* fan activism. Rather, at the point fan behaviors become activism, they are no longer merely independently expressed desires; instead, they are clearly marked social desire paths. What these same texts do demonstrate is that the MCU and its long-term plan, one that does not currently include a Black Widow film, is not meeting the needs and wants of some audience members. In response, they are creating their own artifacts to meet their own desires.[5] Views on YouTube, in turn, could suggest that not just a few, but many other people agree that their desires are also not being met. In sum, the opening credits and trailers may be read as evidence of collective interests. As Nichols points out, however, researchers in her field would not deem a handful of individual yet similar behaviors as "influential on or instructive to formal structures such as policies, organizations, or programs, *unless* collective action through social movements ensues" ("Social Desire Paths: A New Theoretical Concept" 647–48, emphasis added). The goal of social desire path analysis is not to wait until individual choices accumulate into collective awareness and then social movements. Not that there is anything inherently wrong with social movements. The goal is to be proactive. Social entities—whether public schools or transportation systems, businesses or non-profit organizations—that do not pay close attention to repeated individual choices to work around or against existing structures are missing an "opportunity to apply social scientific observations and insights to create more responsive … structures" (648). Simply put, when Marvel refuses to be schooled by audience desire for a Black Widow film, they are missing an opportunity to develop an MCU that is more responsive to and, thus, more representative of a notable portion of the people Marvel has cultivated as devotees.

Not surprisingly, when a group of individuals recognizes that they are in fact a group, they are likely to organize and create a social movement. Examples range from class-action lawsuits to political protest to, in the case of media fandoms, fan activism in its various forms, including but not limited to save-our-show-from-cancellation campaigns or food drives by lovers of *The Hunger Games* novels and films. It is the work of social scientists to recognize these emerging desire lines and ascertain the reasons they have been drawn (Nichols, "Social Desire Paths: An Applied Sociology of Interests" 167). Likewise, it is the work of media and fandom scholars to notice fan desire paths and investigate why they arise and what they mean. In both cases, these patterns of behavior reveal the values of those cutting the paths (Nichols, "Social Desire Paths: A New Theoretical Concept" 649). As I mention above, the desire for a Black Widow film is embroiled with a society-wide socio-political conversation about gender. The discussion has just as much to do with who gets to identify as a "real" science fiction and fantasy fan as it does with what defines a complex female character and how she is depicted on screen. One reading of the fan opening credits and trailers I introduce earlier is that the texts are concrete forms of resistance to sexism, both in fandom and in the entertainment industry. At the very least, such artifacts created by admirers of Black Widow, Natasha Romanoff, and even Scarlett Johansson herself express the value of gender equality. Thus, the fans I am talking about in this essay could be seen as a subgroup of a much greater one, a true social movement opposed to sexism in popular media, media fandom, and geek culture at large. And the conversation about that topic has at its core two main groups of interlocutors: fans and producers. Their relationship is vital to changing the structures that fan texts indicate are simply not working.

The Fan-Producer Relationship

The relationship between media consumers and media makers has experienced notable changes in the last several decades, particularly with the emergence of the Internet and digital social networks. With good reasons, the scholars examining this relationship have focused almost exclusively on the interaction between audiences and producers of television (Askwith; Benecchi; Benecchi and Colapinto; Benecchi and Richeri; Bennett; Bury,

Deller, Greenwood, and Jones; Chin; Collier; Cubbison; Larson and Zubernis; Hadas and Shifman; Macklem; R. Williams). One of those reasons includes the fact that each medium works differently. As an episodic or serial medium, most television shows are written and produced in ways that allow showrunners to gauge audience interests—likes and dislikes—as well as respond to audience feedback through alterations to the narrative, if showrunners so choose, particularly the narrative's arc. My colleague Meghan K. Winchell and I have observed and chronicled this kind of fan-producer relationship between Olicity (Oliver Queen + Felicity Smoak) fans and the executive producers of The CW and DC Comics series *Arrow* (2012–).[6] In contrast, film does not lend itself to the involvement of audience members in the composition, production, and distribution process. In the case of movie franchises such as the MCU, there is certainly an opportunity to note audience responses to earlier installments, but not in the ways television viewers communicate their feedback, largely through social media and often directly with the people who have power to make changes to a storyline. Filmmakers are much less likely than showrunners to engage with fans through these platforms.[7] In fact, they are not made by the studios to do so. Not true for their colleagues who create for the small screen.

In the television industry, it has become common—by choice and, more and more commonly, by contract—for showrunners (and cast members) to communicate with viewers via Facebook, Twitter, Tumblr, and the like. For example, Marc Guggenheim, an executive producer for *Arrow* joined Tumblr in 2014. Since that time, he has kept devoted audience members engaged by "leaking" set photos or cell phone snapshots of the script he is working on at a particular time, posting links to entertainment articles about the show, and answering viewers' questions for a day or two after an episode's airing. Occasionally, he also uses his Twitter account (started in 2007) to live-tweet episodes. The main purpose for fostering this interactive relationship, of course, is a promotional one. Particularly, in television, shows still depend on ratings and, thus, advertising revenue to survive—even as tie-in or transmedia texts and products have also become part of a series' chances for renewal. At the same time, this kind of fan-producer relationship, argues media scholar Suzanne Scott, suggests to viewers "a more dialogic relationship" (47). In other words, fans who regularly participate in online communities and conversations with showrunners are likely to feel a greater sense of intimacy or proximity to the people making decisions regarding the narrative itself, and in turn, they may feel a greater sense of agency and reciprocity with those showrunners. This simply does not describe the relationship—if it can be called a relationship at all—film audiences have with filmmakers.

The suggestion of a more intimate, proximate, reciprocal relationship can, in turn, easily lead fans to assume they have power to influence the course of the story they love so much. That assumption is complicated, of course. It is at times true—as Winchell and I have shown elsewhere—and at other times false. Also, the logistics of television production itself, as with film, can stand in the way of showrunners responding to viewers' desires. For example, in an interview with *OK! Magazine*'s Kaitlin Menza, Guggenheim explains,

> We love the fans, and we love that the fans are active on Twitter and are constantly giving us feedback. The practical matter is, by the time an episode airs, we're far down the road in writing. I would say the fan feedback tends to have the most influence in terms of educating as to what it is working about the show, and what's resonating. I wouldn't say there's a specific example I could point to, but I would say that *the fans are present in the writers' room* [emphasis added].

Presence, of course, does not imply power. Showrunners and filmmakers alike are actually in a difficult position as they juggle the demands of their employers, of the production process, and of viewers—all the while trying to be true to themselves as artists. This is one of the main complications for understanding the fan-producer relationship and the significance of fan-fashioned texts: the metaphors we use. Is a television episode, is a film a *product* to be purchased or a work of *art* to be admired? Obviously, I have posed my question as a binary opposition. One could argue that a Marvel film is both. (Yes, film is art. Are Marvel movies art? That is an entirely different argument, I admit, and an argument for another time and place.) Therein lies the complicated nature of this discussion. Again, to repurpose Norman, using barriers to block people from accessing a more efficient, more intriguing, more pleasurable route is not user-centered design. "Unless it is a work of art [to be admired but not *used*]," insists Norman, "a public space is for people…. for the benefit of the people who use it, taking into account their true needs and wants" (129–30). The fact is Marvel's audience is so massive in number and so diverse in composition that it is impossible to take into account everyone's needs and wants. This reality, though, does not make Marvel less accountable for the narratives they produce.

My claim about accountability rests on the foundation of a particular assumption: stories matter. Though I do not have the space in this essay to elaborate on that assumption, I have done so at length in the journal article "By Beholding, We Become Changed: Narrative Transubstantiation and the Whedonverses." Suffice it to say that stories—whatever their form—are more than just a pastime we use for entertainment purposes. They reside at the heart of who we are as human beings. They are the mythologies we live and die by; they define us and mold us. As we create them, they create us. Storytelling, therefore, is powerful and is power. As Marvel itself has taught us, "with great power comes great responsibility." Literary theorists, narratolgists, cognitive psychologists, and media scholars confirm that power over and over again. Narratives have a profound impact on our minds and bodies, our identities, and our behaviors. That is why it is a problem that Marvel's leading superheroes so narrowly represent the global audience. Throughout this essay, I have also used the expression "fans' needs and wants." I have done so on purpose. This topic is not just about what some viewers *want* to see; it is also about what some viewers *need* to see. With Marvel's great power to tell stories comes its great responsibility to tell them in ways and with characters that meet the needs of as many of its fans as possible. A more dia-logic relationship—however that might look, however that might happen—would honor a more diverse and complex MCU and the desires of many of its devotees.

Final Words

Despite fan-made opening credits and trailers, "We Want Widow!" flash mobs, and the critiques of entertainment news outlets and media scholars, Marvel unfortunately does not appear attentive to sociable design, to working *with* the interests and desires of some audience members—even though they have had "offers of proposed screenplays, talented directors actively coveting the job, and lots of evidence that [a Black Widow movie] could be great" (McCown). Perhaps we should not be surprised by Marvel's lack of attention. After all, the company has not even prominently featured the female Avenger in its action figure collection or toy lines, yet another reason there have been public outcries. At the same time, declares McCown, "it's a bit bizarre that one of the most recognizable Marvel heroes at this point is an afterthought when it comes to a standalone film." Bizarre indeed, especially considering that there appears to be a significant market for it. Black Widow might as well have a dollar sign rather than a red hourglass emblazoned on her belt buckle, yet for now Marvel remains fixed on its "master" plan that does not include her in a title role.

Regardless of what choices Marvel makes or does not make, noting and understanding the significance of fan-made texts is the charge of media and fandom scholars. Both physical and social desire paths allow us to look closely at an individual fan's or a fandom's interests, passions, and desires as well as to consider the meanings and importance of self-selected pathways of activity, behavior, and agency. These lines, however faint, can suggest collective inter-ests, revealing a clearer picture of the wider fandom. Nichols states that "polit-ical scientists focus on interests solidified in the formation of interest groups, … groups that can directly challenge and change existing social structures" ("Social Desire Paths: An Applied Sociology of Interests" 167). This concept,

I believe, is essential to seeing the worth of both a handful of artifacts created by only one, two, or three fans and a massive, organized fan-driven campaign. The single fan needs a community or fandom just as a fandom needs each fan. Together, they have the potential to "challenge and change" the objects of their desire.

Physical and social desire paths can also help scholars assess what values underlie fan activities and discover what behaviors mean in terms of new models for not only film production, distribution, and marketing, but also the fan-producer relationship. As K. A. Williams asserts by citing Tiessen, "desire lines express the excess that premeditated constructions cannot foresee or contain." Fan-made Black Widow opening credits and trailers simultaneously "express the excess" of fan desire and expose the structural weaknesses of the MCU's architectural design, a design that for whatever reason cannot or will not "foresee or contain" a movie devoted to contemporary cinema's first female Avenger. "Studios wish to direct audience's excitement, but audiences are also capable of directing and marking their own desire and anticipation," asserts Williams (para. 4.12). Even if a standalone Black Widow film continues to elude those who desire it, what remain are the fan-made texts and an array of other tactics that anticipate such a film. These tactics and texts can be called a social desire path for good reason. They are the tangible evidence that such a desire exists.

NOTES

1. The term *fanvidders* refers to fans who create "vids" or music videos by using footage from film or television and splicing it together often to create a variation on the original narrative. According to Francesca Coppa, the art "began with slide shows over music in 1975, and was then developed into a high art by VCR vidders in the 1980s and 1990s" (58). Of course, digital editing software has revolutionized the practice. Today, almost anyone can create a vid, though some fans retain a kind of celebrity status among their peers because of their highly-honed skills in vidding.

2. *Cosplay* is portmanteau of *costume* and *play*. It refers to the fan practice of dressing up as a beloved or admired fictional character. Though the term originated within the context of Japanese anime and manga, it is widely used today to refer to any form of costume play and is an especially popular pastime at fan conventions.

3. "Grass grows by inches, but dies by feet" was coined by Henry Archer Diehl, Jr., around the mid–20th century.

4. Thanks to Sherry Ginn, editor of this collection, for directing me to the psychological theory of reactance so that I might better explain one of the many reasons humans create desire lines.

5. I cannot help but think of the medical and psychological term "self-consoling behavior" when I think of fans creating texts to satisfy their own desires. If we understand the power and importance of narrative (or myth) for human beings, it makes sense that when stories do not fulfill our needs and wants we may turn to making up our own as a form of solace.

6. At San Diego Comic-Con International in July 2014, actor Stephen Amell, who plays Oliver Queen on The CW's *Arrow,* stated, "There's one woman in Oliver's

life this year.... It's Felicity." The statement upset some fans and thrilled others as it foreshadowed a significant shift away from the DC Comics' canon, wherein Oliver, the Green Arrow, is paired romantically with Laurel Lance, the Black Canary. Instead, the television series moved toward a pairing that was lobbied for by a particular group of fans within the wider fandom surrounding the series. In our book chapter on this shift, Meghan K. Winchell and I argue that "social media engagement by fans, particularly those who desire an Oliver-Felicity romantic relationship ('shippers' who refer to themselves as Oliciters), have played a—if not *the*—defining role in this shift away from canon" (n. pag.). What Oliciters did early on was note the screen chemistry between actor Emily Bett Rickards and Stephen Amell, chemistry he does not share with the actor cast to play Laurel Lance, Katie Cassidy. This recognition and social media activism to make their desires clear to executive producers only reinforced what the showrunners themselves were noticing. As a result, Rickards became a permanent cast member. By the fourth season, Oliver and Felicity had gotten engaged. Winchell and I insist that evidence points to Oliciters giving "writers permission to free themselves from a canon developed for the comic book page and take the story in a direction that was best for the televisual incarnation of the Oliver Queen/Arrow character" (n. pag.). Direct and indirect communication by way of social media platforms was the tactic fans used to accomplish that alteration to the narrative.

    7. Social media engagement with viewers has actually become very popular with and helpful for independent filmmakers. However, those at the helm of blockbusters are quite removed from such direct contact with audiences.

WORKS CONSULTED

Anderton, Ethan. "VOTD: Fanmade Opening Credits for the Black Widow Movie We Deserve." slashfilm.com. /*Film*, 15 May 2015. Accessed 14 Feb. 2016.

Askwith, Ivan. TV 2.0: Turning Television into an Engagement Medium. MA thesis. Massachusetts Institute of Technology, 2007. Print.

Baker-Whitelaw, Gavia. "These Fan Trailers Will Make You Wish the 'Black Widow' Movie Were Real." dailydot.com. *The Daily Dot*, 16 Apr. 2015. Accessed 14 Feb. 2016.

Benecchi, Eleonora, and Cinzia Colapinto. "Engaging with Glee: Transmedia Story-telling for a Television in Transition." *Business Models for a Digital Economy: The Value of Contents*. Ed. Enrique Guerrero. Navarre, Spain: University of Navarre Press, 2010. 210–18. Print.

_____. "Television and Social Media in the Era of Convergence and Participation." *Managing Media Economy, Media Content and Technology in the Age of Digital Convergence*. Ed. Zvezdan Vukanovic and Paulo Fuastino. Lisbon: MediaXXI Publishing, 2011. 321–44. Print.

_____. "TV Series Go Beyond the Screen." *Previously On: Interdisciplinary Studies on TV Series in the Third Golden Age of Television*. Ed. Miguel A. Perez-Gomez. Seville: Frame, 2011. 433–46. Print.

Benecchi, Eleonora, and Giuseppe Richeri. "TV to Talk About: Engaging with American TV Series through the Internet." *The New Television Ecosystem*. Ed. Alberto Abbruzzese, Nello Barile, Julian Gebhardt, and Jane Vincent Fortunato. New York: Peter Lang, 2013. 121–40. Print.

Benecchi, Eleonora. "Online Italian Fandoms of American TV Shows." Ed. Anne Kustritz. *European Fans and European Fan Objects: Localization and Translation*.

Spec. issue of *Transformative Works and Cultures* 19 (2015): 9 secs., 80 pars. Accessed 10 Mar. 2016.

Bennett, Lucy. "Tracing Textual Poachers: Reflections on the Development of Fan Studies and Digital Fandom." *The Journal of Fandom Studies* 2.1 (2014): 5–20. Print.

Burks, Robin. "Fan-Made Title Sequence for 'Black Widow' Movie Hits All the Right Notes." techtimes.com. *TECHTIMES.com*, 14 May 2015. Accessed 14 Feb. 2016.

Bury, Rhiannon, Ruth Deller, Adam Greenwood, and Bethan Jones. "From Usenet to Tumblr: The Changing Role of Social Media." *Participations* 10.1 (2013): 299–318. Accessed 10 Mar. 2015.

Chin, Bertha. "The Fan-Media Producer Collaboration: How Fan Relationships Are Managed in a Post-Series X-Files Fandom." *Science Fiction Film & Television* 6.1 (2013): 87–99. Print.

Cochran, Tanya R. "By Beholding, We Become Changed: Narrative Transubstantiation and the Whedonverses." Ed. K. Dale Koontz and Ensley F. Guffey. *Joss in June: Selected Essays*. Spec. issue of *The Journal of the Whedon Studies Association*, 11.2/12.1 (Summer 2014): 20 pars. Accessed 17 Mar. 2016.

Cochran, Tanya R., and Meghan K. Winchell. "When Fans Know Best: Oliciters Right the Ship." *Arrow and Superhero Television: Essays on Themes and Characters of the Series*. Ed. Jim Iaccino, Cory Barker, and Myc Wiatrowski. Jefferson, NC: McFarland, forthcoming. N. pag. Print.

Collier, Cassandra M. *The Love That Refuses to Speak Its Name: Examining Queerbaiting and Fan-Producer Interactions in Fan Cultures*. MA thesis. University of Louisville, 2015. Accessed 10 Mar. 2016.

Coppa, Francesca. "A Brief History of Media Fandom." *Fan Fiction and Fan Communities in the Age of the Internet: New Essays*. Ed. Karen Helleksen and Kristina Busse. Jefferson, NC: McFarland, 2006. 41–59. Print.

Cubbison, Laurie. "Russell T. Davies, 'Nine Hysterical Women,' and the death of Ianto Jones." *New Media Literacies and Participatory Popular Culture across Borders*. London: Routledge, 2012. 135–50. Print.

Hadas, Leora, and Limor Shifman. "Keeping the Elite Powerless: Fan-Producer Relations in the 'Nu Who' (and New YOU) Era." *Critical Studies in Media Communication* 30.4 (2013): 275–91. Print.

Jenkins, Henry. "How the Extended Marvel Universe (and Other Superhero Stories) Can Enable Political Debates." *Confessions of an Aca-Fan: The Official Weblog of Henry Jenkins*. Henry Jenkins, 6 May 2015. Accessed 14 Feb. 2016.

Larsen, Katherine, and Lynn Zubernis. *Fandom at the Crossroads: Celebration, Shame and Fan/Producer Relationships*. Newcastle upon Tyne: Cambridge Scholars, 2011. Print.

Macklem, Lisa. *We're on This Road Together: The Changing Fan/Producer Relationship in Television as Demonstrated by Supernatural*. MA thesis. The University of Western Ontario, 2013. Accessed 10 Mar. 2016.

McCown, Alex. "A Fan Made Great Opening Credits for the Black Widow Movie We're Not Getting." avclub.com. *A.V. Club*, 14 May 2015. Accessed 24 Feb. 2016.

Menza, Kaitlin. "Arrow's Executive Producer Shares the Secret to Felicity and Oliver's Chemistry." okmagazine.com. *OK! Magazine*, 14 May 2014. Accessed 19 June 2015.

Nichols, Laura. "Social Desire Paths: A New Theoretical Concept to Increase the Usability of Social Science Research in Society." *Theory and Society* 43 (2014): 647–65. Print.

_____. "Social Desire Paths: An Applied Sociology of Interests." *Social Currents* 1.2 (2014): 166–72. Print.

Norman, Donald A. *Living with Complexity*. Cambridge: MIT Press, 2011. Print.

Pantozzi, Jill. "Watch the Black Widow Title Sequence for the Black Widow Movie You've Always Wanted." themarysue.com. *The Mary Sue*, 13 May 2015. Accessed 14 Feb. 2016.

Romano, Aja. "Fan Creates the Perfect Spy Movie Credits for Our Nonexistent Black Widow Movie." dailydot.com. *The Daily Dot*, 15 May 2015. Accessed 14 Feb. 2016.

Scott, Suzanne. "Who's Steering the Mothership? The Role of the Fanboy Auteur in Transmedia Storytelling." *The Participatory Cultures Handbook*. Ed. Aaron Delwiche and Jennifer Jacobs Henderson. New York: Routledge, 2012. 43–52. Print.

Tiessen, Matthew. "Accepting Invitations: Desire Lines as Earthly Offerings." *Rhizomes: Cultural Studies in Emerging Knowledge* 15 (Winter 2007): n. pag. Web. 14 Feb. 2015.

"What Is Reactance Theory?" psychologydictionary.com. *Psychology Dictionary*, n.d. Accessed 13 Mar. 2016.

Williams, Kathleen Amy. "Fake and Fan Film Trailers as Incarnations of Audience Anticipation and Desire." Ed. Fancesca Coppa and Julie Levin Russo. *Fan Remix/Video*. Spec. issue of *Transformative Works and Cultures*, 9 (2012): 9 secs., 44 pars. Accessed 28 Jan. 2015.

Williams, Rebecca. "Good Neighbours? Fan/Producer Relationships and the Broadcasting Field." *Continuum: Journal of Media & Cultural Studies* 24.2 (2010): 279–89. Print.

Videography

Angel. Created by Joss Whedon. The WB, 1999–2004. TV.

Ant-Man. Dir. Peyton Reed. Marvel Studios, 2015. Film.

"Ariel." *Firefly: The Complete Series.* Writ. Jose Molina. Dir. Allan Kroeker. Twentieth Century–Fox, 2002. DVD.

Arrow. Created by Greg Berlanti, Andrew Kreisberg, and Marc Guggenheim. The CW, 2012–present. TV.

The Avengers. Dir. Joss Whedon. Marvel Studios, 2012. Film.

Avengers: Age of Ultron. Dir. Joss Whedon. Marvel Studios, 2015. Film.

Avengers: Infinity War Part 2. Marvel Studios, in production.

"Belonging." *Dollhouse: The Complete Second Season.* Writ. Maurissa Tancharoen and Jed Whedon. Dir. Jonathan Frakes. Twentieth Century–Fox, 2010. DVD.

Buffy the Vampire Slayer. Created by Joss Whedon. The WB (1997–2001) and UPN (2001–2003). TV.

Captain America: Civil War. Dir. Anthony Russo and Joe Russo. Marvel Studios, 2016.

Captain America: The First Avenger. Dir. Joe Johnston. Paramount Pictures, 2011. Film.

Captain America: The Winter Soldier. Dir. Anthony Russo and Joe Russo. Marvel Studios, 2014. Film.

Captain Marvel. Marvel Studios, in production.

Catwoman. Dir. Pitof. Warner Brothers, 2004. Film.

"Doppelgangland." *Buffy, the Vampire Slayer.* Season 3, episode 16. Writ. and Dir. Joss Whedon. First broadcast 23 February 1999.

Elektra. Dir. Rob Bowman. Twentieth Century–Fox, 2005. Film.

Firefly. Created by Joss Whedon. Twentieth Century–Fox, 2002–03. TV.

"Ghost." *Dollhouse: The Complete First Season.* Writ. and Dir. Joss Whedon. Twentieth Century–Fox, 2009. DVD.

"The Hollow Men." *Dollhouse: The Complete Second Season.* Writ. Michele Fazekas, Tara Butters, and Tracy Bellomo. Dir. Terrence O'Hara. Twentieth Century–Fox, 2010. DVD.

The Hunger Games: Mockingjay Part 1. Dir. Francis Lawrence. Lionsgate, 2014. Film.

The Incredible Hulk. Dir. Louis Leterrier. Universal Pictures, 2008. Film.

The Incredibles. Dir. Brad Bird. Disney, 2004. Film.

The Inhumans. Marvel Studios, in production.

"The Iron Ceiling." *Agent Carter*. Writ. Jose Molina. Dir. Peter Leto. Season 1. Episode 5. First broadcast 3 February 2015.

Iron Man. Dir. Jon Favreau. Paramount Pictures, 2008. Film.

Iron Man 2. Dir. Jon Favreau. Paramount Pictures, 2010. Film.

Iron Man 3. Dir. Shane Black. Marvel Studios, 2013. Film.

Lost. Created by J.J. Abrams, Jeffrey Lieber, Damon Lindelof. ABC, 2004–2010. TV.

"A Love Supreme." *Dollhouse: The Complete Second Season*. Writ. Jenny DeArmitt. Dir. David Straiton. Twentieth Century–Fox, 2010. DVD.

"Man on the Street." *Dollhouse: The Complete First Season*. Writ. Joss Whedon. Dir. David Straiton. Twentieth Century–Fox, 2009. DVD.

Marvel's *Agent Carter*. Created by Christopher Markus and Stephen McFeely. ABC, 2015–2016. TV.

Marvel's *Agents of S.H.I.E.L.D.* Created by Maurissa Tancharoen, Jed Whedon, and Joss Whedon. ABC, 2013-present. TV.

Marvel's *Daredevil*. Created by Drew Goddard. Netflix, 2015–present. TV.

Mission Impossible: Ghost Protocol. Dir. Brad Bird. Paramount Pictures, 2011. Film.

"Needs." *Dollhouse: The Complete First Season*. Writ. Tracy Bellomo. Dir. Felix E. Alcalá. Twentieth Century–Fox, 2009. DVD.

"Prophecy Girl." *Buffy, the Vampire Slayer*. Season 1, episode 12. Writ. and Dir. Josh Whedon. First broadcast 2 June 1997.

"Safe." *Firefly: The Complete Series*. Writ. Drew Z. Greenberg. Dir. Michael Grossman. Twentieth Century–Fox, 2002. DVD.

Serenity. Dir. Joss Whedon. Universal Pictures, 2005. Film.

"A Spy in the House of Love." *Dollhouse: The Complete First Season*. Writ. Andrew Chambliss. Dir. David Solomon. Twentieth Century–Fox, 2009. DVD.

"Stop-Loss." *Dollhouse: The Complete Second Season*. Writ. Andrew Chambliss. Dir. Felix E. Alcalá. Twentieth Century–Fox, 2010. DVD.

Thor. Dir. Kenneth Branagh. Paramount Pictures, 2011. Film.

Thor: The Dark World. Dir. Alan Taylor. Marvel Studios, 2013. Film.

Timberlake, Justin, Tim Mosley, and Nate "Danja" Hills (lyrics). "What Goes Around Comes Around." Prod. Justin Timberlake, Timbaland, Nate "Danja" Hills. [Video Dir. Samuel Bayer.] Jive Zomba, 2006. Music.

"Trash." *Firefly: The Complete Series*. Writ. Ben Edlund and Jose Molina. Dir. Vern Gillum. Twentieth Century–Fox, 2002. DVD.

"True Believer." *Dollhouse: The Complete First Season*. Writ. Tim Minear. Dir. Allan Kroeker. Twentieth Century–Fox, 2009. DVD.

"Vows." *Dollhouse: The Complete Second Season*. Writ. and Dir. Joss Whedon. Twentieth Century–Fox, 2010. DVD.

"The Well." *Marvel's Agents of S.H.I.E.L.D.: The Complete First Season*. Writ. Monica Breen. Dir. Jonathan Frakes. ABC Studios, 2014. DVD.

"The Wish." *Buffy, the Vampire Slayer*. Season 3, episode 9. Writ. Marti Noxon. Dir. David Greenwalt. First broadcast 8 December 1998.

About the Contributors

Jillian Coleman **Benjamin** graduated summa cum laude with a master's degree in humanities and religious studies from Sacramento State University. Her research interests are feminism in popular culture, representation of women and minorities in literature and media, Chinese literature and Modernist literature.

Lewis **Call** is an associate professor and the chair of history at California Polytechnic State University, San Luis Obispo, and the author of *Postmodern Anarchism* and *BDSM in American Science Fiction and Fantasy*. He has written extensively about representations of alternative sexualities in the works of Joss Whedon.

Tanya R. **Cochran** is a professor of English and communication at Union College in Lincoln, Nebraska. Her interests include composition, rhetoric, narratology, fandom studies, gender studies, and the intersection of faith and learning. An editorial board member for *Slayage: The Journal of the Whedon Studies Association* and its undergraduate partner *Watcher Junior*, she is also the past president of the Whedon Studies Association (2012–14) and one of its co-founders.

Malgorzata **Drewniok** is a teaching fellow at Winchester School of Art at Southampton University. Her research has focused on how the language of *Buffy the Vampire Slayer* TV series is manipulated to show the change in identity among the vampires. She is also interested in stylistics, pragmatics, gender and language, popular culture, television studies, and contemporary gothic.

Valerie Estelle **Frankel** is the author of many books on pop culture, including *Doctor Who—The What, Where, and How*; *Sherlock: Every Canon Reference You May Have Missed in BBC's Series 1–3*; and *History, Homages and the Highlands: An Outlander Guide*. Many of her books focus on women's roles in fiction, from her heroine's journey guides *From Girl to Goddess* and *Buffy and the Heroine's Journey* to *Women in Game of Thrones* and *The Many Faces of Katniss Everdeen*.

Sherry **Ginn** has published numerous research articles in the fields of neuroscience and psychology, but more recently has focused on the intersection of popular culture with psychology and neuroscience. She is author or editor of books on women in science fiction television, sex in science fiction, and *Farscape* and *Fringe*. In addition to a book collectively examining the television series of Joss Whedon, she has co-edited a book on Whedon's series *Dollhouse*. A collection on time travel in science fiction television, co-edited with Gillian I. Leitch, was published in 2015.

David **Kociemba** serves as the president of the Affiliated Faculty of Emerson College Union and as a committee member on the AAUP Committee on Contingency and the Profession. He has taught courses in media history, television studies, disability studies, digital media and culture, video art, and fandom studies. His writing focuses on the work of Joss Whedon and Jane Espenson, disability representation in *Glee* and the films of Todd Haynes, and paratexts like spoilers and opening title sequences.

Samira **Nadkarni**'s publications trace her interest in postmodern poetry and performance, Whedon studies, hermeneutics, ethics, neo/colonialism, fan studies, and digital texts. Her writing on the Whedonverses focuses primarily on issues of humanistic ethics such as memory, race, and intersecting power structures. She serves on the editorial board of *Watcher Junior: The Undergraduate Journal of Whedon Studies* and is a guest contributor to the *i love e-poetry project*.

Heather M. **Porter** is a member of the Producers Guild and the Academy of Television Arts and Sciences and has worked on five seasons of *Hell's Kitchen* and four seasons of *RuPaul's Drag Race*. A Whedon scholar and charter member of the Whedon Studies Association, she has presented at all six Slayage Conferences. Her research interests include quantitative analyses of images of violence, intelligence, and sex in the science fiction and fantasy genres.

Index

9 780786 498192